WRITER'S GUIDE TO
CHARACTER TRAITS

second edition

includes profiles of human
behaviors and personality types

LINDA N. EDELSTEIN, PH.D.

WRITER'S DIGEST BOOKS

writersdigestbooks.com
Cincinnati, Ohio

Visit our Web site at www.writersdigest.com for information on more resources for writers.

To receive a free weekly e-mail newsletter delivering tips and updates about writing and about Writer's Digest products, register directly at our Web site at http://newsletters.fwpublications.com.

14   13   12   11   10   10   9   8   7   6

Distributed in Canada by Fraser Direct
100 Armstrong Avenue
Georgetown, ON, Canada L7G 5S4
Tel: (905) 877-4411
Distributed in the U.K. and Europe by David & Charles
Brunel House, Newton Abbot, Devon, TQ12 4PU, England
Tel: (+44) 1626 323200, Fax: (+44) 1626 323319
E-mail: postmaster@davidandcharles.co.uk
Distributed in Australia by Capricorn Link
P.O. Box 704, Windsor, NSW 2756 Australia
Tel: (02) 4577-3555

Library of Congress Cataloging-in-Publication Data

Edelstein, Linda.

Writer's guide to character traits : includes profiles of human behaviors and personality types / by Linda Edelstein.-- 2nd ed.

p. cm.

Includes bibliographical references and index.

ISBN-13: 978-1-58297-390-6 (pbk. : alk. paper)

ISBN-10: 1-58297-390-3

1. Fiction--Technique--Handbooks, manuals, etc. 2. Characters and characteristics in literature--Handbooks, manuals,etc. 3. Typology (Psychology)--Handbooks, manuals, etc. 4. Human behavior--Handbooks, manuals, etc. I. Title.

PN3383.C4E34 2006
808.3'97--dc22

2006008083

Edited by Michelle Ehrhard
Designed by Claudean Wheeler
Production coordinated by Robin Richie

F+W PUBLICATIONS, INC.

Acknowledgments

Thanks go to my small, wonderful writing group, Margit Kir-Stimon and Nancy Newton for their ideas and for listening patiently week after week. And to Karen Drill for her willingness to help me bring ideas to life.

Dedication

For Jennifer and Keira, always with love

About the Author

Linda N. Edelstein received her Ph.D. from Northwestern University. She teaches there and maintains a private practice in Evanston and in Chicago. She has previously published two books in psychology and has written widely on loss and mourning, women's identity, and creativity.

TABLE OF
contents

introDUCTION

Writers ask me all kinds of questions: "What makes a man have an affair?" "Why would a woman stalk her former lover?" "How can I learn what motivates a person's behavior?" Rarely is there one answer to questions like these. But psychological research can provide vast amounts of data that can help writers, beginners and accomplished authors alike, gather accurate information about personality and behavior in order to create believable and authentic characters. My goal in writing this book has been to create a friendly reference for just that purpose. It is a crash course in psychology for writers. I describe the inner workings and behaviors of ordinary—and not-so-ordinary—people in lists, charts, and descriptive paragraphs. All this information is not a substitute for your imagination, but a way to inspire your mind.

In my work as a clinician and teacher, I don't deal with fictional characters; I work with people. I have been in psychology since the early 1970s, so I have had a lot of time to understand the interior lives of individuals, couples, and groups: what makes them feel happy and sad, what motivates them, and what events bring them to a screeching halt. Daily, I tiptoe my way through the many layers that exist in each of us and marvel at how impenetrable most of them remain, both to ourselves and to those around us. I am continually impressed—not always positively—by the strange ways people behave. Just when I tell myself that I have heard it all, I am humbled again by the intrigues people manage to create. Dorothy Parker was right: "People are more fun than anybody." To understand people, to write about them, and to read about them is endlessly engaging. When we unravel their psychological puzzles, we ultimately shed light on our own lives.

As a psychologist, I am the ultimate reader. I sit in an armchair and read people all day long, always moving through an unfolding story, worrying, trying to understand, making sense, cheering, unraveling mysteries, and bearing witness to the search for a happy ending. This book is a synthesis of my reading, real and imagined, over the years; I wrote it because I thought it would be fun for me and helpful for others to have easy, accurate lists of qualities that hang together in personality types. In this book you will find more than four hundred lists describing individual personality types, traits associated with stages of normal child development, types of criminals, patterns of sexual behavior, dynamics of life events, family processes, responses to traumas and disasters, group and organizational dynamics, characteristics associated with people in various careers, descriptions of abnormal behavior, and other assorted informational tidbits. The lists presented here contain traits that are not my own creation, but are usually mainstream ideas accepted in psychological theory and research. Some material is on the edge, especially when I describe disorders about which little is yet known. Footnotes point you to more articles and books if you want to go deeper into any of the material.

One of the strange features about being a psychologist is that everybody else is also a psychologist. People know a great deal about psychology; we as a society have become very well informed on human emotions and behaviors. The ever-increasing array of talk shows, reality TV, interview shows, and magazines reveals both the unending desire to know about other people's lives and the genuine sophistication of the man or woman on the street with regard to psychological matters. One-dimensional, uninteresting characters have become unacceptable to the reading public.

Writers hate stereotypes because they are usually unfair, often insulting, and always boring. But stereotypes are popular because they provide us with a language shortcut.

They jolt our memories; they give us a quick, if imprecise, way of knowing, even if entire classes of people—fat people, depressed women, post office workers—are reduced to shallow mental pictures. This book is intended to help you create deeper, more coherent identities for your characters. We all see the outside of people; we see their behavior. To construct compelling characters, we need to reach inside. We need to answer questions about our characters: Why don't people leave a building when the alarm sounds? (See page 246.) Why do people fail to keep New Year's resolutions? (See page 226.) What does a childhood of poverty do to personality? (See page 50.) Why do leaders of corporations fail? (See page 316.)

Individuals are complex; mere labels, such as "depressed," are inadequate. Two people suffering from the same trauma or dealing with the same emotional disorder are very different human beings with different personalities that influence their responses. For example, one parent whose son died in a senseless car crash may go to work silently each day, emotion escaping only through sobs in the privacy of a scalding morning shower. Another parent may cry and express grief openly with friends, finding solace in companionship; a third may simply want to pretend that life will soon return to normal. All three parents are grieving; no way is right and no way is wrong. Good characters break out of stereotypes; they capture our attention; they move; they get into life. Pick and choose from the traits on the lists to develop your characters, make them plausible, and enrich the personalities you have so carefully developed, so they can go on to hatch plots and make mischief.

The following is a breakdown of the information provided in each chapter:

- Chapter one briefly discusses the creation of believable characters.
- Chapter two gets into the traits of adults. The types described in this chapter are fairly complete. The traits are those normally found clustered together and are demonstrated in attitudes, reactions, patterns of living, and feelings. No one person has all the traits, and individuals have the traits to differing degrees on a continuum from mild to moderate to strong. In mild form, most of these traits are ordinary. In the extreme (marked by →), the trait is transformed into a strong, often pathological version.

- Chapter three provides the traits associated with child and adolescent development, year by year. Children are still works in progress; therefore, children and adolescents do not fit easily into defined types. However, they show certain traits based on age and stage of development.
- Chapter four describes psychological disorders and the traits that define significant deviations from normal development.
- Chapter five examines different types of criminals and crimes, from the mild to the most extreme.
- Chapter six lists sexual behaviors, including common and uncommon sexual disorders. Sexual disorders that have a predominantly physical basis are described in chapter ten.
- Chapter seven is about love, marriage, and other arrangements from the usual to the less common dynamics in adult relationships.
- Chapter eight continues to examine relationships with traits relating to creating a family and all that entails, from adoption to birth order to in-laws.
- Chapter nine offers many examples of life's predicaments. No matter how many plans we make for our lives, ordinary and extraordinary events intervene; this chapter lists the variety of ways in which individuals can cope with these situations.
- Chapter ten describes physical problems that influence appearance, personality, and behavior. Disorders that are primarily physical in nature can have grave psychological consequences. This chapter also includes certain neurological disorders, substance abuse, and eating disorders.
- Chapter eleven reports the findings about traits shared by people in similar professions.
- Chapter twelve sheds light on group influences, characteristics of group membership, specifics associated with selected groups, traits of specific groups, gangs and cults, and the needs that are fulfilled by group membership.
- Chapter thirteen presents some information on physical appearances and nonverbal and verbal communication.

- Chapter fourteen is "The Big Index." You can look up a trait (e.g., sleeplessness, impotence, cruelty to animals, or arrogance) and be directed to the different disorders or situations where you could expect to find it.

How to Use This Book

Molly, an aspiring writer at twelve years of age, spent the summer writing stories in her journal. Molly's mother fielded a million questions: "What kind of job would this person have?" "What do you think she would say when …?" "What do you think he would do if …?" Well, Molly, the answers to some of those questions are in this book. Here are a few tips on how to use the material:

- Leaf through the lists and let them spark your imagination about major and minor character development or situations created by certain types of characters.

- Look up a trait that interests you (in "The Big Index," chapter fourteen) and find its complementary traits. Use them to generate a new character or enrich one of your existing characters. For example, the trait of *blame* offers *blame of others* or *blame of self*. Let's choose *blame of self* and refer to the pages that mention blame of self. Eliminating the page that notes self-blame in children, two adult personality types offer different presentations of self-blame—the Flamboyant (page 33) covers up self-blame; the Victim (page 46) advertises it. Self-blame is also present during depressed moods (page 89) and when certain events occur, like parents' divorcing (page 204) or being in the throes of bulimia (page 270). Those pages will provide information on the main trait—in this case self-blame—as well as other, complementary traits usually found in that type of individual. You can also use these lists to double-check traits in order to see if they are likely to be found within the same character.

- Check the lists to see how a character would behave in difficult circumstances. I have tried to provide a continuum of behavioral possibilities from normal to extreme.

- Play up opposite traits to have a character act against type. People break out of patterns when they are desperate or pushed to extremes, but they usually revert back to type when life settles down again.
- Choose some traits at whose existence you merely hint. For example, paranoia is ugly when it shows up in full force, but a couple of low-level paranoid traits (see Suspicious Type, page 126), such as a bit of suspiciousness or the vigilant search for "truth," will add some dark spice.
- Add extreme or abnormal traits to a character.
- Create external attributes, like clothes, interests, or mannerisms; give characters accurate careers and interests.
- Construct a character's history. Many times, the history will appear in your story as a flashback or memory, but it could also serve as a historical guide only for you, so you understand your character better.
- Get ideas about ways the characters grow and develop from the constellation of traits.
- Depict authentic adult flashbacks to childhood by using chapter three.
- Create complex characters: show a character's "other side," or add abnormality.
- Create multiple characters who can play off each other. For example, bring together an Eccentric Adult (see page 28) and a Conventional Friend (see page 25).
- Create effective minor characters to serve as catalysts, or bring information.

Reminders About Psychological Traits

Traits are only bits and pieces of people's behaviors and personalities. As you create your characters, the following tips may prove helpful:

- Traits—specific qualities of thinking, feeling, behaving, and reacting to frustration or problems—cluster together to describe personality, but are rarely exclusive to one personality. For example, most traits of an Adventurer differ from those of a Conventional or a Loner, but some may be alike.

- Emphasis of different traits within the same type creates very different characters.
- Character can be made more extreme and given degrees of abnormality by choosing heavily from either negative or positive traits.
- Personality, by definition, is stable; but put a character in extraordinary circumstances, and certain traits come to the forefront while others recede.
- Change and out-of-character behavior do take place in our lives, but not as often as we would like to believe.
- Different periods of life give rise to predictable issues—identity for teenagers, mortality for mid-lifers—so certain traits may be exaggerated.
- Personal, idiosyncratic issues, such as abandonment or anger, tend to be worked and reworked throughout life.
- The divide between normal and pathological behavior is not sharp and clear; we exist on a normal → pathological continuum. People can be fairly normal in certain areas of psychological functioning, yet disturbed in others: Certain phobias may never become noticeable if the individual avoids the stimulus, be it heights, snakes, or bridges. We can behave conventionally in many areas and still have hidden oddities or deviances. For example, most child abusers are known to the child and are able to behave appropriately when other people are around.
- Strategies that prove adaptive at one time may fail at another. A child growing up in an abusive alcoholic home may cleverly learn to be invisible as protection. That ability, necessary in childhood, may prove disastrous for the married adult who has no other way to interact during stressful periods.
- People tend to show the same traits when placed in similar situations: A highly competitive man will likely show ambition in the office, on the softball field, or playing Monopoly with his family.
- And, most importantly, characters are all more than any constellation of traits.

This book, therefore, is geared toward a psychological construction of character, comprehending the character, understanding the myriad of traits that combine differently each time to make each of us unique, and constructing a person with internal consistency, so that certain elements run through the whole characterization even when some traits are out of view.

The Revised and Expanded Edition

Much has happened in the six years since the original edition of *The Writer's Guide to Character Traits* was published. I have added information about terrorism, gangs, extremist groups, trauma, families, marriage, and more. There is a great deal of new, specific information integrated into most of the chapters. This expanded and revised edition is being written to make the material easier to use and to provide even more information for writers. The format and design of the book have been revised: I have rearranged some material, hoping that it flows more easily; other material has been removed, either because it seemed tired or to make room for more exciting information. Also, for fun, this revised and expanded edition has three new character-construction aids sprinkled throughout. First, there are sidebars of statistics called "Fact and Figures." Whether your character is in the majority or dances to the beat of his or her own drummer, numbers are fun. You will find statistics, numbers and percentages that jumpstart your plot, subplot, thoughts, or conversation between characters. A second new feature is "New Information." These sidebars contain facts that one of your characters might find helpful. The third addition is the exercises or "Warm Up." These are stimulants for the slow writing day, designed to get your imagination going: push-ups for the mind. Don't brood over the prompts; they are there only to get your fingers going, to overcome a writer's block, or to free yourself from some old pattern.

Comments on the First Edition

The original edition came out in November 1999, has gone into paperback, and continues to sell well. To my delight, *The Writer's Guide to Character Traits* received some honors. The literary journal the *Believer* (December 2003/January 2004) selected it for inclusion among the top forty "How-to-Write" books written since

1913, alongside Natalie Goldberg's *Writing Down the Bones: Freeing the Author Within* and Julia Cameron's *Artist's Way*. The original edition was chosen as one of the "Books for Writers" on the Web site of Writers' Bookshop, an imprint of British publisher Forward Press in 2004. Readers Read (www.readersread .com) ranked it third on their A-List for writing books in April 2000, and www .OneOfUs.co.uk listed it in 2004 with Stephen King's book as a good book to help "with your creative writing."

I also received some criticisms, which generally fell into one of three categories: the book was difficult to use; some traits were listed and others were not; and the traits felt like stereotypes, causing resentment of the lists. I take the first criticism seriously and have reworked a lot of material to improve the flow, and the book designers have improved the visual ease. I hope this helps. Regarding the material that was included or excluded: I included material that had been researched, and not every topic, career, or disorder has produced research useful to writers. Finally, the question of stereotypes is addressed on pages 2–3.

I cannot teach anyone how to write; I am providing lists of reliable information that came from the thousands of studies I read in order to put the book together. The dictionary has all the words you need—it does not write your sentences. The refrigerator has shelves of ingredients—we cook them up differently. You can find the depth and uniqueness in your character. I have provided some people elements; as writers you will put them together in ways that create stunning, fresh characters. Enjoy!

CHAPTER **one**

Real People and Believeable Characters

The traits compiled in the following charts and lists, descriptions of life events, and discussions of psychological development are designed to help you create believable and engaging characters. What are the elements of believable characters? Believable characters possess cohesiveness and consistency. They have histories and internal lives and they play multiple roles. We identify with them and they engage our empathy. And finally, believable characters are diverse.

Cohesiveness and Consistency

My neighbor makes a marvelous six-layer faux Mexican appetizer. She arranges colorful levels of cheese, avocado, sour cream, beans, lettuce, and tomato—all acceptable ingredients individually, but the complementary flavors working together make the dish a real hit. I have tried to assemble something similar on the pages that follow: "people ingredients"; components that work together naturally, coherently, and authentically. The lists can help you imagine the depth of the character's personality. Use some of the traits, or use them all; display some traits to the reader and hold others in your own mind. Using all the traits strongly might overwhelm a character (and numb a reader), but you can play with the traits to create a character who is mild or extreme, sympathetic or repellent. The people ingredients invite you to be a gourmet, to construct a unique character; not to whip up a fast-food dish for which the point is "recognizability" with no surprises.

Even when a writer's imagination soars to places more fascinating than reality, characters must possess an internal cohesiveness: They must make sense. Cohesiveness means that the diverse elements of personality and behavior hang together in a way readers can follow and believe. The aspects of personality must stick together. For example, a client once admitted to me that she had stolen money. I was surprised by her confession; it seemed unlike the person I assumed her to be, but after we talked, I understood. I could see how personality traits that I already knew she possessed—such as arrogance, the need to impress people with a high lifestyle, the belief that her hard work ought to get her more praise, and low self-esteem—combined with easy access to money could result in embezzlement. Her history contributed, too: She had successful parents who overvalued money and openly preferred her high-flying older brother. Would she have gone out with a gun and robbed a liquor store? Never. She was not violent; she had certain rules by which she lived, and she considered herself above common burglary. There was a certain logic to her behavior, including the grandiose notion that she could pay it all back and no one would ever know. These diverse traits, once revealed, hung together and explained why a woman who was a pillar of the community wound up in trouble. I never could have predicted it; my understanding was retrospective, a story unfolding.

More often than not, people are consistent. My friend Carolyn can be depended on to provide a cynical response; I get impatient when I wait in line, either on foot or in the car; my daughter retreats into silence when she is furious with the family; and my client Steve falls asleep when his wife says, "Let's talk." Personality traits tend to show up repeatedly, especially when people are faced with similar events. But roles that we play, situations in which we find ourselves, and people with whom we interact elicit different traits. At work as an attorney, Carolyn compassionately explains federal regulations to an aging client with no editorializing; on vacation, I am appointment-free and patient; with her friends, my daughter expresses herself directly and eloquently; and in therapy, where Steve enjoys the safest hour of his week, he loves to talk and shows no signs of drowsiness. These character traits can all be true; none have to be false.

Character can be consistent and still hold surprises: Shift the supporting players or the circumstances and different traits are revealed. Character is like looking at a box I hold up in front of your eyes. You clearly see the side facing you. You can know everything there is to know about that side—but you are naïve if you think that one side is all there is. You know that the box has other sides, and you make assumptions about the unseen sections of the box. Some of those guesses will be correct, like the size and shape of the other sides. Other assumptions will be wrong, because those sides are presently out of view. People are like the box. We see them at work and learn a bit about one side. They tell us some of their history, and we learn a bit more. They share their feelings about an event, or we watch them react and infer their feelings, and we learn still more. We see them embedded in this context or that and, over time, we learn about the sides that previously had been out of view.

Roles Influence Traits; Traits Influence Roles

Roles are a blend of personality traits and the work that a person does, whether that work is company president, hit man, or new mother. Different roles emphasize different aspects of an individual. I am more reserved and listen more attentively to my clients than when I am teaching, lecturing, or teasing students. Sometimes—not often—I don't listen at all; I only look alert. My work as a psychologist has trained me to listen clearly to all that is said and much that is not said; my love of a good story, my curiosity about people's secret lives, and even my voyeurism probably influenced my choice of career. Those traits led me to the role, and the role has professionalized the traits.

Situations Influence Traits; Traits Influence Situations

Just as our roles vary, so do the situations in which we find ourselves. All situations have the possibility of drawing out traits, good or bad, that might remain hidden in other situations. Laura may be wonderful and companionable in one-on-one situations, but in a group she feels intimidated and withdraws. Many athletes are powerfully aggressive on the field, but passive in the rest of their interactions. These are examples in which the situation—a crowd or a playing field—influences the traits that are displayed. It works the other way, too. Sometimes traits influence the situation: A relaxing party is changed by the intrusion of a drunk neighbor, or a work project goes nowhere until someone with organizational skills joins the team.

Relationships Influence Traits; Traits Influence Relationships

People elicit certain traits in each other, and the dance can become habitual. One goal in couples therapy is to make this dynamic obvious so that people can change their behavior. Sue says, "If you didn't always pursue me for sex, maybe I would have the time to desire you." Her husband, Bob, answers, "If I waited for you to initiate sex, we would be celibate." In other areas of their relationship, these traits can be seen in a more positive light. Sue is easygoing and optimistic. She has always admired Bob's drive and tenacity in his career, and thinks he's the world's best salesman. Bob is uptight and worries excessively, so he finds Sue's buoyant, relaxed outlook on life reassuring. Because of her confidence in him, Bob is closer to becoming the office star than he ever imagined possible.

The same dynamics go on at work. Amir enjoys the last word on hiring and firing. His assistant, Fred, works hard to please him and is always personable—at least to Amir. As a reaction to his obligatory amiability to his superiors, Fred shows his less pleasant qualities to those below him who in turn, whenever possible, sabotage his projects. The exhibition of power in this chain of relationships influences the feelings and behaviors that are displayed. The traits, feelings, and possible behaviors already exist in the individuals involved, are drawn to the surface by events, and create the subtleties of the relationships.

Some of the traits included in this book are internal, some are behavioral, and some are reactions to others, but rarely are they situation-specific. You can move your character from the bedroom, to the supermarket, to the shower.

Character consistency is more effective than inconsistency because we begin to recognize the person's "voice." We believe that we know someone; we know what to expect, or we think we do. Playwright Edward Albee is said to have tested his characters by imagining them in situations other than those he had created. He wanted to see if the characters would stand up outside his play. Consistency of personality does not argue against change. In literature, as in life, development comes from events and growth working on a character's structure. Because you know the expected behaviors, consistency also allows you to choose to have characters act against type some of the time, like the overly cautious fellow who falls hard for the wrong woman because he feels momentary freedom.

Consistency doesn't mean that we show everybody everything at once. Occasionally a client, sad and complaining, will say apologetically to me, "I'm not always like this. When I'm at work [school, with others, etc.] I am strong and confident." I know. Sometimes I want to answer, "I'm not always like this—kind, calm, focused, and intelligent. Sometimes I am anxious, dopey, sarcastic, short-tempered, and tired."

Empathy

In my work, I understand people by what they tell me about themselves and their lives, but also by establishing an empathetic connection. Empathy is that elusive exchange whereby, for a fleeting moment here and there, I walk in someone else's shoes. I get a glimpse of the universal elements in another person's struggle, feelings that we all know—love, hate, despair, shame, loneliness, fear, joy. It isn't only psychology that tries to understand and communicate universals. In his lectures at Harvard University, artist Ben Shahn (1898-1969) described his goal in painting a particular image as trying to create "the emotional tone that surrounds disaster" more than painting a picture of a literal disaster.[1] When he succeeds, people respond to the feelings of disaster in the painting. We understand people similarly when we connect to some universal quality in them that finds its counterpart in our own private world. In literature, as in life, we move closer to characters when we resonate with their emotional lives.

Understanding a character's emotional world is not the only way to generate interest. We can use a hobby, like growing orchids, to make a character stand out. We can use a physical characteristic—like four tattoos, each of which spells "Mother"—to make a point about personality, but the personality itself is more compelling. Props are eye-catchers, but complexity of personality is what sustains the reader's interest.[2] If a character engages our feelings, we care about what happens to him or her; we wonder how the conflict will be resolved. To know and be conscious of the character is to remain connected and involved, even if the character's experience is far from our own.

Believable Characters

Believable characters are essential in fiction and nonfiction—in books and on the screen. Characters must be durable, fallible, and able to grow and change. Writers in all disciplines strive to create realistic characters. Authors of juvenile and adult mysteries need a fully formed hero or heroine to provide the tension because he or she is pitted, often alone, against a personal adversary. Short-story writers need to develop characters' emotions to capture the reader quickly. Minor characters, too, require attention, so they can stand on their own. Unless characters are realistic, you will intrude on and inhibit their development. You will meddle with a vacant character until believability is gone. Realistic characters tell you how they will behave.

[1] Shahn (1957). [2] Burns (1988).

In Jane Austen's work, we can appreciate her characters' conduct in particular situations when they are set out in the book, even if it doesn't make sense in today's world or in our lives.[3] When we are absorbed in the material, we feel emotion. And when we are emotionally moved, we believe. Character is "a paradigm of traits," more than simply a series of actions.[4] A character acts because … In this way, the reader becomes conscious of the character's reality, even when that reality differs from his own.

Characters work best when you create a virtual identity for them. The character can then inhabit an imaginative space in the reader's mind, a space that you have created. Readers go along with characters as long as the characters remain coherent.[5] The reader doesn't need to be similar to a character to be interested in him or her. The reader needs to understand and be engaged by the person, whether characteristics are shared or not. I see many people in treatment who are not like me, and I don't see myself reflected in them. But, as they develop and unfold, when they allow me to know their world, I feel connected and very concerned about their "story" and its outcome.

Character History

All characters have unique personal histories and childhoods upon which social/historical events have a huge impact. Events that occur in a person's childhood shape the individual's background assumptions about life and the world, while those occuring in late adolescence shape the individual's conscious identity. Events in adulthood may affect the opportunities available to an individual, but do not shape their values or their identities. For example, the four-year-old in New York City who experienced 9/11 may grow up with ideas about terror, violence, separation, or stability that come directly from this event. The nineteen-year-old fireman who drove in from Iowa to help and the twenty-five-year-old woman who counseled survivors think of themselves in certain ways that were shaped by their conscious behavior during those weeks. The fifty-year-old owner of a

[3] Charlton (1984). [4] Chatman (1978). [5] Cohan (1983).

company who trains and supplies security guards may have prospered, but his basic identity is probably untouched.

Diversity

Traits are not confined to people; cultures also have characteristics. Contrast, for example, the individualistic nature of the citizens of the United States with the appreciation for the collective in Japan. Conflict can exist between the cultural values of individuals; the competitive drive of an Anglo boy differs from the cooperative beliefs of a Native American boy. Talking to the dead is acceptable behavior in many cultures, while in the mainstream United States, a person could find herself confined to a hospital and medicated for the same activity. Many, many other differences exist: Some are subtle. These kinds of differences provide further opportunities for character and relationship development.

CHAPTER two

Adult Personality Types

Each of the twenty-three adult personality types in this chapter refers to an individual's enduring pattern of inner experience and behavior. Personality development begins early and remains remarkably consistent throughout life. Yes, we change and behave out of character, but not as often as we would like to believe. Therefore, it is useful to think about personality types and the ways people ordinarily behave before we imagine how they might behave against type, grow, change, and react under extraordinary conditions.

The types described in this chapter are fairly complete and, for the most part, normal. In mild form, the majority of these traits are ordinary, though in the extreme (marked by →), traits can become exaggerated, even pathological. Information on the fundamentally abnormal types can be found in chapter four.

Traits emanate from a blend of life experiences, internal ways in which we organize ourselves, and inherited temperament. Characters demonstrate their traits in attitudes, reactions, patterns of living, and feelings. Traits are also influenced by the context in which people find themselves. For example, a solitary person may be effective at work as a researcher, but ineffective and odd at a holiday party. Individuals are reactive beings, so different situations influence how many traits are seen and how strongly people respond. Also, over time, environment and life circumstances will enrich or distort personality, and will cause an individual to behave in healthier or more pathological ways.

The combinations of traits listed on the following pages are generally found clustered together. Rarely would one person have all the traits, and individuals have the traits in differing degrees on a continuum from mild to moderate to strong. In creating your characters, you can pick and choose from the traits on the list and decide on the strength of each trait.

Each type in this chapter is subdivided into sections called *Internal* and *Interpersonal*, depending on whether the emphasis of the trait is more emotion and attitude (Internal) or behaviors and reactions to others (Interpersonal). For example, a character who exemplifies the first adult type, Adventurer, often remains unaware of the feelings of others, primarily an internal quality. He may demonstrate that trait interpersonally, by ignoring social conventions or exhibiting behaviors that show him to be oblivious to others.

Following many of the lists is a short section called Normal → Extreme. Traits that can deteriorate into abnormality usually fall on a continuum ranging from normal to extreme rather than existence or non-existence. Let's look at the Adventurer again: The wonderful, normal quality of self-confidence, which allows the Adventurer to take risks, can deteriorate into poor judgments and lead to disaster.

To get more information and further ideas about character development, choose a trait from any list in adult types (for example, in the Adventurer type) and refer to chapter fourteen, "The Big Index", where it will be listed under Traits. The index points you to other places where that particular trait appears.

There are six virtues and their component character strengths[1] that research has found to be important for a healthy adulthood. These traits can be incorporated into many types.

VIRTUE	CHARACTER TRAITS
Wisdom and knowledge	Creativity, curiosity, open-mindedness, love of learning, and perspective
Courage	Bravery, persistence, integrity, and vitality
Humanity	Love, kindness, and social intelligence
Justice	Citizenship, fairness, and leadership
Transcendence	Forgiveness, humility, prudence, and self-regulation
Temperance	Appreciation of beauty and excellence, gratitude, hope, humor, and spirituality

Traits of Adult Personality Types

THE ADVENTURER

The themes of the Adventurer are excitement and boldness. He may look and sound ordinary, but underlying most activities is the need to feel like a warrior, often unknowingly at the cost of others. More men are Adventurers than are women, because culture and socialization inhibit this type in growing girls; however, there have always been daring Adventurer women like Amelia Earhart.

[1] APA Monitor on Psychology (July/August, 2004).

INTERNAL

- Energetic; always on the go
- Bold, dominant
- Often unaware of the feelings of others
- A leader; wants own way
- Competitive
- Fickle, changeable

INTERPERSONAL

- Lives on the edge; needs excitement to feel alive
- Seeks thrills, is prepared to try anything, especially activities with speed or danger
- Enjoys the spotlight; likes to perform
- Is not bothered by rules or social convention
- Has an overt interest in sex; likes having a partner/spouse

NORMAL → EXTREME

- Thick-skinned → lacking in guilt
- Confidence → poor judgment
- Forceful → ruthless
- Extroverted → hostile
- Rebellious → anti-authority
- Assertive → aggressive
- Independent → disagreeable
- Impulsiveness (e.g., in making decisions) → dangerous to self or others

Traits of the Adventurer usually appear in childhood as boldness or risk-taking and mature over a lifetime. On the positive side, the Adventurer type contains fun-loving, entertaining, and gregarious elements. Negatively, this adult may ignore rules, run roughshod over the feelings of others, and bark orders. Not surprisingly, the Adventurer is drawn to careers with excitement—pilot, stock trader, salesperson, or managerial positions—but in the extreme can become a con artist.

NEW INFORMATION Why do people close their eyes to risk? Why do they drive cars without seatbelts, smoke, engage in unsafe sex? Some possible answers include: unrealistic levels of optimism; impaired judgment as the result of drugs, alcohol, or depression; inability to recognize the consequences of their behavior; and certain personality traits, such as sensation seeking or assertiveness.[2]

THE BOSS

The Bossy person wants to be in the limelight, whether at home, work, or play. The themes that run through the life of a Bossy are control (of self and others) and having things her own way.

INTERNAL

- Driven by aggressive energy; competitive
- Confident
- Stubborn; values self-control
- Closed-minded; rigid thinker, dogmatic in opinions
- Serious
- Rarely guilty or ashamed
- Mistrustful of compassion or kindness
- Low tolerance for frustration
- Status-seeker

INTERPERSONAL

- Is not deterred by punishment or pain
- Is thick-skinned and insensitive to social approval, but sensitive to comments or attacks

[2] APA Monitor on Psychology (April, 2003).

- Gets the job done; good at coercion
- Tunes in to the weaknesses of others, then uses that knowledge
- Can humiliate others; sarcastic
- Justifies aggression: "You've got to take care of yourself'"
- Is boastful, brusque, belligerent
- Wants to be the leader in any group
- Does not concede to or acknowledge another point of view
- Wants to get her own way
- Avoids warmth or intimacy
- Does not recognize the impact of her acts
- Sees others as puppets to be manipulated; is domineering

NORMAL → EXTREME

- Aggressive → reckless
- Quarrelsome → combative
- Desire to control others → sadistic
- Headstrong and forceful → abusive
- Quick responses → aggressive if threatened
- Desire to force ideas on others → tyrannical
- Directness → chronic rudeness
- Unwillingness to be a follower → a heckler

As a youngster, the Bossy type can be seen in adherence to doing chores, watching younger siblings, leading activities, or keeping things organized. Later, that same aggressive energy can be positively channeled into leadership or turn insistent and relentless, cold, demanding, or humiliating. The Bossy gravitates to careers like hotel or restaurant management, campaign manager, advertising executive, or school superintendent—jobs that allow dominance but can become abusive. Mild traits are useful in sales, medical, and psychological or psychiatric fields. Often the Bossy is able to cloak negative traits in socially responsible work, such as business takeovers or the military.

WARM UP Globalization is likely to be one of the dominant forces in the psychological development of people in the twenty-first century. Young people all over the world are affected by and aware of a global culture that exists beyond their local culture. Identity used to be created in large part by prescribed social roles. As a consequence of globalization, identity becomes increasingly about individual choice. People see a variety of paths to love and work, not simply those in their family, town, or country. This can be confusing or liberating, but certainly we will see hybrid, complex, bicultural and multicultural identities. Write a scene that shows a young adult struggling with his or her creation of a role different than would have been expected.[3]

THE CONFORMIST

The Conformist is similar to the Conventional (see the following personality type), but has more of a flavor of compliance.

INTERNAL

- Compliant; goes along with others
- Responsible
- Rule-follower; uncreative

INTERPERSONAL

- Follows rather than leads
- Likes laws more than freedom

NORMAL → EXTREME

- Discipline → inflexibility
- Morality → rigid behavior and preaching

The Conformist child will never rock the boat, and neither will the adult. The goal is to live within the rules and the laws. This type runs into trouble when he goes beyond law-abiding citizen to intolerant, unthinking bully. The Conformist makes a fine assistant or second-in-command manager who implements the rules or a worker in a structured environment.

[3] Arnett (2002).

THE CONVENTIONAL

A Conventional lives by the rules and prefers the established ways; the status quo is vastly preferable to change.

INTERNAL

- Conservative in social matters, religion, and morals
- Respectful of established ideas; prefers the familiar to the unfamiliar
- Nostalgic
- Oblivious to the need to try new things or do things differently
- Belief in the motto "If it's not broken, don't fix it" taken to the extreme
- Opposed to change: new food, new technology, or new vacation spots
- Resistant to new styles, fashions, and trends
- Dependent on others; strong ties to family and work

INTERPERSONAL

- Is loyal, has long-lasting friendships
- Is dependable and consistent
- Lacks trust in innovation; prefers the status quo
- Avoids situations that are strange, too easy, or too difficult
- Is baffled by developmental transitions, such as alterations in family dynamics

NORMAL → EXTREME

- Personal identity which depends on sameness → a strange, secret life
- Fear of change → mesmerized by people totally different from oneself

The Conventional is often created as a reaction to lack of consistency or stability in childhood. Chaos and strange experiences can be humiliating to a child, who may grow up to take great solace in predictability. Later in adulthood, distress will come from children or friends who challenge the Conventional's ideas. Careers that are traditional and secure—clergy or teaching—are satisfying.

THE CREATOR

The Creator's life gets meaning from the ability to produce new ideas or products.

INTERNAL

- Artistic, intuitive, sensitive
- Observant; sees the big picture
- Persistent
- Unconventional; does not like conformity
- Brainstormer; easily absorbed by ideas
- Introverted; has an internal focus
- Happy in the internal world: a pleasant place and a respite from the outside
- Tolerant of ambiguity; allows disorder
- Fanciful and enthusiastic
- Imaginative; captured by the innovative
- Content with her own company

INTERPERSONAL

- Can work alone for long periods
- Is forgetful, undependable in areas outside of focus
- Can be impractical
- Can be good-natured with others, but not always sensitive to them
- Reacts to stimuli emotionally and subjectively
- Sees the world in unique ways
- Not swayed by the group; indifferent to "what the neighbors are doing"

NORMAL → EXTREME

- Impractical → accident-prone
- Internal → oblivious to others

The child Creator views the world in unique ways and the need to express herself only gets stronger over time. The Creator's needs may be demonstrated in the arts but could also find outlets in math, puzzles, or projects of her own design.

Creators gravitate to artistic, internal occupations such as poet or writer, or quiet work such as researcher, composer, arborist, or geologist. They are better suited for independent work than corporate life.

 WARM UP Write three paragraphs in which your mother interacts with a character created from one of the types in this chapter.

THE DEPENDENT

The Dependent's world revolves around having his needs met. These traits go beyond what is normally expected for a particular time of life, even in youth or during periods of trauma or illness.

INTERNAL

- Shy, humble, lacks self-confidence
- Troubled by own anger or aggressiveness
- Procrastinator; has difficulty initiating projects
- Easily flustered; becomes fearful and anxious
- Reliant on others, which prohibits development of independence
- Willing to take on unpleasant tasks out of desire to be liked
- Lacking in self-confidence; sees oneself as inefficient and powerless
- Fearful of abandonment

INTERPERSONAL

- Wants to be taken care of, but fears disappointment
- Tries to elicit care from others; feels unable to manage well without help
- Needs guidance: "Tell me what you think I should do"
- Craves reassurance and support
- Allows parent, spouse, boss, or friends to make his major life decisions
- Waits for others to take action; yields to others
- Fears losing approval; fears evaluation

- Acquiescence to others → painfully submissive
- Mild → clingy
- Need of others → a quick and indiscriminate attachment to people
- Difficulty in expressing disagreement → silence
- Consideration → excessive deference and self-sacrifice
- Difficulty making decisions → others governing life

Although some of the Dependent's traits may be inborn, others develop in response to circumstance; for example, a child who is terrified by a parent's illness or threatened abandonment. Some Dependents had an authoritarian parent: This encouraged giving in to maintain relationships. Others had an overprotective parent who inadvertently caused the Dependent to believe that he was unable to function without guidance. The Dependent is willing to listen and obey if she or he gets reassurance in return. They seek work, play, and people who will provide approval and instruction; they rarely show much sparkle or creativity because that is too risky. The Dependent gravitates to work as a bank teller, clerk, or court stenographer, where initiative is not required. The Dependent type is focused on pleasing others, to the exclusion of pleasing him- or herself.[4]

THE ECCENTRIC

The Eccentric marches to the beat of a different drummer. He is genuinely different from the norm and may appear weird to others.

INTERNAL

- Self-absorbed, forgetful, impractical
- Better with abstract ideas than real situations and people
- Conveys the attitude of being burdened
- Engaged in internal dialogue
- "Lone wolf": works well alone; frustrates others
- Usually absorbed in the pursuit of some talent, gift, or skill

[4] Bornstein and Bower (1996).

INTERPERSONAL

- Distorts and misreads the behavior of others; socially inept
- Can be interesting to others
- Picks up and drops conversations at odd points
- Remains out of touch with trends and conventions
- Is uninterested in others in any practical way—and it shows
- Does not intend to harm others, but is oblivious to social cues
- Demonstrates strange and unusual behaviors

NORMAL → EXTREME

- Out of touch → isolated

Eccentric youth do not always do well since childhood is such a time of conformity, but with like-minded friends, they manage. It is easier for adults who can control more aspects of their lives, interests, social settings, and careers. The Eccentric gravitates to careers that are solitary, such as research, or work that is abstract, such as math or computers.

THE EXTROVERT

Extroverts are, if not the most fascinating of characters, among the most normal and least pathological. Extroverts truly like people, enjoy crowds, and flourish in energetic activities.

INTERNAL

- Outgoing, not introspective
- Not easily intimidated
- Talkative
- Optimistic in outlook; sees the hopeful side
- Expressive, enthusiastic, and gregarious
- Immoderate emotionally

INTERPERSONAL

- Belongs to groups and participates in activities
- Enjoys being with others; avoids being alone
- Is friendly; seeks social situations
- May not understand other people's depression or anxiety

NORMAL → EXTREME

- Friendly → flighty, lacking intimacy, superficial

The natural friendliness of Extroverts is an asset from childhood on. The irony of this type is that their love of contact with people requires no intimacy. It works for them—they are happier people than introverts. The Extrovert does well as a youth camp director, counselor, high school teacher, or missionary—any work in which there is a good deal of superficial contact with people.

 NEW INFORMATION Anger is found in most adult types. It is a basic human emotion that can be used to your character's advantage or disadvantage.

Anger has positive value. Historically, where would the civil rights or women's suffrage movements be if people had remained indifferent? On the relationship level, anger can clarify problems in relationships and thereby strengthen them. Anger also increases a person's sense of control compared to people who express fear rather than anger. Anger also seems to have some power in the workplace. People see colleagues who express anger as having higher status than those who express sadness or guilt. Getting angry also seems to have an advantage in deal-making with strangers: When strangers negotiate, the person who appears angry gains concessions; his opponent cannot judge his limits and sees the anger as toughness. This advantage disappears when the negotiation is between people who know each other well.[5]

Unfortunately, being angry simplifies people's judgments and leaves them prone to bias. Also, angry, hostile people are more prone to heart attacks: Their cardiovascular health suffers from the stress of staying angry for long periods. Anger

[5] van Kleef (2004).

and anxiety increase vulnerability to illnesses, compromise the immune system, exacerbate pain, and increase risk of death from cardiovascular disease.

On the other hand, people who cope with their anger constructively, such as working on the problem that made them angry, have healthier blood pressure than people with fewer coping skills.

Men are socialized to express their anger and act it out. They demonstrate more physical aggression and impulsivity. Women, socialized to keep their anger down, have received the message that anger is unfeminine and unattractive. This may lead them to behave in passive-aggressive ways instead of directly expressing anger.[6]

THE FALL GUY/GIRL

The Fall Guy or Girl is notable for being in the wrong place at the wrong time with the wrong people.

INTERNAL

- Trustful of people
- Gullible
- Underachiever; ambition is undirected
- Good humored; rarely hostile
- Narrow in range of interests
- Conventional
- Not analytical

INTERPERSONAL

- Gets taken advantage of by others
- Is socially at ease; pleasant
- Does not exercise good judgment about people; is overly trusting
- Is unaware of motives of others
- Tends to be a follower rather than leader

NORMAL → EXTREME

- Following others → danger from lack of judgment

[6] Tiedens, (2003); Lerner (2003); Davidson (2003).

There is always some kid who doesn't get the joke, who falls for the scam, who remains innocent. The Fall Guy becomes a trusting adult, but is the target for every get-rich-quick scheme around. There are no special careers for the Fall Guy, but he too often gravitates to scams that harm his savings account.

THE FEARFUL

Life for the Fearful is driven by inhibition and fears of rejection. It dominates the internal world and relations with others.

INTERNAL

- Withdrawn
- Sensitive to criticism
- Self-deprecating
- Non-assertive
- Unhappy
- Aversion to stress

INTERPERSONAL

- Is socially inhibited; uncomfortable in social situations
- Feels inadequate and anxious in the presence of others, but longs for closeness
- Is ultrasensitive to others; restrained in intimate relationships
- Concerned about physical appearance
- Has image of self as socially inept and unattractive
- Fears involvement with others unless certain of being liked
- Belongs to few groups

NORMAL → EXTREME

- Fear of embarrassment → avoiding activities that cause discomfort

When a person starts off shy and serious and, over the years, people and circumstance do nothing to help him change, a Fearful is created. Fear, as dominating factor in life, leads to avoidance of any people or activities that might cause embarrassment or shame. The Fearful type will always be a responder, never an initiator, so careers in which he or she takes orders—for example, assistants or domestic workers—are likely possibilities.

FIGURES AND STATISTICS When we think of heroism, what comes to mind? Firemen rushing into the World Trade Center on 9/11, certainly. Maybe racecar drivers or mountain climbers. We see a lot of men. Wait—adventure-seeking and risk-taking is not heroism! Let's figure out a definition: Heroism consists of courageous actions undertaken to help others, despite the possibility that the actions may result in the helper's injury or death. Suddenly we see female heroes. Statistics on the Righteous (those non-Jewish individuals who helped Jews during World War II), living kidney donors, Peace Corps volunteers, and Doctors of the World—all people doing acts that require courage rather than physical strength—show participation of women equal to or greater than that of men.[7]

THE FLAMBOYANT

Life for the Flamboyant contains love, sex, competition, and disloyalty, always with a lack of authenticity, as if the Flamboyant shows or expresses more than is really felt. Flamboyant women lack close relationships with other women.

INTERNAL

- Dramatic, easily upset, and emotionally unstable
- Unaware of own seductive or aggressive behaviors
- Always conscious of a sexual undercurrent; interprets others' behaviors as sexual; then feels like the evil seductress/seducer
- Susceptible to poor self-esteem and self-blame
- Indirect and devious
- Naive and simplistic, immature, excessively emotional, and childish
- Depressed because she feels like a bad person
- Not a clear thinker; feels insubstantial

[7] Becker (2004).

- Vague; has an unclear picture of self; does not see self as responsible for actions
- Attention-seeker; demands nurturing and support
- Dramatic; appears phony; provides an ongoing melodrama for others
- Prone to develop physical symptoms (headaches, weakness, chest pains) under stress
- Emotionally overdone; histrionic; positive and negative feelings are both expressed flamboyantly

INTERPERSONAL

- Seems "flaky," flighty, and insubstantial to others
- May see others as sex objects
- Creates triangulated relationships (as the "other" man or woman)
- Is competitive with individuals of the same gender
- Is exhibitionistic; dramatic in social situations
- Is vain, promiscuous, and jealous
- Has superficial but important relationships because of the need for attention
- Is manipulative; plays games to try to get whatever she wants

NORMAL → EXTREME

- Attention seeking → suicidal gestures without intention to do harm
- Intense feelings → disorganized, overwhelmed, or dysfunctional

Flamboyant traits may be created in childhood if parents have been overly seductive or the child was emotionally or sexually exploited by adults. Normal needs for nurturing are not met, so competitive behavior becomes the norm. The heightened emotion makes others perceive them as insubstantial. The need for attention remains and is channeled into adult flirtatiousness, although Flamboyants are not particularly sexually promiscuous. The Flamboyant gravitates toward careers where emotional experience can be directly shared (art, design, media, show business), or work in which intuition is rewarded.

THE HYPER

The Hyper's life is active, but not always with direction. There is movement, but it can occur without progress.

INTERNAL

- Overactive in thought and behavior
- Grandiose; self-centered
- Careless; changeable
- Easily excitable with unstable moods
- Thrill-seeking

INTERPERSONAL

- Is outgoing
- Is active; energetic
- Becomes poor company because of self-centeredness and overactivity

NORMAL → EXTREME

- Excitement → outbursts of euphoria
- Moodiness → explosive anger

Hyper people are easily picked out of a group. As children, they are the ones who are running and jumping, knocking kids over, and breaking knickknacks; sometimes they have explosive tempers. As adults, they can create lives that allow for a high level of activity and motion that satisfies them. They are not the kind of friend or partner who can easily share emotions. Careers that allow for activity, change, and motion (outdoor recreation, construction) work better than still, intellectual pursuits.

WARM UP Time perception is integral to human motivation. People are driven by questions such as:

Is time running out? Do I have extra time? If time is limited, what activities have little meaning? What has great meaning? If I have limited time, what goals cannot be accomplished later? What do I feel when I realize that I cannot stop time?

Write a scene where two best friends are mildly drunk and plagued by these issues. Would the scene be very different if the friends were thirty years old rather than fifty years old?

THE LONER

The Loner's life seems to be directionless: He drifts with little strong attachment to anyone. The Loner's type is not to be confused with the emotional numbness or freezing of temporary states of withdrawal experienced when individuals are in strange circumstances, such as being an immigrant or reacting to tragedy.

INTERNAL

- Comfortable with solitude
- Reserved; rarely expresses anger or any other emotion
- Passive in the face of tragedy; may appear unambitious
- Inadequate at responding to significant life events
- Unwilling to reveal himself easily
- Harsh toward self
- Prefers hobbies and interests that allow him to be alone: computers, math

INTERPERSONAL

- Appears bland and cold; is indifferent to the approval of others
- Does not engage in the usual social smiles and nods
- Is oblivious to social cues; unable to bond with others
- Is detached; does not want social relationships and lacks skill to deal with others
- Avoids emotional entanglements; very restricted emotionally
- Is uninterested in sex; often does not marry and does not change if he marries
- Appears superficial or self-absorbed due to lack of interest in others
- Has few, if any, close friends; may be close to a sister or brother
- Does not get satisfaction from being a member of a family

- Finds social closeness difficult, maybe even terrifying
- Considers other people a source of pain, not comfort

NORMAL → EXTREME

- Solitary ways → gravitating to a harsh environment
- Detachment → retreating to ensure safety

Loners often feel like they shouldn't exist, so they remain alone, emotionally as well as physically. The world of people is a frightening place. Loners make little eye contact with people; they try to tune out unpleasant experiences and avoid rejection and failure. Even a Loner's demeanor, with dead eyes and stiff posture, tells people that the Loner needs distance. Loners gravitate to careers that have little contact with others, whether it is a guard on the late-night shift or a technical job involving machines.

 WARM UP Write a quick paragraph showing what happens when friendly neighbor invites a Loner to the neighborhood block party.

THE MAN'S MAN

The Man's Man appears one-dimensional because only certain qualities are allowed to emerge. The counterpart to the Man's Man is the Ultra-Feminine (discussed on pages 45–46).

INTERNAL

- Exaggeratedly masculine
- Coarse; demanding and hard
- Fearful of weakness
- Secretive of any powerlessness or impotence
- Adventurous and aggressive
- Worldly and sexually experienced
- Ambitious; needs to win
- Compulsively masculine with no desire to change

INTERPERSONAL

- Lacks individuality and originality
- Emphasizes male interests; likes traditional male pursuits
- Is inflexible about masculinity
- Responds to trouble with aggression
- Is likely to have rocky relationships with women; may look for Ultra-Feminine woman

NORMAL → EXTREME

- Masculinity → being one-dimensional

Masculinity comes first, before tending to emotional needs or family occasions. The Man's Man loves sports, guns, and physical activity of all sorts, regardless of his aptitude. Any relationship that requires much attention will be in jeopardy because he is out being adventurous and aggressive. A Man's Man can work in many fields, as long as they allow time for his real passions; however, bold, risky careers such as racecar driving would be extremely satisfying.

THE MANIPULATOR

This person seeks control through domination of others and usually uses charm to achieve her ends.

INTERNAL

- True self is hidden from others
- Interested in looking good; puts effort into appearance
- Self-justifying regarding her bad behavior
- Cunning and deceptive
- Intent upon exercising and maintaining control
- Verbal, articulate and compelling
- Subtly aggressive

INTERPERSONAL

- Manipulates others in ways that obscure clear, objective evidence of aggression
- Can make others doubt their gut hunches that they're being taken advantage of or abused
- Takes advantage of vulnerabilities of others
- Sees relationships as a game and people as pawns, objects to be used
- Looks for people to deceive and manipulate
- Enforces self-worth through submission from others
- Is terrified of failure
- Desires domination as main goal
- Denies responsibility for actions, blames others
- Expects others to be selfish and manipulative

NORMAL → EXTREME

- Controlling → actions that dominate others and physical abuse

The Manipulator is governed by the need to control people and situations, whether it is done under the guise of charm, sweetness, dependency, or more aggressive deceptions. Domination makes her feel safe and effective; anything else is frightening and threatens a fragile sense of self-esteem. Business, sales, and other careers that have deal-making as their base are ideal professions, but individuals can also gravitate toward law or academics.

THE PASSIVE-AGGRESSIVE

For the Passive-Aggressive, days are lived under a negative cloud. He tries hard, but always feels misunderstood.

INTERNAL

- Jealous
- Reserved, pessimistic, and ill-tempered
- Sulky, resentful, and sour (this may be hidden)

- Hostility is suppressed, leaving passivity on view
- Incapable of remaining passive, so a bad mood erupts
- Willing to try hard, but expects the worst
- Convinced he is chronically misunderstood
- Anxious from the tension that arises from swings between passivity and aggression

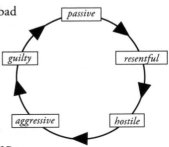

INTERPERSONAL

- Nags others often
- Is not physically abusive but has short-lived bursts of temper
- Has intense relationships
- Dislikes anyone having power over him
- Infuriates other people
- Behaves in indirect ways
- Tries to comply, but cannot keep it up for long

NORMAL → EXTREME

- Passivity → actions against those people who are close

Passive-Aggressive types seem friendly, mild, and easygoing at first, then annoying. They make intense rebellious stands at odd times and are subtly oppositional at other times. They are attracted to tough, controlling partners because that satisfies the passivity, but their aggression eventually emerges against partners or anyone else who has thwarted them. Passive-Aggressive types are found in all professions.

THE PERFECTIONIST

The Perfectionist has the desire to be not excellent, but perfect. Her standards are extremely high, and failure to meet those standards causes great stress.

Many believe that they will be valued only if they are perfect. They experience a sense of pressure coupled with hopelessness and helplessness: "The better I do, the better I am expected to do."

INTERNAL

- Demanding; has exceptionally high standards
- Driven to succeed and to avoid failure
- Very vulnerable to criticism
- Hard worker; tries to avoid criticism and defects
- Unable to turn to others for help
- Susceptible to intense self-scrutiny and self-doubt

INTERPERSONAL

- Constantly attempts to prove herself
- Wants others to meet her standards of perfection
- Believes she must meet the high standards of others to be acceptable[8]
- Advertises her own perfection
- Avoids situations in which she might appear imperfect[9]

NORMAL → EXTREME

- Self-criticism → depression
- High standards → intense faultfinding of others
- Fear of imperfection → lying

Some Perfectionists are born, others are made. Winning love through excellent grades, beauty, or performance can drive the Perfectionist in childhood. By adulthood, the Perfectionist drives herself. This type is attractive because of their energy, ambition, and talent, but they get dark and angry when faced with disappointments. Perfectionists are found in all careers and are great workers—if they can ever complete their "imperfect" projects.

[8] Blatt, (1995). [9] APA Monitor on Psychology (November, 2003).

THE PERSONABLE

A Personable makes for one of the best friends or colleagues around because of all the easy, delightful qualities she possesses.

INTERNAL

- Unruffled, calm, mature, and cooperative
- Flexible, warm, easygoing, casual, and trusting
- Not creative; better with people than with ideas
- Good-hearted; accommodating
- Hardworking
- Not a risk taker

INTERPERSONAL

- Is participatory; sees the good in people
- Is insightful about people and alert to environmental cues
- Likes working in groups rather than alone
- Gets along with everyone; well liked
- Joins groups and clubs to make friends, not for causes

NORMAL → EXTREME

- Fondness for people and dislike of being alone → hasty marriage
- Enthusiasm → hasty, poor decisions
- Ability to see the good in people → gullibility or being manipulated
- Interest in being with people → hypochondria to get attention
- Desire for others' approval → compromising one's own beliefs
- Too much socializing → not getting work done

Personable types have plenty of good friends and are adept at making new ones; this can lead to being overwhelmed and losing sight of her personal priorities. Although they are natural leaders because they understand how to get consensus, they are not usually ambitious or creative enough to be in the top position. They can shine in careers like human resources, real estate, or any work involving public contact.

THE PROBLEM SOLVER

The Problem Solver is someone we all want to have in our corner when we get into a mess, but he can stumble by being too capable for others and not capable enough for himself.

INTERNAL

- Resourceful; reliable and mature
- Able to face reality, but may lack imagination
- Disciplined; can exercise restraint
- Stable; not easily influenced by emotions of others
- Emotionally steady with no wide swings or dips in feelings
- Internally motivated; can achieve goals
- Pleased with himself; little self-blame

INTERPERSONAL

- Sticks to projects; perseveres
- Is not easily disturbed
- Is savvy in relationships; knows how to get his point across
- Does not panic easily; good under fire
- Makes the best out of what life offers

NORMAL → EXTREME

- Coping skills → excessive self-sufficiency

The traits of Problem Solvers are usually in evidence in childhood when their efficiency is notable. In adulthood, their abilities continue to be rewarded in many fields such as engineering or law. Their process goes like this: Recognize a problem → generate options → make choices → follow through.

THE RESILIENT

Life is no different for Resilients than for others, but they have the remarkable ability to recover from life's losses and disappointments.

INTERNAL

- Happy most of the time
- Productive; has good concentration
- Able to cope with adversity with a minimum of stress
- Motivated; effective problem solver
- Willing and able to take responsibility for her own life
- Possesses a good sense of humor
- Ethical; has high standards
- Able to face problems and take personal control

INTERPERSONAL

- Has personal goals: fame, power, money, career growth, community, children
- Is interested in others as well as in self
- Uses physical activity to combat stress
- Maintains a strong support network[10]

NORMAL TRAITS CAN BECOME → EXTREME TRAITS

- Independence → an inability to depend on others

Resilient types suffer disappointments and feel lost just like everyone else, but they remain confident that they will survive and have mastery over their lives. They have goals which keep them on course, strong social supports, and positive attitudes about life.

THE SHOW-OFF

The Show-Off requires an audience; being alone can feel unrewarding. But for others, being with a Show-Off can seem like being trapped in unending theater.

[10] Flannery (1997).

INTERNAL

- Active and alert
- Intolerant of frustration
- Immature and unhelpful
- Expressive with shifting emotions
- Can be undercontrolled and aggressive
- Ostentatious

INTERPERSONAL

- Is often a show-off, which interferes with relationships
- Is effective with people and tasks
- Is socially outgoing
- Can be oblivious to others
- Wants to be admired
- Is sarcastic
- Has trouble sharing

NORMAL → EXTREME

- Expressive can become → aggressive

Show-Offs can be fun because of their active, outgoing natures. They can also get annoying when they demand excessive attention with little regard for others. Many Show-Offs are able to channel their qualities very well: for example, as courtroom attorneys or in theater work.

 WARM UP Write a scene in which two different personality types go on a blind date to an erotic movie.

THE ULTRA-FEMININE

The Ultra-Feminine is to women what the Man's Man (on pages 37–38) is to men. Not surprisingly, they often wind up together.

INTERNAL

- Stereotypical feminine behaviors
- Exaggerated qualities of naïveté and innocence
- Nurturing, passive, and soft
- Tendency to take on traditional feminine roles
- Constricted emotionally; self-pitying
- Helpless and dependent
- Indirect, modest, and coy
- Idealistic

INTERPERSONAL

- Has difficulty expressing anger or handling conflict
- Is accepting of stereotypical male behaviors
- Boosts men's egos; flirts
- Is submissive and yielding; seductive
- May doubt own adequacy as a woman

NORMAL → EXTREME

- Flirtatiousness → loss of herself

Ultra-Feminine types have usually been rewarded for their femininity. Girls and women are not threatened by them; boys and men want to flirt with or care for them. The downside is they are not seen as substantial, so an Ultra-Feminine is seldom the one people turn to for help in a time of crisis. On a personal level, they have avoided negative emotions, so when they are confronted with conflict, they have little experience with feelings of pain and rage. Ultra-Feminines gravitate to nurturing positions like teacher, childcare provider, or dental assistant.

THE VICTIM TYPE

Life for the Victim is filled with themes of lack of self-determination and control. Victims are always convinced that others are more in command than they are.

INTERNAL

- Filled with rage that is buried, and therefore not strongly felt
- Unaware of his own hostile behaviors
- Troubled by feelings of weakness and impotence; wants to feel safe
- Pessimistic and negative about life
- Put-upon; feels and acts burdened
- Rarely happy; pleasure results in anxiety so it must be avoided
- Tendency to turn self-denial into social concerns: "I cannot buy new shoes because others have none"
- Inhibited, serious, responsible, and unassuming
- Emotionally flat; has no deep feelings either of love or hate
- Vaguely depressed and helpless when left alone

INTERPERSONAL

- Feels mistreated; distrustful of others
- Tries to please others, but self-sacrifice leads to bitterness and more suffering
- Is convinced that he is constantly suffering and is proud that he or she is able to "take it"
- Wants to avoid abandonment
- Continues loving others who may treat him badly
- Is unable to be self-protective because of constant self-blame
- Is demanding; inordinate need for affection
- Is unable to receive pleasure; has sexual dysfunction in relationships
- Depends on others, but relationships often repeat humiliation and defeat
- Complains but does not change; displays defeat to the world; says, "No one can help"
- Frustrates those who want to help, makes them ineffectual and arouses their anger
- Is indirect; appears compliant but may be secretly manipulative

- May have learned to enjoy defeat as a way of surviving with pride
- Tries to "be good," and "goes along" to avoid being alone
- Wants to arouse guilt in others, and hopes that guilt will become love

NORMAL → EXTREME

- Lack of self-care → trouble; for example, marrying an alcoholic or sticking with an abusive boss
- Unassertiveness → being endlessly stuck
- Proud of sacrifice, being able to "take it" → depression and suffering
- Fear of being alone → denial of danger from others
- Confusion of mistreatment with affection → poor judgment of abusive behaviors
- Need to avoid abandonment → verbal, physical, or sexual abuse to be endured

The Victim feels impotent from an early age. He has little success with independence so anger grows, but remains hidden. The Victim has no belief that he can succeed alone, gain respect, or make effective changes. Therefore, loyalty to bosses, friends, or partners changes from an admirable trait to a trap that he cannot leave, even after mistreatment.

CHAPTER three

Child and Adolescent Types

IN THIS CHAPTER

- *Traits of Infancy and Early Childhood* • *Traits of Middle Childhood*
- *Traits of Adolescence* • *Early Adult Transition*

Children are not miniature adults; their personalities are not yet fully formed. Therefore, children and adolescents do not fit into defined styles like the adults in the previous chapter. However, children and adolescents can be expected to show certain traits based on age and stage of development. This chapter provides the traits associated with normal development and some of the milder ways in which young people run into trouble. Other chapters provide additional information about children and adolescents: Chapter four describes more severe disturbances; chapter seven includes information about children of divorced parents; chapter eight has facts about how birth order affects children, as well as othr familial relationships; chapter nine contains some child and adolescent traumas; and chapter ten explains adolescent substance abuse, addictions, and eating disorders.

Traits Associated With Childhood Poverty

The following traits of poverty may help plot development and emerging personality traits and explain the backgrounds of one of your characters. Poverty often means:

- Greater levels of violence in the community
- More family separations and more housing relocations
- More neighborhood crime
- Harsher or more punitive parenting
- Less social and emotional support for young parents when they are new at parenting
- Fewer resources in the neighborhood and in the school
- Fewer books and more television; no computers or technology
- Less parental involvement in the school
- Fewer qualified teachers
- Greater exposure to unsanitary drinking water, lead-based paint, and pollution
- Homes with structural defects, rodents, or poor heating. More accidents resulting from lack of smoke detectors, fire extinguishers, gated stairs, or locked storage closets[1]

Traits of Infancy and Early Childhood

THE FIRST YEAR

BIRTH TO TWO MONTHS

Some form of a "self" (a single, distinct, integrated body that experiences feelings and has intentions) probably exists before birth. Other aspects of the

[1] Evans (2004).

self, such as the ability to plan, reflect, put experience into language, and share knowledge, require maturation.[2]

The newborn is far more of a person than many people believe; her days are filled with periods of alert inactivity when she is wakeful but not busy or eating. Babies are born with individual temperaments that can be seen most clearly during times of stress. In the chart below, the different dimensions of temperament are listed in the left column; on the right, the range of temperament gives you a continuum of possibilities from which to choose.

DIMENSIONS OF NEWBORN TEMPERAMENT

DIMENSION	RANGE OF TEMPERAMENT
Motor Activity	Listless/quiet → Restless/Energetic
Mood	Placid/easy to soothe → Quick to cry/Irritable
Approach/Withdraw	Passive/avoids new things → Active/Seeks stimulation
Distractibility	Easy to distract → Stays focused
Attention	Short attention span → Persistent
Response	Shows little intensity → High-energy reactions
Sensibility	Low threshold of response → Tolerates change
Regularity	Regular functions → Unpredictable
Impulsiveness	Restrained → Impetuous

During infancy, the world is a physical place. A newborn's pleasure comes from sucking, feeding, and being held—all physical activities. When hunger grows and sweeps painfully through the infant, he cries out in deep, gasping breaths.[3] Each child is born with preferences about what is pleasing to look at, but sunshine is a common favorite. The stimulation of the light coming through the window combined with the sounds of people moving in the house excites his entire nervous system

[2] Stern (1985). [3] Stern (1985).

and captures his attention. The physical world remains central but expands as baby learns to grasp objects, turn over, and explore his limited surroundings.

We rarely see a young child as the central character in a story (unless it is a story written for children), but the following traits provide accuracy for any minor characters and give you a basis for interaction among characters, such as between parent and child.

Neglect

Rumination disorder—the repeated regurgitation and rechewing of food without an underlying medical condition—may be a sign of neglect, high stress levels, lack of stimulation, or poor parenting. This condition is usually seen in young children three months to twelve months old. Another trait of neglected infants is poor attachments: either the failure to respond to others, or the reverse, the indiscriminate attachment to others.

Physical

- Knows his mother; turns to the smell or voice of his mother
- Prefers seeing faces to looking at patterns
- Likes the human voice better than other sounds
- Actively moves his arms and legs; his eyes examine the world and he seeks stimulation
- Mimics what he sees: if Dad sticks his tongue out, the baby will slowly try to do the same

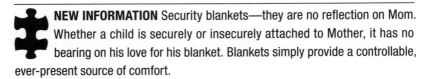 **NEW INFORMATION** Security blankets—they are no reflection on Mom. Whether a child is securely or insecurely attached to Mother, it has no bearing on his love for his blanket. Blankets simply provide a controllable, ever-present source of comfort.

TWO TO EIGHT MONTHS

Physical

- Begins to explore the environment and sits up with the aid of her own hands

- Tries to engage adults in play, where before she was only a passive participant

Interpersonal

- Begins to recognize her separateness as a person from her mother
- Becomes curious
- Seems to know the difference between inanimate objects, such as toys, and people

The infant already seems to be a more complete person; she is beginning to know herself and intentionally moves her body. The baby becomes more social. She smiles, coos, and makes eye contact for long periods. She likes human faces but can be frightened by grimaces. Startled by breezes, high and low noises, and changing sights, she remains calm as long as she senses her family close by.[4]

EIGHT TO TWELVE MONTHS

Physical

- Sits up; crawls
- Grasps objects, hair, and toys
- Manipulates objects with hands; learns through touching
- Is drawn to pictures that reflect his mood: chooses a drawing similar to his own sad face
- Has trouble sleeping due to accumulated stimulation from activity

Internal

- Is fearful; stranger anxiety is shown as distress in the presence of unfamiliar people
- Recognizes other people as separate from himself with distinct bodies and different thoughts

Interpersonal

- Demonstrates ability to share when he points to an object and checks back with his mother

[4] ibid.

- Enjoys and understands teasing; for example, holding a toy out and pulling it away
- Changes into a more sociable person and loves an audience

A noticeable change occurs when the infant gains subjectivity, the knowledge that he has a mind and so do others. This milestone allows him to communicate differently, and life becomes increasingly interpersonal. He also loves to show off his increasing physical accomplishments. Peek-a-boo is a favorite game. He also remembers where toys are hidden and excitedly attempts to find objects.

Strangers are disturbing, but the infant is now firmly attached to his family and babysitter, and not just because they feed him. He wants their company for emotional reasons—soothing, comfort, or help regulate his ups and downs.[5]

WARM UP Girls have more leeway than boys to play with "other-gender" toys. They will even be indulged in this, as long as they also have appropriate feminine behaviors and looks. Write a scene in which a conventional granddad takes an unconventional child to the toy store.

TODDLERHOOD

The ability to walk marks the beginning of toddlerhood with lurching steps usually starting between ten and sixteen months. Now we begin to understand more of the developing internal world of the child.

AGE ONE

Physical
- Has rounded body and walks, or "toddles" with head thrust forward
- Thinks with her feet; walking allows her to have her first taste of independence
- Explores, bumps into people, and knocks into objects
- Loves to run and be caught, climb stairs, and close doors
- Likes to grab things, throw, and pull at objects
- Has improved hand movements but no fine finger abilities

[5] ibid.

Internal

- Is uninhibited; touches and tries things that make this age dangerous
- Is thrilled with self and feels omnipotent
- Has increased tension from interaction with the world and craves reassurance
- Seeks comfort in hair twirling, thumb sucking, a blanket or other security object, rocking, or head banging

Interpersonal

- Still likes to be carried even though she can walk
- Gains separation from caregiver through walking
- Likes to explore, but checks back to be sure Mom is still in sight[6]

The infant can toddle happily across the room until she trips over a cord and brings down the lamp. Then, frightened by the crash, she bumps into a ceramic figurine. Hearing her mother yell, she bursts into tears and crawls back to her blanket.

AGE TWO

Physical

- Is learning to control body; turning sharp corners requires preparation
- Still has trouble going to sleep because of accumulated stimulation
- Loves throwing things
- Deals with toilet training; begins self-control of body

Internal

- Is often overtired and overexcited
- Fears noises from vacuum cleaner, animals, toilet flushes, or draining tub water
- Lives in the present; little sense of past or future

Interpersonal

- Begins to deal with sibling rivalry because he has to share attention and love

[6] Ames, Ilg, and Haber, (1982).

- Throws temper tantrums that include screaming, throwing himself on the floor, hitting, kicking, and biting, often because he is frustrated by his limited ability to communicate

As the toddler ends his second year, he makes the transition from toddler to child. Physical activity gets smoother. An important change, psychologically, is that he now retains an image of his parents in their absence and understands that they will return. The development of language is a major milestone for the young child. Language emerges during the second year, and at twenty-four months, most toddlers have a vocabulary of more than fifty words. During the next six months, they learn to create small sentences. Their favorite phrases are "me do it" and "no." The struggle between independence and dependence occupies toddlers during this period.

Victimization

Unfortunately, not all children are cherished. Children suffer more victimization than do adults because they are weak, small, cannot retaliate, and have little choice about their associates. Some forms of victimization are conventional; others are unique to children. Pandemic (affecting many children) victimization includes sibling assault, bullying, verbal and physical abuse, spanking and other forms of corporal punishment, and witnessing crimes committed against family. Acute (affecting some children) forms include physical abuse, neglect, abduction by a family member, and childhood prostitution. The extraordinary (affecting few but garnering attention) forms are homicide and non-family abduction.[7]

AGE THREE

Physical

- Has command over her body; runs smoothly, walks securely, and loves outdoor play
- Begins to learn gender differences

[7] Finkelhor (1994).

- Develops ways of playing depending on gender: boys play rougher and more physically than girls

Internal

- Wants to do things correctly ("Dis way?") and conforms to routines
- Plays more imaginatively with dolls whether a boy or girl
- Becomes interested in books and music
- Likes humor; for example, enjoys being asked, "Is your coat green?" when it is red

Interpersonal

- Is friendlier to others: "We go for a walk?"
- Is capable of sympathy and is pleased when she pleases others
- Listens, wants to learn, and likes to tell stories of her adventures
- Enjoys language and uses it to ask "How?" "What?" "Why?" and "When?"

The child has become a psychological being. She has reached another landmark: She thinks about and makes up explanations for the things she sees around her. She can now create a story from the diverse details in her life, and she likes to talk about things.

WARM UP Children cope better with the daily stresses of life when they have parents who express more praise, admiration, and gratitude than threats and anger. The children not only feel better, but also learn to regulate their own emotions, and they gain an understanding of others. Write two paragraphs showing a child imitating a parent's behavior.

AGE FOUR

Physical

- Can do some things by himself, such as play outdoors
- Boys grab genitals as tension reliever
- Has good balance, excessive and energetic drive; can move well and quickly

- Has improved motor skills for tasks like buttoning, or catching a ball with his hands
- Can feed, wash, and dress himself

Internal

- Is exuberant, expansive, and highly sure of himself
- Has extreme emotions: loves a lot; hates a lot; laughs loudly; and cries, kicks, and spits hard
- Enjoys newness and loves exaggeration; uses his fluid imagination
- Develops a vastly increased vocabulary and likes language
- Grasps concept of time and seasons and activities associated with each, such as swimming in the summer

Interpersonal

- Realizes that adults are not all-powerful and that he can get away with mischief
- Hates changes made by parents, such as mom's new haircut
- Is intrigued by bodily functions, he tries out "dirty" words and makes "poo-poo" jokes
- Likes to hear true stories
- Enjoys everyone's humor; changes familiar songs and stories into new, silly versions
- Creates strong friendships and learns how to get along with others
- Is resistant to adult commands; knows his own mind and rejects the suggestions of others
- Goes to bed more easily because he likes to play with books and stuffed animals in bed[8]

The child feels a certain amount of power these days. He is expansive and funny, sometimes going overboard and tempting the other members of his family to squash him. He "loves" or "hates" everything, often without any reason that is apparent to anyone else.

[8] Ames and Ilg (1976).

NEW INFORMATION Socialization into traditional gender roles is apparent at an early age. Girls' Halloween costumes depict beauty queens, princesses, and other images of traditional femininity. Boys' costumes emphasize the warrior theme and are more likely to feature villains.[9]

AGE FIVE

Internal

- Is calmer and quieter than a four-year-old; enjoys life: "Today is my lucky day")
- Feels secure; loves Mother; not adventurous or daring
- Is serious and thoughtful; self-controlled; likes to practice skills like printing name
- Is matter-of-fact, factual, and concrete; likes to be certain and accurate
- Is capable of self-criticism
- Believes that if she does good, good happens; if she does bad, bad happens[10]

Interpersonal

- Usually begins kindergarten, so she meets other children and learns new behaviors
- Is conscious of rules and feels rage when punished unjustly

---

Characteristics of Separation Problems at Five and Six Years Old

- Terrible anxiety about separation from home or parents
- Fears about being alone
- Anxiety seen in physical complaints: "I have a stomachache"
- Anxiety seen in school avoidance: "I'm sick"
- More common in closely knit families than in more distant families
- Problems often precipitated by stress

---

[9] Nelson (2000). [10] Ames and Ilg (1979).

Traits of Middle Childhood

Middle childhood occupies the period from the ages of six to ten, and is generally marked by the ever-widening circles in which children move. The world quickly expands from family to school, peers, and playgrounds. The physical world is replaced in importance by the world of activity and relationships.

Imaginary Friends

Imaginary friends appear when a child is between the ages of three and ten years old. Thirty-one percent of children enjoy an imaginary friend; it is a dramatic but normal aspect of childhood and not indicative of psychotic or pre-psychotic disturbance.

TRAITS OF THE CHILD WHO CREATES AN IMAGINARY FRIEND

- May be a boy or a girl (occurs equally with girls and boys)
- Can temporarily stop playing with imaginary friend when playmate arrives
- May share imaginary friend, but often will not
- May be an only child or one of many siblings; may be quiet or outgoing: not just a phenomenon of only children, lonely children, or quiet children
- May use imaginary friend as a playmate, a conscience, or a way to govern behavior
- Blames imaginary friend for misdeeds
- Displays his or her own best qualities through the imaginary friend: love, care, and kindness
- Has a chance to practice behaviors and work on understanding
- Uses imaginary friend for companionship

TRAITS OF THE FRIEND

- May do exotic activities that a good child cannot allow herself
- Is distinct and has set features

- May require a seat and place setting at dinner
- May never appear in public
- May be an animal; may be the same or opposite sex as the child
- May have an ordinary or a fantastic name
- Disappears, often with no explanation

AGE SIX

Physical

- Begins to demonstrate specific abilities: swimming, dancing, or music

Internal

- Experiences tension, evident in wiggling, kicking table legs, and swinging arms
- Has difficulty making choices, especially with small matters: "I want the blue shirt!" and as soon as Mom takes the clothes from the drawer, "No, I want the red shirt!"
- Feels insecure, so he loves praise and flattery

Interpersonal

- Begins building practical relationships
- Begins to need increased independence from parents, which is gained through school and playmates
- Is competitive and stubborn: "Make me!"
- Does what is asked and then does the opposite; for example, picks up the shoe and drops it again

The child now exists in a larger world and is exposed to many new things: at school, at classmates' houses, and during activities. The potential for exciting learning or new fears increases.

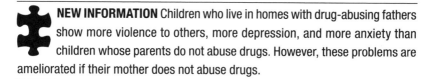 **NEW INFORMATION** Children who live in homes with drug-abusing fathers show more violence to others, more depression, and more anxiety than children whose parents do not abuse drugs. However, these problems are ameliorated if their mother does not abuse drugs.

AGE SEVEN

Physical

- Has an increased awareness of her body; may avoid public bathrooms; dreads exposure

Internal

- Is introverted, absorbed; a time of withdrawal, pulling in, and calming down
- Has worries, inner tensions, and fears: being late for school, the dark, or ghosts
- Becomes aware of herself; wants her own room
- Relieves tension through muttering, mumbling, and wiggling loose teeth
- Plays with pencils; draws and erases
- Can tell time and wants a watch; knows days and months
- Comprehends bad and good as abstract concepts rather than orders from parents

Interpersonal

- Can take other people's needs into account
- Wants mother to listen to complaints, often about dislike for the opposite sex
- Quits telling potty jokes
- Becomes interested in babies and pregnancy but not concerned about sex[11]

At seven, the child is less easily known: There is much life under the surface that is not readily apparent. She watches, her mind rushes, and her hands fidget.

NEW INFORMATION In 2004, US companies spent fifteen billion dollars marketing to children and adolescents—twice the amount spent in 1992. It is not until children are seven or eight years old that they can understand the persuasive intent of advertising.

---

[11] Ames and Haber (1985).

AGE EIGHT

Physical

- Likes to go to interesting places; wants to explore so he walks or bikes
- Is willing to try new food; his world is expanding
- Is physically better coordinated so sports are more rewarding

Internal

- Likes his own objects and money and hoards possessions
- Is aware of his personal qualities, appearance, and others' responses to him
- Evaluates his own failures and mistakes and can think logically
- Is intellectually more curious; enjoys reading
- Is interested in life processes; beginning to understand death as an event in all lives
- Is enthusiastically friendly; less self-centered; recognizes the views of others
- Can picture a series of actions so he can run an errand

Interpersonal

- Is interested in human relationships, even nosy about others
- Becomes jealous of siblings with mother, but has a smoother relationship with father
- Loves to talk and with emphasis: "It was awful!"
- Has a best friend; less play with the opposite gender
- Shares secrets with friends that are not shared with parents
- Likes specific clothes, special brands, board games, dice games, and cards and wants to win
- Has difficulty understanding group compromise: "But I want to play a different game!"[12]

The child suddenly is less afraid. He is expansive; he takes everything he learned at seven and uses it in the world. He has a great love of animals and shows

[12] Ames and Haber (1989).

tenderness to them. Of course, he still feels free to tell his family that "the shirt you bought me sucks!"

Characteristics of the Unpopular Child in Middle Childhood
• Has few social skills for making friends
• Is not adept at managing conflict
• Is aggressive, silly, babyish, and a show-off
• Is anxious; uncertain about own worth
• Is less resourceful than peers; doesn't know how to manage people well

AGE NINE

Physical

- Girls may be ahead of boys in physical development
- Has greater body strength and hand dexterity
- Develops improved coordination and reaction time

Internal

- Lacks self-confidence because of deepening emotions
- Has difficulty making choices and decisions
- Is wrapped up in self and overly sensitive
- Is anxious about health; complains about physical well-being
- Can understand changed rules, but likes standardized rules

Interpersonal

- Resists adult supervision and is critical of others

The child demonstrates what parents call "the sulks." Teasing can no longer be tolerated and parents are often annoying. In return, parents are becoming confused about how to communicate with their child. That is fine with the child, who prefers reading and talking with friends to having conversations and interactions with her parents.

Common Childhood Fears, Ages Six to Twelve

Children between six and twelve years old have many fears, some realistic and others unrealistic. Some common childhood fears for this age group include:

- Animals: fears being attacked by snakes, tigers, or lions
- School anxieties: fears being late for school
- Home and family issues: fears being adopted or that the house will burn down
- Worry for others: fears that a family member will become ill or die or that a friend or family member will have an accident
- Worry for self: fears being followed by a stranger and being kidnapped

AGE TEN

Physical

- Exhibits tension in nail biting or hair twirling
- Puts more emphasis on clothing choice than personal hygiene

GIRL	BOY
• Enjoys activities, such as biking, running, playing sports and table games, collecting things, drawing, writing, and performing plays	• Gravitates to activities such as ball games, biking, table games, collecting things, drawing, and constructing things
• Shows approaching puberty, softening, and a waist; worries about breasts	
• Is more aware of sex than boys; asks more questions	

Internal

- Begins to gain more poise
- Has fewer fears and nightmares[13]

Interpersonal

- Places increasing importance on relationship with friends
- Plays in groups (boys often play in larger groups than girls)
- Learns appropriate competition through organized sports

Peer Groups of Middle Childhood

- Become important around age ten
- Are preferred company to parents
- Give children information about their own roles and status
- Help form attitudes and values
- Shape concepts of adult world
- Allow leadership skills to develop

TRAITS OF ADOLESCENCE

Adolescents authoritatively discuss sex, love, self, friendship, religion, society, justice, and the meaning of life. Conversations are endless, and phones, notes, and e-mail are constant. Beginning at this time, abstract thinking allows adolescents to form concepts so they can think about how one thing relates to another, and about social institutions, and they can question possibilities. The young people are trying desperately to define themselves and gain an identity. For parents, adolescence can be a trying stage because their sons and daughters become egocentric and self-absorbed while they figure out who they are—all very annoying, but normal. For many families, adolescence coincides with parents' midlife issues, an unfortunate collision of events. More dangerously, adolescence brings a sense of invincibility and unlimited

[13] Ames, Ilg, and Baker (1989).

power so young people are more likely to take chances. Accidental deaths are highest for young men between the ages of fourteen and twenty-four years old than for any other age group.

FIGURES AND STATISTICS Forty-eight percent of all Americans between the ages of fifteen and fifty-four experience a psychological disorder during their lifetime. Many begin in childhood.[14] It is estimated that 7.5 million, or 12 percent, of American children and adolescents suffer from mental disorders.[15] Life is stressful, and even when growth and development are normal, kids have a complex world to negotiate.

EARLY ADOLESCENCE

AGE ELEVEN

For most children, this marks the beginning of adolescence.

Physical
- Seems to be in constant motion
- Doesn't like to sleep and doesn't like to wake up
- Is aware of and has definite ideas about clothes
- Shows increased physical development, girls more so than boys
- Experiences physical changes, such as body pains of undetermined origin, growth spurts (especially in boys), and erections

Internal
- Is egocentric
- Is, at best, alert, imaginative, and energetic
- Is, at worst, lying, self-centered, and quarrelsome; has a conscience but may lie or steal
- Begins to think about money and how to spend it
- Experiences intense emotions; anger and tears occur often
- Develops a sense of humor; acts silly

---

[14] "Psychological Sources: Essential to American." American Psychological Association practice directorate. (February 1995). [15] "Report Card on the National Plan for Research on Child and Adolescent Mental Disorders," Archives of General Psychiatry. (September 1995).

Interpersonal

- Is quick to criticize
- Has higher standards of behavior for others than for himself
- Is not helpful to family around the house
- Attempts to become free of parents to gain independence; resistant and rebellious
- Is more critical of mother than father: "*She* says I can't go!"
- Behaves better to others outside of home than in the home
- Is interested in all that goes on; gossips
- Has difficulties with siblings; competitive
- Is less casual and more discriminating about friends
- Realizes people are more important than play
- Becomes more critical of school
- Has close, mutually shared relationships outside the family

Clubs, friends, or secret societies gain in importance. Preteens do not want adult supervision, nor do they believe that they require care. This makes patience and strategy significant parental talents.

Traits of Bullying

- Bullying occurs most frequently in sixth, seventh, and eighth grades.
- Victims have difficulty making friends and are lonely.
- Bullying occurs in rural and urban areas.
- Boys are more likely than girls to be bullies and to be the victims of bullies.
- Girls bully with verbal rather than physical aggression.
- Bullies are more likely to smoke or drink.
- Bullies are also victims of bullying.
- Bullying often occurs without intervention from teachers or other adults.[16]

---

[16] Nansel (2002).

Puberty has begun. There are significant differences in puberty for boys and girls.

PHYSICAL	
GIRL	**BOY**
• Is invested in her own body; some begin to diet	• Experiences changes in hormonal levels as puberty begins
• Is better prepared for menstruation than boys are for ejaculation	• Uses masturbation as a means to control excitement or to soothe himself
• Gains weight, develops widening hips, grows (to age fifteen), and develops sweat glands	• Develops slimmer hips, muscles, facial hair, and sweat glands; will grow and gain weight later
	• Looks like he will break objects with his awkwardness
	• Dreams about buildings with equipment and bombs, tubes, and periscopes
	• Is less comfortable with body changes than girls
INTERNAL	
• Dreams about idealized love and pop stars	• Is lazy; conflicted between being active vs. passive

• Underreacts with indifference, or overreacts with sarcasm, tirades, tears	• Puts on a gruff exterior to cover gentleness that is best seen with pets
• Likes cuddling with family members	• Provokes fights
• Has less need for independence; tolerates connectedness	• Competes with peers over height, competence, spitting, and telling tales
• Demonstrates independence as she borrows mother's clothes and then criticizes them	• Is conflicted between dependent vs. independent means. (Wake him up and he is angry. Don't wake him up and you are uncaring. Tell him to sleep and you are interfering.)

WARM UP Pick an age and write a quick paragraph marketing new shoes to children of that age.

AGE TWELVE

Physical

- Matures at a rate that may be noticeably different than peers; girls are more physically developed
- Experiences body pains of undetermined origin
- May have tried drugs, cigarettes, and alcohol
- Argues less about bedtime, but sleep is more restless
- Cares a great deal about appearance; the "right" clothes become very important

GIRL	BOY
• Has achieved 95 percent of her adult height by the end of the year, the average for twelve-year-old girls	• May be either well ahead of or well behind peers in physical and emotional development: boys show great variation in growth and maturity
• Begins menstruation: twelve is the average age of menarche	• Is puzzled by spontaneous erections caused by sexual stimulation, anger, horseplay, and fear
• Starts to worry about weight	• Is frequently hungry
	• May masturbate: common in boys of this age
	• Bathes, but may still struggle with subtleties such as hand washing

Internal

- Evens out temperamentally, but emotions are shapeless
- Has enthusiastic reactions of all kinds, both positive and negative
- Shows greater moral development
- Exhibits increased sense of humor; humor takes on sarcastic tones; loves double entendres
- Tries to hide feelings, but emotions, especially anger, are not under control
- Knows own positive and negative qualities
- Begins to demonstrate distinct abilities, such as athletics, math, or music

- Is more governed by conscience

Interpersonal

- Is more distinct as a person, so is less critical of parents
- Finds friends a source of pleasure and support: "All my friends have a later curfew!"
- Attends parties: girls hoping for romance; boys to horse around and eat
- Figures out ways to earn money
- Compares self to others; looks for similarities and differences
- Likes the opposite sex; boys and girls notice each other (girls show more interest)
- Influenced by peers: individuals are heavily ruled by the group

Loneliness is common for many kids during these years. Some girls get neatly cut out of a clique without ever knowing what they did wrong. They hide, eating lunch in the school library rather than sit alone in the cafeteria until they find a different group of friends.

Boys also suffer during this time, less from relationships with other boys than from the awkwardness of being a growing adolescent. They dream of being cool and of success at sports, which would bring the attention they crave.

AGE THIRTEEN

Physical

- Continues to experience steady physical changes

> **BOY**
>
> - Continues to grow and change: genitals grow, voice deepens and cracks, nose sticks out of face, and growth still occurs in spurts; 50 percent have experienced ejaculation
>
> - Becomes particular about clothing; notices own grooming; manners improve

- Continues to be a ravenous eater

- Has probably tried cigarettes, drugs, or alcohol

Internal

- Demonstrates physical and emotional withdrawal; wants to get rid of dependency on parents
- Seems to always be pulling thoughts together
- Acts sour and cloudy; has uncertain disposition
- Is ethical and concerned with right and wrong
- Is busy with thoughts and feelings even when she appears indifferent
- Enjoys time in own room
- Does not handle money well; always broke
- Worries about a lot of things
- Has crisp and sardonic humor; sarcasm increases
- Mimics teachers, siblings, and parents
- Scrutinizes outer self first, and then inner self
- Thinks globally about world issues: hunger, peace, animals

Interpersonal

- Needs privacy; doors are closed and locked: "Leave me alone!"
- Replies to adults with one-word answers: "okay" or "nothing"
- Is embarrassed by parents; argues more with mother than father
- Develops different relationships with mother and father; may still talk to mother, but father is easier for homework instruction
- Dates and attend parties; girls like parties better than boys do
- Begins to dislike authority
- Becomes increasingly sophisticated about ethics, right and wrong, white lies, and accepting blame

GIRL	BOY
Experiences closely knit friendships; maybe three friends, with two often ganging up on one	Is still comfortable doing things in groups, but may have a best friend

Family problems and social relationships can take their toll on academic performance and certainly influence their moods. Teens often feel angry and guilty from real or imagined transgressions, and many are willing to punish others and themselves. Failure is an effective self-punishment for real or imagined crimes.

 NEW INFORMATION Psychologists see a new trend in parenting: trophy children. Perfectionist parents are using their children to meet their own needs. This has always existed, but previously had been considered a flaw in parenting. Now it has become acceptable. Why? Parents are determined to make their children competitive in this global economy and will do anything to keep their own offspring on top of the heap. Children are the new status symbols as seen in the schools they attend or the teams they join. They are their parents' latest, greatest projects.[17]

AGE FOURTEEN

Physical

- May use drugs, alcohol, or cigarettes
- Continues to be particular about clothes
- Is involved in activities, sports, and groups

GIRL	BOY
• Looks like a young woman; physical development is well underway	• Experiences greatest growth spurt this year; looks masculine, and has deeper voice

[17] Marano, *Psychology Today* (2005); Mintz, S. (2004).

• Is well-groomed: girls at this age are cleaner than boys	• Continues to develop at a different rate than peers
	• Goes from unselfconscious to modest
	• Probably masturbates regularly and understands ejaculation

Internal

- Shares emotions more; less turning inward
- Wants more freedom; willing, sometimes eager, to argue
- Experiences more drive toward the other—or same—gender
- Knows right from wrong even when doing wrong

Interpersonal

- Is highly critical of parents; family is the problem more than school or friends
- Feels parents don't understand; father now joins mother as an object of criticism, though teens obey father better than mother
- Is, according to parents, easily insulted; demands everything and appreciates little
- [Girl] experiences disturbance in the father/daughter relationship as she matures and dates
- Finds that same-sex and opposite-sex friendships may be dissolving and reforming; boy-girl relationships shift rapidly
- Is more pleasant with people outside the family
- Understands money better but cannot hold on to it; many expenses
- May find work

After puberty, when hormones settle down, boys and girls have boundless energy directed into appearance and social relationships. Unfortunately, social relationships are also the cause of shame as having different clothes, being ridiculed, or coming from a dysfunctional family can make life miserable.

WARM UP New research finds sons and daughters similarly subjected to parental disclosures after a divorce. Parents confide in their children for several reasons: the desire for the adolescents' support; the desire to express their emotions; and the desire to teach, socialize, or change their adolescents' opinions. However, there are problems with parents turning their adolescent children into confidants. Such parental disclosures may violate rules that define generational boundaries, or distress the child, placing her at risk for emotional difficulties. They increase the adolescents' sense of lack of control over events and feelings that precipitated the disclosures. They also worry the children: They want to help their mothers; at the same time they want to defend the other parent or stop their mothers from talking. Overwhelmed by these conflicting feelings, they may act out in disobedient ways.[18]

Write a scene showing a son's reactions after his mother has confided damaging information about his beloved father.

MIDDLE ADOLESCENCE

AGE FIFTEEN

Physical

- Shows minimal response to stimuli; restricted energy
- Is sexually active to varying degrees

Internal

- Has a deepening capacity to reason
- Has limited emotional and intellectual expression
- Is thoughtful and reflective rather than expansive and expressive
- Is able to organize thoughts and perceptions
- Tries to evaluate and hold on to a perspective
- Is unadaptable and unhappy

[18] Susan Koerner, et al. (2004).

Interpersonal

- Demonstrates individualistic and often unpredictable responses to others
- Craves conflict with authority; rebellious; negative toward family
- Looks for things to do with friends as they become very significant
- Experiments with friends; likes getting away with things
- Pushes family limits; evokes anger in parents

This is an age that finds teenagers having run-ins with parents, police, and authorities. Good kids are pushing the limits, some with alcohol, sex, or drugs.

> **NEW INFORMATION** Fathers play a special role in children's lives as their mentor, play partner, and the one who encourages them to competently meet the challenges of the world outside the family. Children whose fathers sensitively support their autonomy gain emotional security that persists into adolescence.[19]

AGE SIXTEEN

Physical

- Regains coordination as body growth stabilizes

Internal

- Becomes future oriented
- Is more self-sufficient
- Is introspective; daydreamer
- Becomes more straightforward with others
- Develops deeper interests; is more creative and imaginative

Interpersonal

- Shows interest in and sensitivity towards others
- Is concerned about relationships with others
- Gains independence by receiving a driver's license

The sixteen to twenty-one year old moves in the direction of continuing to become a more clearly defined individual. The conflict becomes "I want to be independent, but I don't want the pain of separation."

[19] National Institute of Child Health and Human Development Journal of Family Psychology 1994.

Early Adult Transition

AGES SEVENTEEN TO TWENTY-ONE

These years mark the period when individuals move from their adolescent structure and initiate preliminary steps in the adult world. There are major developmental tasks to accomplish whether they are in college or have begun to work.

PHYSICAL

- Has completed changes

INTERNAL

- Is beginning to separate emotionally from parents
- Feels the vacuum created when parents' rules disappear and there are no replacements
- Experiences greater autonomy
- Is forced to take more ownership of own body
- Is forced to make decisions
- Wrestles with vocational choices

INTERPERSONAL

- Tries to establish a more adult relationship with parents
- Feels receptive to new people and ideas, for better or worse
- Experiments with relationships and behaviors

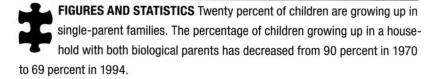 **FIGURES AND STATISTICS** Twenty percent of children are growing up in single-parent families. The percentage of children growing up in a household with both biological parents has decreased from 90 percent in 1970 to 69 percent in 1994.

The Twenty Most Common Dreams of College Students

1. Falling
2. Being attacked or pursued
3. Trying repeatedly to do something
4. School, teachers, and studying
5. Sexual experiences
6. Arriving too late
7. Eating
8. Being frozen with fright
9. A loved person is dead
10. Being locked up
11. Finding money
12. Swimming
13. Snakes
14. Being inappropriately dressed
15. Being smothered
16. Being nude in public
17. Fire
18. Failing an examination
19. Seeing oneself as dead
20. Killing someone[20]

[20] Griffith, Miyagi, and Tago (1958).

CHAPTER **four**

Psychological Disorders

IN THIS CHAPTER

•Early Influences That Shape Personality • Mild Childhood Problems • Moderate and Severe Childhood Problems • Skill Disorders • Adolescent Problems • Problems in Adult Development • Severe Disorders of Adulthood

Disorders, by definition, are conditions that make people deviate in substantial ways from the norm; they differ in ways that make life tricky. Some of the problems described have strong biological, as well as psychological, components. However, disorders exclude behaviors that are a result of cultural differences or that are acceptable actions elsewhere. For example, *ataque de nervios*, a strange collection of physical symptoms that may include mutism, catatonic posturing, hyperventilation, and even self-mutilation is acceptable in Puerto Rican culture as an intense grief response to the death of a loved one. If a woman presented this reaction in a United States hospital, she might well be administered heavy medication. Another example is provided by the Bedouins of Western Egypt. Their fiercely independent culture prizes mastery and self-control, so a Bedouin man's public reaction to death is anger or apparent indifference. Their sadness however, is expressed in poetry. These fascinating, diverse responses are cultural differences, not disorders.

Early Influences That Shape Personality

Even when an individual cannot remember early events, those experiences often influence later behaviors. If a newborn lies neglected in a dark room, his cries unanswered and his needs unmet, he will have no substantive memory of those early months. However, the influence of mistreatment may be seen years later in issues of trust and care. A girl conceived and born after the death of an older sister has no knowledge of the tragedy, yet her upbringing and her parents' reactions to her will be influenced by the event that occurred before her birth. Problems unsolved by one generation are passed down to the next.

Some problems seen in childhood and adolescence can occur during any time of life. Children, like adults, can be depressed or psychotic and can have an addiction or eating disorder. In this chapter, disorders are described alphabetically under general headings of Mild Childhood Problems, Moderate and Severe Childhood Problems, Skill Disorders, Adolescent Problems, and Disordered Adult Personality Types.

Each child is born with a basic temperament that is shaped by life events. When a child fits nicely with her parents and her environment, she flourishes. When circumstances are adverse, the child suffers. Some circumstances are innocent; for example, I treated a young woman who was an artist. Unfortunately for her, she was born into a family of accountants—nice people, but they had no idea what to do with her, and she suffered from feeling different and unvalued. In a more serious instance, a young man had been born with heart defects that required repeated surgeries before the age of fifteen. His mother had already nursed her own parents through fatal illnesses and hated taking care of him. Whatever normal shyness he started with became distorted; by the time I met him he was a withdrawn, ashamed, and angry young adult. In these ways and innumerable others, childhood personality and past experiences shape the present.

Mild Childhood Problems

Childhood problems are those that begin early and are seen primarily in young people. Some disorders end after childhood or adolescence; others continue throughout life.

Several of the disorders below could have been appropriately included in chapter ten, Physical Disorders, but because they are so closely tied to youth, they have been listed below. These include common difficulties of childhood, such as tics, stuttering, and enuresis (bed-wetting). Less ordinary problems that have a strong physical-emotional link are also here: skill disorders, autism, and encopresis (involuntary bowel movements).

ANXIETY

The anxious child doesn't behave badly; in fact, she is too withdrawn and fearful to get into any trouble. Many children outgrow their anxiety completely; others control it enough to become only mildly anxious adults. Some, however, go further into themselves and have no peer relationships, are cold and unresponsive, secretive, like to be alone, and refuse to communicate very much. This last group may become the adult Loner personality.

TRAITS OF THE ANXIOUS CHILD

- Is shy, timid, and tense
- Is depressed and sad
- Is hypersensitive and easily hurt
- Feels worthless
- Is self-conscious; easily embarrassed
- Lacks confidence
- Cries frequently
- Is aloof and worried[1]

Anxious children's difficulties go beyond shyness and can hamper their normal social development. Their problems with separation may cause them to refuse

[1] Achenbach (1982).

to go to school, or come home with stomachaches and nausea; playing at other people's homes can be a problem.

WARM UP Anxious people's attention is actually drawn to threatening stimuli, and they have trouble disengaging their attention from such stimuli.[2] Write a quick paragraph describing a young boy as he watches an approaching storm.

DEFIANCE

A defiant child has difficulty being appropriately assertive, so she overdoes the rebelliousness. An extreme version is the conduct-disordered child, described in the next section, Moderate and Severe Childhood Disorders. Conduct disorder is more worrisome because violence is present and the future possibilities are more negative.

TRAITS OF THE DEFIANT CHILD

- Is negative and hostile; loses her temper
- Is argumentative; refuses to listen to parents and teachers
- Is touchy and easily annoyed
- Blames others; does not want to accept responsibility
- Has low self-esteem
- Finds it difficult to be properly assertive
- Swings from being withdrawn to bullying[3]
- Has difficulty appropriately separating from parents
- Uses defiance to gain emotional control and regulate distance from parents

Defiance is frustrating and perplexing to parents who feel disregarded. And they are right: The child is negative, unable to listen, unable to work, and feeling lost. The defiant child sees running away as a solution.

[2] Fox (2002). [3] Mones (1988).

ENURESIS (BED-WETTING)

Enuresis is of little concern until after the age of four. At that time, it begins to interfere with a child's ordinary life. He cannot engage in activities without fear of wetting his clothing.

TRAITS OF THE BED WETTER
- Usually wets at night; wetting is less common during the day
- Wets involuntarily
- Does not mind being wet
- Suffers from negative self-esteem
- Is regarded badly by peers
- Is subject to teasing
- Is often aggressive: bedwetting is less common in easygoing children
- Has difficulty adapting to new situations: bedwetting is more common in maladaptive children
- Does not respond to punishments from parents or teachers

Enuresis usually occurs during the night or, occasionally, when the child is engrossed in an activity, during the day. Often, it runs in families and one of the child's parents was also a bed-wetter. Once a child passes his fifth birthday, the other kids become more aware of the problem. Sleeping at a friend's house becomes impossible; the child is teased and becomes ashamed and fearful.

A more disturbing scenario is the child who intentionally urinates in inappropriate places. This is often the result of confusion and anger over personal or family matters.

Encopresis (involuntary bowel movements) is less common than bed-wetting. It occurs at inappropriate times, more often during the day than at night, and is often a sign of stress.

OBSESSIVENESS

Children go through normal phases of worry, but the obsessive child is chronically fearful without a justifiable cause. This can become more severe as time goes on.

TRAITS OF THE OBSESSIVE CHILD

- Is anxious, tense, filled with worry and fear
- Seems mature; conforming
- Needs reassurance; very sensitive
- Learns to control feelings, especially joy
- Uses guilt to keep anger under control
- Models himself on parents' authority

Obsessive children are often appreciated because they are serious and try very hard. They are conscientious and usually do well in school. Parents forget that good behavior and adherence to rules can mask anger, and overcontrol leads to restrictions in emotional development.

 WARM UP Write two paragraphs following an obsessive child getting ready for his final exam.

OVERATTACHMENT

Although attachment is essential, overattachment is problematic. For the overattached child, themes of fear about separation run through every day.

TRAITS OF THE OVERATTACHED CHILD

- Is anxious about any separations from parents
- Worries that bad things will happen to parents: "Don't have a car crash!"
- Worries excessively about being taken from parents, such as being kidnapped
- Avoids school because bad situations could happen while she is away
- Has trouble going to friends' houses; cannot sleep at a friend's house or at camp
- Reacts to threats of separation from parents with a tantrum, terror, or begging
- Experiences physical symptoms at an imminent separation: nausea, vomiting, or headaches

- Has fantasies and nightmares about separation
- Calls or writes excessively when she has to be away

The overattached child is not demonstrating love when she wants to be with her mother; she is showing fear. Any suggestion of separation, such as camp or visiting relatives, results in panic. Often, this problem occurs after the threat of loss or abandonment has raised the child's fears to unmanageable levels.

Tics

Tics—sudden, recurrent, repetitive motor twitches that cannot be controlled for any period of time—can be a sign of childhood distress. There are two types of tics: motor and vocal. Motor tics include behaviors such as repeated blinking or smelling things; vocal tics include coprolalia (repeating "bad" words), barking, or echolalia (the imitation of someone else's words or sounds). Childhood tics generally disappear unless they mark the onset of a disease such as Tourette Syndrome. This disorder includes one vocal tic, such as echolalia, in combination with several motor tics, such as jumping and grimacing.

Moderate and Severe Childhood Problems

Any of the following disorders can range from mild to severe. The traits below are descriptive of the severe forms of each disorder. To create milder forms of these problems, use few traits, mild forms of the traits, or demonstrate that the behavior can be easily controlled.

ATTENTION-DEFICIT HYPERACTIVITY

The term "ADH" is often used incorrectly to describe behaviors that are unattractive and to gloss over different problems, such as pervasive anxiety or anxious depression, that show similar symptoms.

TRAITS OF THE ATTENTION-DEFICIT HYPERACTIVE CHILD

- Fidgets or squirms in a seat at school or at home
- Has trouble remaining seated when instructed to do so

- Has trouble concentrating; easily distracted; short attention span
- Fails to finish things that he starts
- Acts before thinking; is impulsive
- Needs a lot of supervision
- Cannot wait for his turn in games or in groups of other children
- Talks out of order; calls out in class
- Has trouble following instructions even when he intends to do so
- Shifts from one activity to another
- Interrupts other people; intrudes into conversations or activities
- Has trouble playing quietly; runs and jumps on furniture
- Does too much talking and not enough listening
- Loses things such as books, assignments, toys, or equipment
- Is sluggish, lazy, and drowsy

Attention-Deficit Hyperactivity always begins in childhood before age seven and is often first pointed out by a teacher. The problems don't begin at school age; rather, as the child begins school, classroom and school standards of behavior highlight already existing problems.[4] ADH children are usually noisy and very active, but going out to school, restaurants or other people's houses makes things worse, and the children are next to impossible to manage. Other kids respond badly to the annoying behaviors, so ADH children become some of the less popular children. The constant fighting, the child's need for attention, and aggressive behavior strain many families.

AUTISM

One of the saddest disorders of childhood is autism. It always appears first in childhood and rarely gets better. Autism is a severe and pervasive impairment in communication with delay of or lack of language and poor social interaction: In its severe forms, there are no relationships and no reciprocity.

[4] Garber, Garber, and Spizman (1990).

TRAITS OF THE AUTISTIC CHILD

- Is unaware of others; treats people like objects
- Has no awareness of another person's distress; no ability for empathy
- Possesses no ability to play and has no reciprocity
- Prefers solitary activities and is passive
- Has no ability to make friends, share, or take turns
- Suffers from an absence of the need for attachment
- Does not come to caretaker for comfort when hurt or tired
- Has no concept of privacy
- Makes repetitive sounds; monotonous, screeching, or melodic
- Has little or no verbal communication; 50 percent never speak
- Has little or no nonverbal communication: no smiles; has a steady stare,
- Exhibits characteristic strange, restricted, repetitive body movements: head banging on walls, flapping, or hand-twisting
- Insists on sameness; reacts badly to any change, such as rearranged furniture
- Follows same dull routine day after day; unchangeable rituals
- May attach to one object; for example, may carry a paper bag around

Autistic children are born, not made. Parents usually recognize a problem before doctors are able to make the diagnosis: The infants do not want to be held; they don't babble or respond in expected ways. As they grow, they often spend hours each day in some solitary activity, such as rocking or thumping, and are difficult to distract. Some autistic children learn to be more relational; other more severely autistic children never do.

CONDUCT PROBLEMS

A child with conduct problems persistently violates rules and disregards the rights of others. The child can change with increased maturity, or can become the Boss adult personality, or much harsher, in adulthood.

TRAITS OF THE CHILD WITH CONDUCT PROBLEMS

- Dislikes social rules; is disobedient and defiant
- Can be violent and aggressive
- Fights; behaves cruelly to people and pets, bullies and threatens
- Is loud, attention-seeking, and a show-off
- Is destructive; vandalizes property
- Has temper tantrums; blows up easily
- Hates to take directions; is impertinent, smart, and impudent
- Has school problems and lacks self-control; is boisterous and noisy
- Is not deterred by fear
- Lacks desire to please others; is uncooperative and inconsiderate
- Lies; is mistrustful and untrustworthy

Children with conduct problems believe that others are bad and harmful. This belief allows destructive behavior, which can be seen early on at school (hitting other kids, showing disrespect to teachers, or cheating) and at home (destroying family members' property or harming pets). These children cannot follow rules, so sports and games are not a solution.

When child conduct problems also include bad companions, gangs, truancy from school, running away from home, stealing, lying, and cheating, the odds go up for future trouble and run-ins with the law.[5]

 NEW INFORMATION Advertising separates children from their parents by encouraging them to reject anything associated with the older generation.

DEPRESSION

We do not like to believe that children can be depressed. Childhood depression is also one of the most difficult disorders for adults to identify. The predictable symptoms of guilt, self-blame, feelings of rejection, low self-esteem, and negative self-image are often not evident: In children, depression is often marked

[5] Quay and Werry, eds, (1979).

by physical complaints, refusal to go to school, emotional outbursts, fears, underachievement, insomnia, anger, or isolation.

Children get more notice when they behave badly than when they are lethargic and uncommunicative, which can make depression an unrecognized threat. Even when adolescents report severe depression, parents and teachers are often dangerously unaware of the situation. Depression can be mild, but I have included it in the moderate and severe listings because it can lead to child and adolescent suicides. For a list of traits, see *Depression* under Problems in Adult Types on pages 99–101.

Fire-Setters

- Fire-setters have a variety of motivations:
- Juvenile curiosity: Many five to ten year olds do not understand the consequences of playing with fire
- Cry for help: Children who are depressed or suffer from family troubles may try to call attention to the stress in their lives
- Lack of empathy: Some delinquent eleven to fifteen year olds have little empathy for others and don't care about causing property damage
- Fire fixation or death wish: Children may be psychotic or paranoid and have a fixation on fire. They may want to kill themselves.
- Lack of judgment: Developmentally disabled children do not want to harm others, but may lack judgment
- Peer pressure/showing off: Children may set fires primarily to gain support from their peers, such as those set during riots or in a religious fervor[6]

MENTAL RETARDATION

Mental retardation is a physical disability, often with psychological consequences. It can be a result of a genetic abnormality, a birth defect, or trauma during or after birth. The child's capability depends on his level of retardation—mild, moderate, or severe; each has different levels of ability. Down Syndrome is a

[6] APA Monitor on Psychology (July/August, 2004).

common cause of retardation and has specific physical features, but 30 to 40 percent of the causes of retardation are unknown. Other causes for mental retardation include: hereditary factors (Tay-Sachs, phenylketonuria or PKU, fragile x syndrome), prenatal problems (alcohol consumption or infection during pregnancy), birth and perinatal problems (prematurity, malnutrition, trauma, or lack of oxygen), physical disorders (lead poisoning, trauma, or infection), and environmental problems (deprivation).

TRAITS OF THE MENTALLY RETARDED CHILD

- Is significantly below average in intelligence
- Has significant trouble in adaptation; for example, with social skills, communication, and daily living
- Has trouble reaching adult levels of independence and responsibility
- Cannot progress in some areas, such as speech skills

Children with mild mental retardation go to school, learn trades, and make friends. Their adaptation not only depends on the level of their disability but also on personality, motivation, education, and opportunities.

MUTISM

There are rare children who are able to talk but refuse to do so.

TRAITS OF THE MUTE CHILD

- Is usually willing to talk at home
- Is able to speak and understand language
- Refuses to speak in several important settings; for example, school or a friend's home
- Begins behavior early before school years
- May appear normal until school or settings outside the home make mutism evident
- May have an overprotective mother
- May have had an early trauma such as hospitalization

Children who elect to be mute often have only this one strange behavior. It isn't shyness at work; in fact, the mute child is bold and very much in control when she remains silent. It can last for weeks or years.

 WARM UP Write two paragraphs having a defiant child assigned to work with a mute child on an art project.

SCHIZOPHRENIA

Schizophrenia is rare in children—only about 5 percent of cases of this disease begin before puberty—but it does occur and has all the same characteristics found in adults. Schizophrenia can disappear, recur intermittently over the lifetime, or progressively get worse. See pages 114–117 for a list of traits.

SKILL DISORDERS

There are children who have a marked inability to do a certain activity, but have normal abilities in other areas. These disorders are not indicative of mental retardation, and children perform adequately in other areas. The following list provides some of the idiosyncratic disorders.

- Arithmetic Disorder: Cannot develop arithmetic skills such as math operations, copying numbers, counting objects, or reading math signs
- Writing Disorder: Cannot adequately spell, use written grammar, punctuate, or organize paragraphs
- Reading Disorder: Cannot adequately recognize written words or comprehend written words
- Speaking Disorder: Cannot adequately express herself in words; uses limited vocabulary, has trouble acquiring new words, or uses short sentences and simple grammar

Adolescent Problems

The disorders described previously may continue into adolescence; the disorders described next generally begin in adolescence. Other problems that begin in adolescence, such as eating disorders and substance abuse, are fully described in chapter ten under Physical and Mind/Body Disorders.

Alcohol Abuse in Teenagers—A Major Problem in the US

- Young people who excessively use alcohol are three times more likely to have had suicidal thoughts and five times more likely to have made suicide attempts than their peers who did not use alcohol.
- Substance abuse can spark suicidal behavior by increasing impulsivity and decreasing inhibition.
- Substance abuse can be a method for attempting suicide.
- People abuse substances to escape from or dampen experiences of distress.

CUTTING

Self-cutting is repetitive, nonlethal cutting of the body usually beginning in adolescence. Cutting indicates problems, usually trauma or a personality disorder, but does not involve major mutilation.

TRAITS OF AN ADOLESCENT WHO CUTS

- Is usually female (males self harm is seen in accidents or dangerous behavior)
- Often has an eating disorder
- Is secretive; cutting is done in isolation and repeated until blood flows
- Transforms emotional pain into physical pain
- Feels removed from her own body during the cutting: "I watched myself cut" or "It was like I wasn't there"
- Does not want to die: this is not a suicide attempt; in fact, she fears inadvertent death
- Feels self-hatred
- Is angry at herself for having needs and feelings, and for lack of control in life

- Feels calmer and relaxed afterward
- Feels shame: "I'm a freak"
- Is trying to be independent
- Reaffirms identity and boundaries of skin through cutting: "I exist if I bleed"
- Often stops cutting spontaneously

There are competing explanations for the causes of self-cutting. Some individuals are manipulative or attention seeking ("I wanted someone to ask what was wrong."). Others cut as a result of rape or childhood sexual abuse ("I'll show you how bad you made me feel!"). Some people are punishing themselves and others are discharging anger ("See what I can do!"). Still other explanations include self-purification ("I had to get rid of the badness.") or pleasure or tension release ("The feelings were building; then afterwards, I was calm.").

Any of the above explanations may be at the root of the behavior. As the stresses of adolescence pile up, some individuals begin to cut themselves. When they watch the blood flow, they feel relief. Cutting is not about death as much as it is about rage and pain.

SUICIDE

Suicide is the third leading cause of death for people between the ages of fifteen and twenty-four. From 1980 to 1997, the suicide rate among fifteen to nineteen year olds increased by 11 percent, and among ten to fourteen year olds, it increased by 109 percent.

It may be an impulsive act; for example, an adolescent reaction to spurned love or severe rebuke.

Adolescent suicide also may result of copying from friends or being exposed to media coverage.

TRAITS OF A SUICIDAL ADOLESCENT: WARNING SIGNS
- Talks about committing suicide
- Shows abrupt changes in personality
- Gives away prized possessions

- Has previously attempted suicide
- Harms herself in less obvious ways
- Increases the use of alcohol and drugs
- Shows an inability to tolerate frustration
- Becomes sexually promiscuous
- Withdraws; shows an inability or unwillingness to communicate
- Becomes rebellious; runs away from home
- Becomes truant; neglects academic work and has difficulty concentrating
- Shows hostile behavior; is unruly at school and fights with friends
- Is involved in theft or vandalism
- Is depressed
- Neglects personal appearance
- Shows an unusually long grief reaction to loss, sadness, or discouragement
- Is inactive and bored; shows extended apathy
- Is careless; has accidents
- Shows occasional evidence of bizarre thinking, such as delusions
- Has eating disturbances and weight change
- Suffers from sleep disturbances such as nightmares or insomnia

Adolescents change their personalities when they become suicidal. Often, a first sign is dropping grades. They increase substance abuse, borrow a car and have an accident, and withdraw from friends and family. The spiral downward requires intervention.

 WARM UP Write a scene in which an adult remembers one of the previous disorders causing a problem in his or her childhood.

Problems in Adult Development

The following problems can range from mild to severe depending on the number of traits and the severity of them.

ANXIETY/NERVOUSNESS

Anxiety is very common in normal proportions and as a disorder. Individuals are usually quite adept at knowing when they feel that it has gotten out of control.

TRAITS OF A PERSON WITH ANXIETY

Internal

- Constantly worries that life cannot be controlled
- Worries may shift from one thing to another; for example, from child's welfare to own incompetence
- Feels restless, tense, or irritable
- Feels like danger is always around the corner
- May have sleep problems

Interpersonal

- Is likely to come from a fearful family: anxious parents create anxious children
- Is easily reactive and sensitive to others' approval or disapproval
- Is affected by worry in other areas of life: relationships, work, or play

SUBTYPES OF ANXIETY

Anxiety has three distinct subtypes. These three subtypes are unrelated to each other but are all manifestations of severe anxiety problems.

Agoraphobia is marked by fear of places or situations where one could be trapped and help would not be available.

Traits of a Person With Agoraphobia

- Avoids situations that might bring on fear
- Becomes increasingly limited as more places/situations are threatening
- Increasingly relies on others
- Fears to do activities alone
- Avoids situations in which it is difficult to escape, such as crowds or travel in vehicles
- Changes behaviors to avoid fears

Panic is marked by expectations and occurrences of panic attacks (sudden onset and short duration) that make a person feel like she is dying and wants to flee.

Traits of a Person With Panic Attacks

- Has a pounding heart
- Experiences shortness of breath; fear of dying
- Fears losing control: incontinence, fainting, or going insane
- Becomes dizzy, sweaty
- Experiences attacks when life is disrupted by moves or losses
- Becomes ashamed and embarrassed about fear
- Changes behaviors to avoid fear

Specific *phobias* are marked by fears of special things such as snakes, speaking in public, or flying, and are more common in children than adulthood. Common phobias are heights, flying, close spaces, being alone, storms, animals, blood, and water. People with phobias rarely have just one during their lifetime. Fear of heights is the number one phobia of men and fear of animals is number two. With women, the reverse is true.[7]

Traits of a Person With Phobias

- Sweats profusely
- Has the desire to escape
- Responds to stimuli irrationally and excessively
- Has clear, limited, immediate, and persistent fears

[7] Curtis, et al. (1998).

TYPE OF FEAR	AGE AT ONSET	TRAIT
Animals: spiders, snakes	Age seven	High excitement
Natural environment: heights, storms	Age nine	High excitement
Blood/injection/ injury type: dentists, injections	Age nine	Low excitement, fainting
Situational: tunnels, flying, claustrophobia	Twenties	Anxiety; fear of going crazy

 WARM UP The term "nervous breakdown" is not used in psychology but resonates well with people generally and seems to mean overwhelming stress, depression, self-doubt, or problems with personal adjustment. People report that "nervous breakdowns" are caused by health problems, stressful life events, work or school problems, or financial or housing problems. Write a scene in which the character is on the verge of a "nervous breakdown."

BORDERLINE PERSONALITY DISORDER

People with Borderline Personality Disorder show marked instability in life. Adolescents often appear to have these traits, but a major distinction between youth and adulthood is that in adolescence, much of the instability is due to hormonal changes and identity development, which is temporary. In adults these traits are not temporary, and are very difficult to change.

TRAITS OF A PERSON WITH BORDERLINE PERSONALITY DISORDER

Internal
- Swings between fears of abandonment and engulfment
- Has shifting image of self and others

- Is impulsive, which can be seen in acts of self-harm: cutting, self-mutilation, reckless driving, sex, or substance abuse
- Engages in self-destructive acts when feeling the threat of abandonment
- Has intense but easily shifting moods; despair can pass into calm within hours
- Holds grudges about perceived hurts
- Sabotages success; for example, destroying a relationship that is healthy
- May attempt suicide in the swings of feeling, especially to ward off loss or abandonment
- Is poor at tolerating stress

Interpersonal

- Wants to be one with someone else to avoid feeling alone and empty
- Has unstable relationships that, at the extreme, are chronically dysfunctional
- Begins to lose attention of others because even crises get repetitive, and so they become boring to others
- Swings from love to hate of others over small events
- Vacillates about plans, career, and decisions
- Switches sexual choices easily, including sexual relationships with both men and women
- Thinks others are wonderful; admires them, then suddenly sees them as worthless
- Has history replete with parental loss, neglect, abuse, or serious conflict

DEPRESSION

When a mood is pervasive and defines a way of life, we can think of it as defining a personality type. Everyone experiences periods of sadness, pessimism, grief, and other difficult and negative emotions. When these emotions are not experienced for a matter of weeks or months, but become the norm, it can be characterized as depression. There are two basic types of depression:

- Dependent: Defined by strong feelings of loneliness, helplessness, weakness. Longs to be loved, protected, and cared for; fears abandonment. Separations cause apprehension; may search for substitutes.
- Self-critical: Experiences feelings of self-criticism, unworthiness, inferiority, guilt. Engages in harsh self-evaluation, can be competitive, can attack others as well as himself; wants approval.[8]

TRAITS OF A PERSON WITH DEPRESSION

Internal

- Is pessimistic; sees a dark future
- Has poor morale; dissatisfied
- Is apathetic; lacks energy for coping
- Is irritable
- Lacks joy
- Is distracted by fears, worries, or self-analysis
- Overestimates difficulties; feels insufficient; underestimates self
- Is excessively sensitive and easily wounded
- Feels helpless, exhausted, trapped, or blocked
- Sees death as a way out; wants to die
- Has somber, slow, or flat speech; tone may be discouraged

Interpersonal

- May use drugs or alcohol to help negate feeling alone
- Is overly optimistic in the throes of a new love or interest
- Despairs and longs for relief and love
- Seems resentful about having to be a responsible adult
- Is sexually weak; wants contact and snuggling but no passion
- Seems normal for periods but inevitably crashes
- Has difficulty sustaining an adult adjustment to people and work

[8] Blatt (1974).

- Passively withdraws from or makes excessive demands on others
- Seeks nurturance from others; wants to be assured of others' devotion
- Openly discusses own worthlessness and demonstrates helplessness; evokes guilt in others
- Displays anger and resentment subtly to avoid rejection
- Persists in demands, needs, bitterness, and worthless protests
- Is preoccupied with self
- Obsessively worries about troubles
- Sees life as a well of hopelessness
- Considers suicide as an increasing possibility of escape from pain or humiliation
- Fears abandonment and therefore may rush into relationships even while silently raging at all past abandonments

PHYSICAL SYMPTOMS OF DEPRESSION
- Sleep difficulties and early morning wakening
- Proclivity to illnesses and fatigue
- Lowered drives for food, sex, and pleasure
- Physical complaints: bodily aches and pains or headaches

ADULT SUICIDE

Suicide is the ninth leading cause of adult death in the United States. Twenty to sixty-five percent of people who commit suicide have made at least one previous attempt, and 80 percent of individuals who succeed gave warning of their intention.

Suicides can often be predicted by:
- Presence of a specific plan
- Access to a specific weapon
- Preparation: making a will or giving away personal items
- History of suicide in close relatives; prior attempts
- Feelings of hopelessness
- Disorders: depression, alcoholism, or schizophrenia

Not all people are certain of their desire; it is common to have mixed feelings and still proceed. More women than men attempt suicide, but they are generally less successful because they use less guaranteed methods, like overdosing on pills. More men than women complete suicide because they use more lethal weapons, like guns. Older people commit suicide more often than younger people; older white males have the highest success rate. Married people have the lowest rate of attempted suicide. Suicide may be carefully planned and calculated; for example, an elderly man who saves his medicine to get a lethal dose. Motives for suicide include desire for revenge (a man whose wife leaves him for his brother); desire for attention (a wife whose husband and children have lost interest in her); or desire for sympathy (a person who is suffering from lack of appreciation or recognition).

TRAITS OF AN ADULT WHO COMMITS SUICIDE
- Has fantasies about suicide
- Does not believe suicidal thoughts are irrational, so they do not look for help
- Cannot reconcile past image of self with present situation: a failed marriage or business
- Suffers from psychosis or severe depression or manic depressive illness
- Sees suicide as an escape from responsibilities of (continued) life
- Feels complete hopelessness[9]

GRIEF

Most people feel sad from time to time. Where does grief end and depression begin? Grief refers to the normal, albeit intense, range of emotions that accompanies loss.

TRAITS OF A GRIEVING PERSON

Internal
- Feels emotions such as shock, numbness, sadness, temporary depression, helplessness, confusion, inability to concentrate, anger, and even the fear of going insane

[9] Clinard (1963).

- Experiences grief as a response to a genuine loss: unemployment, the death of a loved one, illness, disaster, or rejection
- Experiences grief only temporarily, as a result of certain events
- Moves through a process of intense feelings and eventually joy returns
- Has patterns of poor sleeping, over- or undereating, or crying that eventually cease

Interpersonal
- Finds solace in company or may isolate himself
- Is passive with others
- Is unable to concentrate on or attend to others

Grief becomes a disorder under two conditions: chronic grief and absent grief. Chronic grief is a disorder in which the survivor never lets go, never moves forward in the emotions or in life. The loss is always as fresh as it was in the beginning, and the adaptation is to freeze life at that day. Miss Havisham in *Great Expectations* may be the classic example of chronic grief. More subtle instances can be seen in rooms left forever untouched, or deceased people forever spoken of in the present tense. One woman continued to write and mail letters to her son who had died in Paris; she pretended that he had extended his stay. Chronic grief may result in suicide for the survivor, who sees death as the only path to reunion.

Absent grief is also a disorder in which the survivor never lets go, but on the surface the disorder looks very different from chronic grief because no emotion is displayed; no outward signs of normal grief reactions can be seen. This does not refer to the earliest days of grief, when the survivor may be in shock or may need to put personal feelings aside to help others (for example, during natural disasters) or get tasks done (planning the funeral). Absent grief does not refer to privacy issues and personal beliefs about decorum; it goes beyond the stiff upper lip and means that the emotional nature of the loss is not acknowledged. For example, the father whose twenty-year-old daughter was killed forbade her name to be mentioned, took her violin and locked it away, and expressed no feelings to anyone either in public or private.[10]

[10] Edelstein (1984).

WARM UP Create a character who suffers from one of the psychological problems described in this chapter and show him or her preparing for a large Thanksgiving feast.

NARCISSISM

The hallmark of narcissism is that these individuals are less than meets the eye. The key to understanding a person with narcissism is that, whatever it is, it is always about them.

TRAITS OF A PERSON WITH NARCISSISM

Internal

- Expresses grandiose feelings
- Shows off
- Has low self-esteem
- Lacks empathy for others
- Needs admiration

Interpersonal

- Projects feelings onto others: "You are envious of me!" when really he is feeling envy inside
- Resorts to extreme views of others, self, or life when under pressure; for example, partner is seen as *all bad* and self as *all good*

The Narcissist gravitates to careers in which attention and admiration are available. Politics is a good choice because it allows competition and manipulation. Religious careers are satisfying because there is a built-in audience.

OBSESSIONS

Life for the person with obsessions is a series of preoccupations with order, schedules, cleanliness, and perfectionism.

TRAITS OF A PERSON WITH OBSESSIONS

Internal

- Has long-term anxiety

- Uses intellectualized ways of thinking and relating to protect against anxiety
- Needs to be in control to feel safe
- Is insecure; has difficulty relaxing; is reserved
- Is realistic, logical, and level-headed
- Is skeptical and critical of self; harsh inner voices guide actions
- Looks for rules to guide decisions because of uncertainty; is plagued by self-doubt
- Is inflexible, rigid, tense and high-strung
- Is overly attentive to rules, details, and lists
- Is precise; stubborn
- Collects things and is reluctant to discard objects
- Has a self-image as industrious and hardworking

Interpersonal

- Is overly strict about ethics and morality
- Misses the big picture; focuses on the details
- Feels that love has heavy obligations; expresses affection in a controlled manner
- Turns fun and leisure into work; not good with pleasure
- Tends to be logical and intellectual; hides aggressive feelings
- Fears loss of control or going crazy, which rarely happens
- Looks for sanctioned ways of being judgmental and controlling; is critical of others
- Manages time poorly, so others are delayed and inconvenienced
- Often values work and productivity to the exclusion of everything else
- Wants others to do tasks his way; gives detailed instructions to others
- Expects subordinates to be deferential; wants to please superiors
- Believes there is only one way to do things

- May be stingy with money, compliments, and ideas; finds it difficult to acknowledge others' viewpoints
- Is contemptuous of frivolous people
- Gets angry when control is taken away
- Appears stilted or dull; speaks in a formal manner; dresses with restraint
- Does poorly in new situations

Extreme Traits of a Person With Obsessions

- Has compulsive and ritual behaviors, such as washing, checking, hoarding, excessive arranging, or cataloging; habits such as having shoes tied perfectly or walking through the center of a doorway
- Develops eating disorders from perfectionism
- Develops addictions or hypochondriasis because of lack of emotional expressiveness
- Responds with occasional impulsiveness in order to avoid feeling anything too long

The Obsessive gravitates toward careers in which systematic or technical skills are rewarded, "driven" qualities are appreciated, and emotional response is limited. They are very successful in careers if their traits remain mild. They are excellent at rational, detailed, disciplined work (accounting, technology, research) and superb at enforcing rules (judge, dean, or soldier).

 NEW INFORMATION Obsessiveness may be partly inherited.[11] Obsessions often focus on body, food, safety, or cleanliness; common obsessions include hand washing or repeatedly checking to see that the door is locked. Extreme obsessions are more unusual; for example, an obsession with shoes, fire trucks, or even bowels.

When obsessiveness gets extreme, we also often see compulsions as an integral aspect of the problem. Compulsions are repeated behaviors geared toward simplifying the environment in order to make the world feel safer and less distressing. Common compulsive rituals are:

[11] Clifford, Murray, and Fulker (1984).

- Cleaning: hand washing, housecleaning
- Ordering: straightening objects
- Checking: stove, garage door, keys
- Demanding reassurance: asking questions repeatedly
- Mentally repeating: prayers, numbers, words
- Magical acts of protective behavior: saying particular numbers, wearing certain clothes, touching a talisman
- Avoiding: particular objects

Differences between normal and abnormal rituals are not about the ritual itself, but about the severity of performance, excessiveness, and the extent to which the compulsions interfere with functioning.

Severe Disorders of Adulthood

The following disorders are some of the most extreme in psychology. Severe abnormality is recognized by: degree of disturbance, duration of disturbance, severity of feelings and symptoms, loss of awareness of reality, and exhibition of behaviors that are very different from norms of society. Although the personality types in chapter two offer traits that can create a severe or pathological character, the range is broad. These are disorders, so, by definition, they do not have a normal counterpart. Many individuals with these disturbances can lead normal lives by using medications and learning how to cope with the problems and suffering.

BIPOLAR DISORDER (MANIC DEPRESSION)

Manic depression, or bipolar disorder, is a disability that can exist in any personality type. Of all the mental or emotional disorders, bipolar disorder has the greatest genetic component, meaning that in the families of individuals who suffer from manic depression, there is a likelihood that some relative also has manic depression or depression without highs. At least 1–2 percent of Americans (approximately two million) suffer from bipolar disorder.

It may take years to correctly diagnose this illness. Men usually start with a manic episode and women with a depressive episode, and years can pass between episodes. Stressful life events often precipitate the first and second episodes, but after that little correlation exists between events and episodes. Both the manic and depressive cycles can last for days, months, or even years. When out of control, bipolar disorder can take over a person's life. Medications (usually lithium carbonate) are almost always needed to stabilize the mood swings; when the medications are effective, a person leads a very normal life and the problems are imperceptible.

TRAITS OF A PERSON WITH BIPOLAR DISORDER

Internal

- Feels shifting moods that may be dramatic
- Suffers from depression (see pages 99–101 for more traits) with cycles of regular or irregular manic highs
- Dislikes the depressed feeling that ranges from mild "blues" and increased need for sleep to hallucinations, delusions, or suicide; but enjoys the mania which is usually a "high" with euphoria, little sleep, and vast amounts of energy
- Has feelings during mania that include wild thoughts and reckless behaviors, but can also be chronic irritability

Interpersonal

- Has unstable interpersonal relationships that mirror internal world
- Experiences associated problems: job failure, divorce, or substance abuse
- Jeopardizes relationships with erratic behavior
- May behave angrily or impulsively with others

DELUSIONS

A person with delusions is, in most ways, very much like anyone else. He has no particular personality oddities or traits—except for delusions. Delusions can be bizarre and unlikely, such as being the long-lost daughter of a Russian czar, or more reasonable, such as being watched by a nosy neighbor. Either way, bizarre or possible, the event is not genuine, but it is impossible to convince the person suffering from the delusion of this.

FIVE TYPES OF DELUSIONS

TYPE	TRAITS
Danger delusion	Believes oneself to be in danger: being followed, poisoned, or abducted by aliens
Love delusion	Believes a particular person is in love with her
Jealous delusion	Believes one's partner is unfaithful
Body delusion	Believes oneself to have a disease or a defect
Grand delusion	Believes oneself to be a famous person, or has inflated worth or power

And people behave in accordance with their beliefs, whether they kill their partner for imagined infidelities or visit many specialists to cure their imagined disease.

Alien Abduction

There are many kinds of delusions, but the common ones are of persecution, religion, and fame. One interesting delusion is having been captured by aliens and taken to a space ship. This one holds particular interest because a good number of the people who make these claims are not delusional.

Contactees usually fall into one of two categories: those with mental problems and the others, who are more difficult to figure out because they are nonpsychotic and respected members of the community.

Alien abduction experiences have been reported by thousands of people. All report being taken by nonhuman entities and subjected to experiments or procedures. Many cannot be classified as psychotic.

MULTIPLE PERSONALITY DISORDER

This is a complex, chronic, uncommon dissociative disorder that can develop as a result of trauma. Dissociative states often develop as protection against negative stimuli. One in five cases resists detection; 50 percent can have no symptoms for a year or more. A small percentage brag about the disorder. This is a very hard disorder to figure out and may take months to recognize.

TRAITS OF AN INDIVIDUAL WITH MULTIPLE PERSONALITY DISORDER

Internal

- Has significant disturbance of identity and memory

[12] ibid.

- Has two or more distinct personalities; may be unaware of other personalities and terrified at their emergence
- Is fully controlled by other personalities during fugue state
- Reacts to crises with spontaneous emergence of other personalities
- Suffers from amnesia
- Has medical history of headaches, unexplained pain, and complaints of a sexual nature
- May have attempted suicide or self-mutilation, or had hallucinations or symptoms of post-traumatic stress disorder
- Has extensive psychiatric history with treatment failures
- Sees the world as unsympathetic, overwhelming, and frightening

Interpersonal
- Displays inconsistent personality traits in interactions with others
- Often continues in relationships in which he or she is abused or neglected
- Has difficulty with stable relationships
- Has a chaotic family history
- May have strange interactions with and reactions from others because of disturbance in identity and memory: losing track of time, forgetting, or experiencing a reactive mild dissociative phenomena

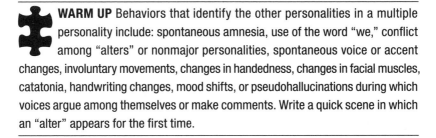 **WARM UP** Behaviors that identify the other personalities in a multiple personality include: spontaneous amnesia, use of the word "we," conflict among "alters" or nonmajor personalities, spontaneous voice or accent changes, involuntary movements, changes in handedness, changes in facial muscles, catatonia, handwriting changes, mood shifts, or pseudohallucinations during which voices argue among themselves or make comments. Write a quick scene in which an "alter" appears for the first time.

SUSPICIONS

A suspicious person is always looking for the "truth." They see nothing as benign; malevolence exists in all actions. The actions of a suspicious person are not to be confused with the cautious behavior of immigrants, refugees, or minorities who must navigate an unfamiliar or unfriendly society.

In childhood or adolescence, this problem may be manifested as odd or solitary behavior with few close relationships; this kind of young person attracts teasing. In the extreme or under stress, individuals can become temporarily psychotic or may have delusions.

TRAITS OF A PERSON WITH SUSPICIONS

Internal

- Is evasive
- Is stubborn and dogmatic
- Dwells on his own frustrations
- Is anxious
- Is preoccupied by doubts
- Sees self as different from others
- Is guarded; always alert, so may appear quiet or cold
- Feels self-righteous
- Cannot tolerate criticism; is very sensitive to others

Interpersonal

- Is suspicious with no basis in fact; suspiciousness impairs relations with others
- Is argumentative
- Feels persecuted; always distrustful so needs to be self-sufficient
- Suspects plots; scrutinizes actions of others
- Assumes that others will cause intentional harm; feels injured and retaliates angrily
- Is suspicious of interference of others
- Blames others; distrusts motives of others; finds it difficult to believe in loyalty of others
- Does not confide in others because of fear that others will share information
- Interprets honest mistakes as intentional harm

- Misinterprets jokes and distrusts compliments
- Holds grudges; is unforgiving
- Can be pathologically jealous
- Collects "evidence" to support beliefs
- Is very controlling in relationships; poor at collaboration
- May be argumentative because of suspiciousness
- Is often involved in legal disputes
- Is very aware of power and rank
- Prefers simplistic formulations

Suspicious people may be successful in large organizations where intrigues are always in motion or in careers like law in which adversarial relationships are part of the fabric of the work. They can also succeed as cost estimators or investigators, where the ability to quarrel is an asset.

 FIGURES AND STATISTICS There are mental health differences between men and women. Ten to twenty percent of women will experience depression, as compared to 8–10 percent of men. Depression in women is often accompanied by anxiety. Eating disorders are more common among women, although they are on the rise in men. Women have a greater incidence of panic disorder and agoraphobia. Schizophrenia is kinder to women; women have later onset, fewer symptoms and respond better to treatment.[13]

PSYCHOPATH

This type is mentioned again in chapter five because the disorder is frequently the basis for criminal activity. A psychopath has no conscience, so behaviors that are forbidden in others, he cannot control.

TRAITS OF A PERSON WITH PSYCHOPATHIC DISORDER

Internal

- Is easily bored
- Has no conscience; is amoral and deceitful

[13] APA Monitor on Psychology (December, 2001).

- Is motivated by money
- Is aggressive and reckless
- Has no guilt about poor treatment of others
- Has no strong feelings
- Is impulsive and irresponsible
- Ignores conventions
- Feels no sense of belonging to family or community
- Is a nonconformist; rationalizes own behavior

Interpersonal

- Does not react to a sense of right or wrong
- Can be violent if thwarted but is generally indifferent toward others
- Is socially maladjusted; fails to conform to social norms or laws
- Has a history of irresponsible performance in school, jobs, and financial obligations
- Is alienated from others
- Dislikes and resents authority
- Has trouble with the law; may have been delinquent when young
- Is charming with others
- Makes a good initial impression; others are dismayed when traits are revealed
- Disregards and may violate the rights of others

 NEW INFORMATION People with schizophrenia may suffer from inability to smell certain things, specifically cheese and bananas.[14]

SCHIZOPHRENIA

Of all the adult types of problems, schizophrenia is one of the most abnormal. Contrary to popular belief, individuals who suffer from schizophrenia are rarely

[14] Minor (2004).

violent or homicidal. They may appear very bizarre, even frightening, but are nearly always harmless to others. The first schizophrenic "break" usually occurs when an individual is in her late teens to early thirties.

There are three types of schizophrenia, paranoid, catatonic, and disorganized. In paranoid schizophrenia, the person is preoccupied with delusions or hallucinations about persecution or grandiosity: "The FBI has planted bugs in the showerhead," or "I am Napoleon." A person with this type of the disorder does not seem as strange as other types of schizophrenics; she may even seem normal at first.

A catatonic schizophrenic is often immobile or mute, but may also be victim to compulsive, excessive, and strange motor movements that lead to bizarre postures.

A person with the disorganized form of schizophrenia has few delusions or hallucinations, but shows irresponsible and unpredictable behaviors, such as inappropriate affection or rambling speeches.

EARLY WARNING SIGNS OF SCHIZOPHRENIA

None of these signs by themselves indicate any mental illness.

- Sleep disruptions; inability to sleep or unusual waking hours
- Paranoid behaviors
- Withdrawal from family and friends
- Difficulty concentrating and paying attention
- Deterioration of personal hygiene
- Rambling or disorganized speech
- Flat or expressionless gaze
- Unusual sensitivity to stimuli such as light or noise
- Smelling or tasting things differently
- Steady, noticeable decline in school or work performance
- Threats of self harm or harm to others
- Can demonstrate sexual promiscuity
- Opposition to authority; truancy, vandalism or theft
- Feelings that others are watching and laughing at him

- Extreme preoccupation with religion
- A growing sense of déjà vu
- Believing that independent events are connected
- Irrational fear or anger[15]

TRAITS OF A PERSON WITH SCHIZOPHRENIA

Internal

- Experiences bizarre delusions; alien thoughts are inserted in the mind
- Has disorganized speech: rambling, incoherent, wanders from topic to topic, provides answers that do not respond to questions
- Has bizarre thinking patterns: unusual associations, illogical connections
- Experiences disturbed moods: may go from very stubborn to peaceable
- May exhibit peculiar behaviors: disheveled appearance; lack of hygiene; inappropriate sexual behavior; agitation; talking to self; jumping around
- Is confused; responds to internal stimuli, not to cues in the outside world
- Hallucinates; any sense can be affected but the most common is auditory: hearing voices that comment, threaten, or instruct
- Is anxious, apprehensive, and plagued by self-doubt
- Is socially alienated and feels misunderstood
- Is usually expressionless in speech with little body language
- Shows inappropriate affect; laughs or cries without reason, or shows no emotion
- Feels estranged from self; does not feel real
- Has difficulty concentrating; poor memory

Interpersonal

- Avoids new situations
- Can be out-of-control and impulsive
- Withdraws from others; is secretive and inaccessible

[15] Health Canada.

TRAITS OF CHILDREN AND ADOLESCENTS
WHO HAVE LATER BECOME SCHIZOPHRENIC

This disorder is rarely seen in children, and there are few definitive hallmarks in childhood that can predict a later schizophrenic problem. Though there are several characteristics that might indicate a predisposition toward schizophrenia, most children who display some of these traits will not go on to develop a mental illness.

POSSIBLE EARLY WARNING SIGNS OF SCHIZOPHRENIA IN A CHILD:

- Is unresponsive, withdrawn in infancy; has poor muscle tone
- Is irritable in childhood; flat in affect; easily distracted
- Has low reactivity in childhood and adolescence; poor motor functions such as coordination and balance
- Is shy and introverted; rarely joyful (girls, all ages)
- Is disruptive; displays inappropriate behavior (boys, all ages)
- Is unresponsive in adolescence; has poor eye contact, little facial expression, and lack of voice inflection
- Is socially incompetent in adolescence

SIGNS OF RELAPSE IN AN INDIVIDUAL WHO SUFFERS FROM
SCHIZOPHRENIA BUT IS IN REMISSION

- Is anxious and irritable
- Is withdrawn, depressed
- Exhibits strange, uninhibited behaviors
- Changes in thought and speech
- Begins to sound suspicious or have delusions

UNUSUAL DISORDERS THAT CONTAIN PSYCHOSIS

Brief Reactive Psychosis is characterized by delusions, hallucinations, catatonic symptoms, and strange speech, but the symptoms last for a very short period (one day to one month) after which the individual returns to full, normal functioning. This disorder often occurs after an overwhelmingly stressful event.

Shared Psychosis is a disorder that is shared by another individual (for example, a spouse or parent) which develops as a result of close living with a person who has schizophrenia or suffers from delusions. The new, shared disorder is similar to the delusional person's original problem.

Drug-Induced Psychosis is diagnosed when hallucinations or delusions are caused by the physiological effects of drugs such as alcohol, amphetamines, cannabis, cocaine, inhalants, and the effects of withdrawal from drugs or alcohol.

CHAPTER five

Criminal Types

This chapter examines criminal types and lists the traits associated with specific types of criminal activity. To enrich a character whose criminal behavior is designed from this chapter, you can refer back to chapters on childhood, adolescence, or adulthood. It is easy to see how some adult types lend themselves to criminal behavior. For example, a character exemplifying the Dependent type (page 27) might make a fine accomplice because she was afraid to speak up. The Fall Guy (page 31) is ripe for becoming a victim in a confidence scheme. A Narcissist type (page 104) could be caught up in his grandiosity and embezzle money because he thinks, "I'll pay it back. I can always make money." When he is caught, he tells his wife, "Other people do much worse, or "I'm entitled to a bigger share of the profits." And he tells himself, "I'm a successful man who needs to maintain a certain lifestyle so others have confidence in me." He also blames others: "They interfere with my ability to do my job."

In this chapter, first we have the types of people who commit non-deadly, nonsexual criminal acts, listed in alphabetical order. Second, we examine types of rapists and others who commit sexual crimes. Third, we examine types of murderers. And last, we look at people in organized crime.

Motives of Perpetrators, From the Mildly Awful to the Genuinely Evil

- Ridding oneself of obstruction; a person is in the way
- Passion, resentment, dislike, or hatred
- Belief that the outcome merits the deed
- Revenge: setting things right from past injustices
- Defense against perceived threat or attack: "I had to beat my wife; she was going to leave!"

Humans have a remarkable capacity to justify their actions, especially the bad ones. Some evil deeds are seen in a greater picture of good. Often, perpetrators see outside influences as having great power ("It wasn't in my control!") or they don't feel fully responsible (for example, temporary insanity: "I couldn't help it!"). Bad deeds always seem less wrong to the perpetrators than to the victims ("It wasn't so bad!"), and perpetrators have no desire to remember for very long, espousing "Let bygones be bygones," until events vanish into the past. Perpetrators remember events very differently than victims, but both memories are distorted.

Types of People Who Commit Nondeadly, Nonsexual Criminal Acts

ARSONIST

Arson is the malicious setting of a fire in order to destroy a specific place or building. (Also see Pyromaniac, page 134)

TRAITS OF AN ARSONIST

- Is usually a juvenile male
- Has a poor school record; often still lives with parents
- Commits the crime as a member of a group
- May be a spontaneous act
- Sets fires out of malice
- Chooses a place near home
- Does not return to the scene of the crime if situationally motivated

CONFIDENCE SPECIALIST

A confidence trick or confidence game (also known as a scam) is designed to intentionally mislead a person (the mark) with the goal of financial or other gain. The confidence trickster, con man, scam artist, or con artist often works with an accomplice called the shill, who tries to encourage the mark by pretending to believe the trickster. In a traditional con, the mark is encouraged to believe that he will obtain money dishonestly by cheating a third party, and is stunned to find that, due to what appears to be an error in pulling off the scam, he is the one who loses money. Some confidence tricks exploit the greed and dishonesty of their victims. Victims of scam do not always go to the police because they may have skirted the law in the deal.

TRAITS OF A CONFIDENCE SPECIALIST

- May work "short con" or "long con" depending on how much time and money are needed for scam
- Is presentable, personable, and well dressed
- Has the ability to gain confidence of others; intuitive
- Is patient, congenial, and a good talker
- Is determined; has good ability to withstand anxiety
- Has little in common with the petty criminal

 WARM UP Write a paragraph in which a nonviolent criminal justifies a crime to a therapist.

COUNTERFEITER OR FORGER

Copies, replicas, reproductions, and pastiches are legitimate works. They become forgeries when someone intentionally tries to pass them off as genuine items even if they know better. Sometimes the difference between legitimate copy and deliberate forgery is blurred. Guy Hain used the original molds to create copies of Auguste Rodin's sculptures. What made them forgeries was that he signed them with the name of Rodin's original foundry. Buyers, dealers, and experts do not like to believe they can be duped, so they can become ideal marks.

TRAITS OF A COUNTERFEITER OR FORGER

- Is often a creative artist
- Draws inspiration from others' work and bases forgery on someone else's technique
- Intends to deceive the buyer/receiver
- Has good technical ability
- Justifies actions: "If I can paint a picture that people buy as a Monet, I must be as good as the original"
- Is usually male
- Is motivated by a battle of wits against the expert
- Bolsters self-esteem through success
- Desires the creation of a sensational object, not financial gain
- May be a one-time event or a career
- Is motivated by envy, jealousy, inferiority, and desire for attention
- May have desire to "prove" a theory

FORGING SPECIALTIES

Archaeological

- Forged items may include skulls, weapons, pottery, or engravings. Another scam is selling a real piece but trying to pass it off as being of earlier origin. Most of the archaeological forgery is made for reasons similar to art forgery—for money. The monetary value of an item thought to be thousands of years old is higher than a similar one sold as a souvenir. However, archaeological or paleontological forgers may have other motives; they may try to manufacture proof for their point of view or favorite theory, or to gain increased fame and prestige for themselves. If the intent is to create "proof" for religious history, it is pious fraud.

- To detect forgeries, investigators of archaeological forgery rely on the tools of archaeology in general. Since the age of the object is usually the most significant detail, they try to use carbon dating or neutron activation analysis to find out the real age of the object.

Artistic

- Forged items include paintings, drawings, furniture, sculptures, ceramics, gems, ivories, or lace. The forger may run a reputable business in restoration, and may be a respected dealer. Another scam is to age pieces by knocking a nose off a statue, adding wormholes, or creating patina so an item looks older. A different tack is to present a piece as an entirely new discovery; such as an "early work of so-and-so."

- Art forgery dates back more than two thousand years to Roman sculptors producing copies of Greek sculptures. Before the commercial art market, copying a work of a master was considered a tribute, not a forgery. In the previous centuries, many painters like Rembrandt had workshops with apprentices who studied painting techniques by copying the works and style of the master.

- An art forger must be at least somewhat proficient in the area he is trying to imitate. Many forgers have been fledgling artists who tried to break into the art market and eventually resorted to forgery. Some forgers have borrowed the original item, copied it, and given the copy to the original owners. Although many art forgers are in the business solely for money, some have claimed that they have created forgeries to expose the credulity and snobbishness of the art world.

- In detection, art experts try to discover its provenance by studying catalogues of previous auctions to find out whether it has been for sale elsewhere. If the item has no paper trail, it is probably a forgery.

Investigators may try to use carbon dating to find out the real age of the item, but this is useful mainly in very old items. They may analyze pigments to find out if the paints used are too modern. They can use X-rays to find whether a painting had been painted on old canvas, or over some other painting (not a surefire method since a genuine artist may have also reused old canvases if they could not afford new ones). X-ray fluorescence can also reveal if metals in metal sculpture or even in the pigments are too pure. Sometimes they may be able to check the artist's fingerprints left in the paint.

Checks

- Check forging is no longer the elaborate business that it once was so the artistry is not needed. Now it can be spontaneous; not carefully planned; exploiting situations as they arise.

- Check forgers are suspicious, distrustful, impulsive, and rapid workers; they are manipulative and may impersonate others if required. They tend to be migratory but stay within a region. They are loners avoiding personal relationships and other criminals. They are tense, blundering when tension gets high. They expect to get caught somewhat regularly. They spend money fast when they have it, for example, by gambling. They may be well educated and come from a professional family.[1]

Criminal

- Forged items include coins and paper money, false and altered checks, wills, deeds, copyrights, letters, postage stamps, or false identity papers. This is very popular during wartime. The forger's hope is to get rich quick; the goal is financial gain or, in the case of forged currency, to flood the market and cause political chaos.

- Criminal forgers may be gamblers. They may also forge identities to gain position, title, or money: For example, a son who is believed drowned "reappears" and is accepted years later by a grieving, wishful mother.[2]

[1] Lemert (1958) [2] Cole (1956)

Identity

- Identity theft is a newer brand of forgery. It is the deliberate assumption of another person's identity, usually to gain access to their finances or to frame them for a crime; these days it is also used to enable illegal immigration, terrorism, or espionage. It may also be a means of blackmail, especially if medical privacy has been breached. Identity theft is usually the result of serious breaches of privacy.

- In many parts of the world, identity theft is the fastest growing offense, although a 2005 study showed that the crime had leveled. Still, 4.25 percent of all adults in the U.S. are victims of identity fraud on an annual basis.

- Identity theft is often assumed to be accomplished through sophisticated methods such as infiltration of organizations that store information, but illegal access to personal information often happens through traditional means (paper financial statements, checks, or credit cards), and the perpetrator is often someone previously known to the victim, such as a "friend," family member, or acquaintance.

Literary

- Forged items include manuscripts, autographs, first editions, or "new" works. Like other forgers, the literary forger must be extremely knowledgeable about materials and possess a remarkably adaptable mimetic ability without giving himself away by allowing his own personal mannerisms to infect his fakes.

- Some work that is sold may have been created with innocent intent many years ago, or the forger may have political motives: he may forge documents to incriminate a person. Literary works, like artistic pieces may be presented as an entirely new discovery.

 WARM UP Write a humorous obituary for a nonviolent criminal.

DELINQUENT

Delinquent is a term that usually refers to a young person who is breaking laws. There is debate about the treatment of delinquency: whether to simply punish the crime or, because the perpetrators are young, to address the forces that contribute to delinquency, such as abuse, poverty, and peer pressure. For female delinquents, research shows that the father is usually absent and the mother may be addicted to drugs or alcohol, offers no protection to the daughter, and chooses men over her.[3] This may account for some of the traits.

TRAITS OF A FEMALE DELINQUENT

- Is comfortable on the street
- Is unforgiving
- Is violent toward and competitive with other girls
- Sees prestige in sex, boys, and older men; brags about sexual prowess
- Gains a sense of power from sex
- Feels betrayed by mother but hopes for reunion with her
- Angry at mother, but fiercely attached to her

TRAITS OF A MALE DELINQUENT

- Is poorly socialized; assertive and aggressive
- Is unafraid; impulsive
- Is unconventional
- Is defiant, hostile, and suspicious
- Is sadistic with mental problems
- Is destructive[4]

 WARM UP Judgments about women's violence against men are less harsh then judgments of men against women. Write a quick scene of domestic abuse with the expected roles reversed.[5]

---

[3] Berger (1989); Calhoun, Jurgens, and Chen (1993) [4] Wilson and Herrnstein (1985).[5] Sorenson and Taylor (2005).

DOMESTIC ABUSER

Domestic Abuse is commonly thought of as synonymous with "wife-beating," but battering can occur between female partners, male partners, or women against men. The following lists deal with spousal abuse: men who batter their wives and women who batter their husbands.

WIFE-BATTERER

A Wife-Batterer is a man who consistently physically abuses his female partner. There are three distinct types of Wife-Batterer: Emotionally Volatile; Family Violent (most common); and Violent Psychopath (differs from Psychopath, page 113).[6]

Traits of a Wife-Batterer

Batterer, Emotionally Volatile

- Violent only within family
- Socially isolated; few friends
- Socially incompetent; doesn't know how to behave with others
- Depressed; feels inadequate
- Emotionally volatile

Batterer, Family Violent

- Majority of spouse abusers
- Less severe and less aggressive
- Suppresses angry emotions
- Feels remorse

Batterer, Violent Psychopath

- Violent to everyone; in many situations
- Belligerent; contemptuous
- More use of alcohol
- Psychopathic traits

[6] Holtzworth-Munroe and Stuart (1994).

WARM UP Battered wife syndrome is a recognized psychological condi-tion to describe a woman who, because of constant and severe physical abuse by a male partner, becomes depressed and unable to take any independent action that would allow her to escape the abuse. The condition explains why abused women often do not seek assistance from others, fight their abuser, or leave the abusive situation. Sufferers have low self-esteem and often believe that the abuse is their fault. Such women usually refuse to press charges against their abuser and refuse all offers of help, often becom-ing aggressive or abusive to others who attempt to offer assistance. Although the condition usually affects women, children and, more rarely, men can also exhibit the syndrome.

More controversially, continual abuse has been used, at law, as a defense for abused persons who subsequently attack or kill the abuser, or engage in violence or sexual abuse against others at the behest of the abuser.

Write the closing argument for either the defense or the prosecution in a bat-tered wife (who retaliated) case.

HUSBAND BATTERER

New research suggests more and more that women can be just as violent as their male counterparts. Women also express violence toward their intimate partners. Ten percent of all couples report mutual violence.

Traits of a Husband Batterer

Responds to aggressive moves with increased aggression

- May have stalked her partner before the relationship developed
- May have been abused as a child
- Has often witnessed abuse
- Uses violence to control her partner's behavior
- Is unable to verbally express herself in a satisfactory way
- Is reacting to being abandoned or being threatened with abandonment[7]

[7] Frieze (2005).

Values and Traits of Violent People

- Have overwhelming need to express intense feelings at anyone
- Crave excitement: planning, implementing, and escaping is thrilling
- Need to flee from pressured situations
- Want justice or retribution for perceived wrongs
- May justify violence with religious or political beliefs
- Are selfish, personally entitled; they want material gain and disregard others
- Have poor self-esteem: any threat of inferiority, blame, or humiliation evokes a violent response
- Are self-indulgent: want others to cater to their needs
- Have history of abuse that teaches violence as acceptable punishment
- Have always believed that they were defective
- Want social acceptance and violent behavior may satisfy a gang[8]

HABITUAL PETTY CRIMINAL

The habitual petty criminal is firmly entrenched in the world of crime, although she never seems to get very skilled at it and remains on the low rungs of the criminal ladder.

TRAITS OF A HABITUAL PETTY CRIMINAL

- Is easily caught
- Is often arrested; has long criminal record
- Rarely commits felonies; always sticks to petty crime
- Begins at an early age
- Has extensive connections in the underworld and thinks of herself as a criminal
- Is unsophisticated, lazy, and irresponsible

[8] Flannery (1997)

- Is a failure in social situations
- Is eventually unable to get legitimate work[9]

IMPOSTER/PRETENDER

An Imposter or Pretender is a criminal involved in a disputed identity claim. Imposters often appeal to romantic sensibilities but these days, with sophisticated medical science, this type of crime may be increasingly difficult to successfully pull off. Some Imposters can make a career out of pretending; many take advantage of an opportunity for some kind of gain.

TRAITS OF AN IMPOSTER

- Is intelligent
- Is verbal; a good talker
- Delights in deceiving people
- Has one type of deception; for example:
  - A child disappears; a lost heir returns (Lindbergh baby)
  - A lost adult reappears (Anna Anderson as Anastasia)
  - A world-weary adult plots to make people think that he is dead
  - A mysterious simple person appears from nowhere; cannot explain himself; people speculate about his/her origins[10]

KLEPTOMANIAC

People with this disorder are compelled to steal things, often things of little or no value, or things that they could easily pay for. They are often unaware of performing the theft until some time later. Rarely, this obsession leads to sexual arousal, and then the term kleptophilia is used.

TRAITS OF A KLEPTOMANIAC

- Cannot resist impulse to take things; steals habitually
- Is not stealing for financial gain; does not need the items

[9] Clinard (1960) [10] Bondeson (2004).

- Does not plan beforehand; mostly situational, taking place in a store
- Often gives items away as gifts
- Sometimes hides items or throws them away
- The need to steal builds beforehand and is reduced by the theft
- Is not dangerous; does not lead to more severe stealing

LATE-BLOOMING CRIMINAL

The Late-Blooming Criminal is interesting because he has led a law-abiding life. For different reasons, the external structure that has kept him in check has weakened, and, without those controls, criminal behaviors are free to emerge.

TRAITS OF A LATE-BLOOMING CRIMINAL

- Has no history of criminal behavior
- Was kept in check during first part of life by domineering mother or religion
- Is freed by old age to express the existing, but suppressed, criminal attitude
- Has had a foundation laid for crime early but it remained dormant until controls broke
- Is intrusive to others; likes to control others
- Is self-indulgent and irresponsible[11]

LOOTER

Looting is often opportunistic, with a lapse in authority fostering the belief that one can violate private ownership with impunity. After a disaster, a looter may believe that if he doesn't secure the property it will be taken by someone else. Looters are often locals of the site of the disaster, and as such, are likely directly impacted by the disrupting event.

[11] Walters (1990).

TRAITS OF A LOOTER

- Becomes aggressive when frustrated
- Strikes out indiscriminately
- Is opportunistic
- Is usually an employed person; not the poorest individual
- Often loots with a partner or with a family member
- Stays in own neighborhood and rarely loots elsewhere
- Acts out during natural disasters and civil problems
- Can be a person of any race, man and woman, adult or young person
- Commits crimes in public in full view of others[12]

OCCASIONAL OFFENDER

The Occasional Offender does not think of himself or herself as a criminal and does not make a living from crime.

TRAITS OF AN OCCASIONAL OFFENDER

- Sees crime as fortuitous, a chance opportunity
- Likes the thrill
- Acts when she needs money (check forgery is common with occasional offenders)
- Unsophisticated in criminal techniques
- No knowledge of "fences" or organized underground
- Makes no effort to progress to crimes of greater skill[13]

ORDINARY CAREER CRIMINAL

For some people, crime is the consistent way they obtain an income; it is a way of life. They repeat crimes over and over and commit large numbers of crimes, usually with a nonviolent specialization.

[12] Quarantelli and Dynes (1970). [13] Clinard (1963).

TRAITS OF AN ORDINARY CAREER CRIMINAL

- Commits conventional crimes: burglary, forgery, embezzlement, or theft
- Seeks to gain something: money, property
- Is most comfortable with others who are similar to herself
- Plans minimally and with little forethought
- Begins crime at an early age
- Shows early signs of predatory behavior
- Has a constant tension and high level of awareness
- Spends time trying to gain status in life and in prison
- Comes from a family with history of criminal activity
- Often abuses drugs or alcohol
- Is often unemployed
- Justifies behavior: "Everyone is more or less dishonest"
- Is irresponsible
- Is self-indulgent, proud of success[14]

PROFESSIONAL CAREER CRIMINAL

The Professional Career Criminal, as compared to the Ordinary Career Criminal, is the upscale version, although not as classy as the White-Collar Criminal. As compared to the Ordinary Criminal, this man or woman is more sophisticated in every way.

TRAITS OF A PROFESSIONAL CAREER CRIMINAL

- Is intelligent and polished
- Uses efficient and intricate techniques; has array of technical skills and manual dexterity
- Commits crime with higher stakes
- Considers himself skilled

[14] Walters (1990); Korn and McCorkle (1963).

- May have had a regular job; not criminal by origin
- Begins later in life; has some social skills
- Plans carefully and commits more complex crimes
- Prefers crimes such as stealing from jewelry stores by substitution; confidence games; passing illegal checks or money orders; shakedown (using force) or extortion; or "grifting" (swindling by use of deception).[15]
- Is migratory
- Rarely uses violence; relies on verbal skills and charm
- Is isolated from general society; feels like an outcast
- Is always suspicious of people[16]

PSYCHOPATH

A psychopath is not necessarily a criminal but the traits make it easy to become one. See pages 113–114.

PYROMANIAC (FIRE SETTER)

Pyromania is a rare obsession with fire and starting fires, in an intentional fashion, usually on multiple occasions. Unlike arson, the fire is not done for personal gain, money, or revenge.

The fire or its aftermath and process is the intent. There is gratification in the act of setting fires and in fire stations, firefighters, fire equipment. (Also see Arsonist, page 120.)

TRAITS OF A PYROMANIAC

- Is usually a young adult man, often unemployed
- Becomes interested in fire in childhood
- Is socially inadequate, particularly in heterosexual relationships
- Sets fires deliberately
- Is excited by the fire; thrilled and satisfied seeing the results
- Often stays to watch the fire; experiences sexual undercurrent

[15] Korn and McCorkle (1963). [16] Sutherland (1937).

- Doesn't set fire for any particular reason, like revenge or gain
- Likes everything about fires: creation and destruction
- May look for work near fires, such as forest ranger or volunteer fireman

SKYJACKER

Skyjacking has become a rare crime; security has made it very difficult to gain control of an airplane. Skyjackers take over airplanes, not with a terrorist intent, but to control the airplane's flight path, usually demanding safe passage to the country of their choice.

TRAITS OF A SKYJACKER

- Is usually a man
- Is not a very accomplished person; wants to distinguish himself
- Is often unemployed at the time of the crime
- Is shy and introverted; dominated by women
- May have a violent father who is already dead, freeing son's aggression
- Often has religious mother
- Is often his mother's confidant
- Is timid and sexually passive[17]

STALKER

Stalking is an abnormal or long-term pattern of threat or harassment (unwanted pursuit) against an individual. Five percent of U.S. women are or will be victims. It is estimated that 200,000 people in the United States are stalking someone. Stalkers, as children, may have had a history of insecure attachments. Later in life, stalking becomes a way of repeatedly trying to get a person to remain close to them. The stalker first seeks proximity; later, when rejected, the stalker wants to retaliate by hurting, controlling, damaging, or destroying the object of his love.[18]

There are five distinct types of stalking.

[17] Hubbard (1971). [18] Powers (1997).

Obsessional

This is the largest category and includes most batterers. The obsessional stalker:

- Is male; knows the victim who is usually an ex-spouse, ex-lover, or former employee
- Conducts a campaign of harassment
- Wants to get the person back; cannot, so stays close with tormenting punishment

Love Obsessional

This stalker has a deep pathological attachment to the victim. John Hinckley, Jr.'s attachment to actress Jodie Foster and his desire to impress her by shooting President Ronald Reagan falls into this category. The love obsessional stalker:

- Is a stranger to the victim
- Is obsessed; wants to make the victim aware of his existence
- Does not really love the victim, but feels connected
- Is not psychotic

Erotomaniacal

This stalker believes that the victim is willing and in love with her. The erotomaniacal stalker:

- Is usually female, occasionally male
- Has delusion about a (usually famous) victim that feelings are reciprocated
- Can begin with an innocent glance from the other person
- Is usually a loner or withdrawn

False Victimizing

This type makes herself the victim of attention. The false victimizing stalker:

- Has a conscious or unconscious desire to be seen as the victim
- Falsifies physical abuse
- Blames the object of her love for stalking and hurting her

Psychopathic

This is the most dangerous stalker and often a killer (see Serial Murderer). Psychopathy is often characterized by antisocial and impulsive behavior. Psychopaths lack empathy so they cannot feel their victim's distress. Approximately 3 percent of men and 1 percent of women have some form of psychopathic personality disorder (on page 113). The psychopathic stalker:

- Is usually male
- Is a dangerous predator; no love or delusion involved
- Is detached
- Desires to harm, usually to induce fear and kill
- Has no particular motive

 FIGURES AND STATISTICS What happens to the Victims of Stalkers?

94 percent make lifestyle changes

83 percent suffer from anxiety

74 percent develop a sleep disorder

53 percent develop fatigue

45 percent have appetite problems

39 percent relocate

37 percent change work

24 percent have suicidal thoughts [19]

VIOLENT CRIMINAL

A Violent Criminal easily resorts to physical aggression even if it is unnecessary in the completion of his crime.

TRAITS OF A VIOLENT CRIMINAL

- May act with minimal or no provocation
- Does not hide aggression
- Is not deterred from crime by fear of consequences
- Belongs to a culture of violence

[19] Journal Watch Psychiatry (1997).

- Values power
- May have been subjected to violence as a child; may have witnessed violence or subjugation
- May have been coached into violence by peers or mentor[20]

WHITE-COLLAR CRIMINAL

"White-Collar" refers to the characteristic white-collar shirts worn by lawyers, bankers, and other professionals associated with business crimes. The crimes include fraud, bankruptcy fraud, bribery, insider trading, embezzlement, computer crime, medical crime, public corruption, environmental crime, pension fund crime, RICO (the Racketeer Influenced and Corrupt Organizations Act of 1970) crimes, consumer fraud, occupational crime, securities fraud, and financial fraud. It is estimated that a great deal of white-collar crime is undetected. (See Narcissism on page 104 for personality traits of the White-Collar Criminal.)

TRAITS OF A WHITE-COLLAR CRIMINAL

- Is employed in high-status occupations with power, influence, and trust
- Commits crimes in conjunction with work: business, law, labor, labor union official, politician
- Separates business and personal ethics: "Business is business"
- Does not see himself as a criminal
- Justifies actions; rationalizes behavior
- Associates with others like himself, so there is less objective scrutiny
- Feels contempt for law; feels above the law
- Is arrogant
- Often conceals criminal acts through elaborate organization
- Learns potential illegalities, such as insider trading, through business knowledge

[20] Athens (1992).

NEW INFORMATION One of the newer White-Collar crimes is computer related. This is usually done by an ex-computer programmer, engineer, or data entry clerk who knows techniques of erasing information. The goal is to steal money by moving it to an accessible location or to sell information. Additional gain is derived from proving oneself smarter than others and by using one's computer knowledge as power.

Types of Rapists and Others Who Commit Sexual Crimes

EXHIBITIONIST

When done without the consent of the viewer, sexual exhibitionism is generally considered to be a sexually aggressive act, and is a criminal offense. Most indecent exposure is committed by men against female viewers. The statistics on exhibitionism are skewed by society's norms—women who expose themselves in public are rarely arrested as exhibitionists, and it is considered more acceptable. Men who expose themselves in this way generally do not commit more serious sexual crimes. Most exhibitionists are very cautious. Some people like to expose themselves in front of large crowds, typically at sporting events, which has been nicknamed "streaking."

TRAITS OF AN EXHIBITIONIST
- Is usually male and feels manly while exhibiting himself
- Is sexually aroused by urges and fantasies of exposing genitals to women
- Sometimes masturbates while exhibiting himself
- Is not usually physically dangerous
- May hope to arouse observer or may believe the observer will be aroused
- Likes being noticed, even if it is negative attention

SEXUAL ABUSER

Sexual abuse is considered to be any behavior that is sexually inappropriate. It is not confined to acts against underage children. Children, adolescents, or adults can be sexually coerced or abused. Men and women can both be sexually abused. Sexual abuse can also occur within a marriage. The abuse may be violent, such as rape, or it may be manipulative, such as an older brother toward a younger sibling. Victims don't always know whether they have cooperated, especially if the abuse is at the hands of someone about whom they care deeply, such as a parent or sibling. Victims are even more confused about how they should have responded: scream, tell someone, or refuse. Children do not always have words to explain the interactions until they are older, especially if the abuse was limited to nonviolent fondling combined with displays of affection. When the abuse is between an adult and child, 80 percent know the child, and 50 percent have the child in their care at the time.

The impact of abuse on the victim depends on many things: the age of the victim, his relationship with the abuser, the circumstances of the abuse, the amounts of violence used, the support received after the abuse, and the length of time that the abuse has.

TRAITS OF A SEXUAL ABUSER

- Is usually male
- Is coercive, forceful; uses trickery
- Offers privileges, attention, or rewards
- Threatens retaliation and reprisal
- Urges secrecy
- Is cautious in public
- Has poor boundaries; disregards or is unaware of appropriate personal limits
- Makes excuses for behavior

TWO TYPES OF PERPETRATORS OF SEXUAL ABUSE

Tyrannical Type

- "King of the Mountain": His behavior expresses self-centeredness and his lack of respect for others. He is openly into power and may abuse adults or children, depending on his proclivity.

Inhibited Type

- "Mr. Mom": His behavior replaces an adult affair. He prefers to think of himself as friendly and denies either inadequacy with adults or a general rage. The inhibited type may prefer young people because he is afraid of other adults.

Excuses of Perpetrators

- Denial: "It was an expression of love."
- Justification or distortion: "It's not really sex."
- Blame the victim: "The child did not stop me."
- Blame others: "Her mother shouldn't have left her alone."

NYMPHOPHILE

A nymphophile experiences sexual desire for female children, usually prepubescent because he is aroused by lack of pubic hair and other signs of immaturity.

TRAITS OF A NYMPHOPHILE

- Is heterosexual; may also desire women and may marry
- Justifies behavior: "I was teaching her about love" or "I'm better than an awkward boy"
- Usually knows the girl
- Shows interest and gains her trust
- Fondles more frequently than engaging in intercourse
- Feels guilt
- Convinces himself that the desire is mutual
- Convinces himself that child is able to give consent
- Insists that he feels affection
- Avoids violence; takes pains not to frighten the child
- Knows how to behave appropriately in public[21]

[21] Masters (1966).

PEDOPHILE

A pedophile is a person who is sexually attracted, primarily or exclusively, to prepubescent children, boys or girls or both.

TRAITS OF A PEDOPHILE

- Is aroused by urges and fantasies to have sex with a preteen child: some act on urges and have sex with a preteen child; others limit themselves to exposing genitals or masturbating in front of the child without touching the child
- Is often attracted to a child of a particular age (may be as specific as age eight to ten)
- May have been abused in childhood
- Shows attention, generosity, and affection to the child
- May court a woman who has an appealing child
- May, in extreme situations, abduct a child or swap children
- May threaten the child to ensure silence
- May have no preference for boy or girl
- Excuses himself by saying that the child was to blame, or "It was no big deal," or "No harm done"

NEW INFORMATION In the physical world, a child usually knows her molester. Online, the story is different. Children and adolescents are approached in "chat rooms" or with "instant messages." Over time, with continued "chat," children become less cautious. The predator gains more information, builds trust, flatters, and creates an emotional bond. Then sexual photos may begin, paving the way for a meeting.

PORNOGRAPHER

Pornography may use any of a variety of media—written and spoken text, photos, sculpture, drawing, sounds, films, novels, or live performances—in which the goal is sexual arounsal. A pornographer makes sexually explicit material.

Some pornographers are business people who create material with consenting adults and without ever abusing either a child or adult. Others may coerce or abuse adults and children into participation and may engage in sexual activity. Pornographers may use children to create porn, and may use porn to seduce children. Those who involve children usually involve their own child or neighborhood children, and are in denial about the seriousness of the acts. They convince themselves that:

- The child gave consent
- The child encouraged the behavior
- He was kind to the child
- The activities were mutual
- No harm was done because sex or porn was done with patience or love

RAPIST

Rape results from different, often overlapping, motivations, seen in the traits described below,[22] which are found in many of the following specific types of rapists. In addition to the following types of rapist, some men commit rape during the commission of another crime with the rape a secondary motive to the criminal.

Sexual criminals who have strong needs for repetition or ritual cannot change, so they follow a pattern: For example, they may choose victims with similar physical characteristics, engage in the sexual act in certain ways, or use the same words or phrases every time. Because the ritual is a need, the rapist cannot easily vary his behavior.

GENERAL TRAITS OF A RAPIST

- Lacks self-confidence at an early age; does not want to feel helpless
- Is often hypermasculine or macho
- May have been abused as a child; used to be a victim, now is a victimizer
- Has witnessed violence in his family
- Began assaults in childhood and adolescence

[22] Douglas, et al. (1992). .

- Is hostile toward women; discharge of anger, rather than the sex, is satisfying
- Believes that aggression and dominance are aspects of male sexuality
- Relies on peers to support rape
- Justifies behavior: "She didn't behave the way she was supposed to"
- May have trouble with erection or ejaculation during the assault (happens to about 30 percent) [23]

There are six different types of rapists, each discussed in the following pages. Each type exemplifies different traits, but most also contain the traits of a general rapist. If the victim is a stranger, the rape suggests that a compulsion is driving the attack, which may indicate that the perpetrator is a serial rapist. For profiling purposes, serial rapes that increase in the degree of physical force used can signal serial murder potential.[24]

ACQUAINTANCE RAPIST

This type of rape is usually situational. A social relationship exists, often of short duration, and the assault normally occurs on a date, and often begins with consensual interaction. The victim feels she knows the man well enough to be alone with him.

Traits of an Acquaintance Rapist

- Expresses little aggression
- Does no severe physical injury to the victim
- Has good social skills and no involvement in criminal activity
- May use alcohol or drugs to facilitate the assault
- Convinces himself that victim is consenting even if she is unconscious[25]

ANGRY RAPIST

An Angry Rapist may choose either a victim he knows or a stranger. The rape is an expression of anger and rage; sex replaces anger, and the victim replaces

[23] Moglia and Knowles (1993) [24] Holmes and De Burger (1988). [25] Abel and Osborn (1992).

some hated person. The rape can also include behaviors from verbal aggression to murder.

Traits of an Angry Rapist

- Is impulsive; often under the influence of alcohol or drugs
- Has history of perceived slights, insults, and rejections by many people over the years
- Hates women generally; may direct anger specifically toward girls or elderly women
- Insults, humiliation, and punishment of the victim are as important as the rape itself

GROUP RAPISTS

Group rape (sometimes called gang rape) occurs when friends or a gang with allegiance to each other commit sexual assault.

Traits of a Group Rapist

- May plan rape or may act on impulse
- Is susceptible to peer pressure and usually commits rape as an attempt to gain group acceptance
- Is persuaded by the leader of the group
- Goes along with action out of fear of or respect for the group leader[26]

POWER-REASSURANCE RAPIST

A Power-Reassurance Rapist acts out in an expression of a rape fantasy. The core of the fantasy is that the victim will fall in love with him. High sexual arousal and loss of control results in a distorted perception of the situation; For example, he may want to date the victim afterwards.

Traits of a Power-Reassurance Rapist

- Has a history of sexual preoccupation

[26] Revich and Schlesinger (1978).

- Has a history of living out sexual perversions: strange masturbatory practices, voyeurism, exhibitionism, obscene calls, or fetishism
- Feels deeply inadequate as a man: believes no one in her right mind would voluntarily have sex with him

SADISTIC RAPIST

A Sadistic Rapist is not impulsive, but rather plans the rape. He chooses a victim that is usually unknown and unsuspecting. The victim is usually injured moderately to severely during the act.

Traits of a Sadistic Rapist

- Uses more violence than necessary to make the victim comply with his wishes
- Is aroused as a result of the pain or fear inflicted on the victim: whipping, bondage, burning, or cutting
- Has a history of behavior problems
- Is predatory; enjoys taking by force, sometimes uses objects in sex
- Seeks control and power, not sex

SEXUAL RAPIST

A Sexual Rapist acts to express his sexual-sadistic fantasies and may want to physically harm his victim in addition to the rape.

Traits of a Sexual Rapist

- Cannot separate sex from aggressive feelings; aggression heightens sexual feelings, or sexual arousal increases rage
- May begin rape as a seduction
- May have longstanding specific fixation on body parts that have sexual significance: breasts, buttocks, anus, genitals, or mouth

OTHER TYPES OF SEXUAL ASSAULT

In addition to rape, there are other types of sexual assaults that arise from psychological problems. Some people do not have physical contact with their victim, but the motivation is still sexual gratification. At one extreme we have the person who gets an isolated wrong number when dialing the telephone and impulsively blurts out obscenities. At the other extreme there are people who engage in long-standing, patterned compulsive behaviors, such as creating routes for peeping in windows, or carrying a video camera to film people or behaviors that interest them sexually.

Some acts of sexual assault are predominantly coercive because the offender uses power or position—employer, police officer, therapist, teacher, coach, or physician—to get the other person to comply. Force is not needed and no severe physical injuries occur; dominance or authority is enough.

Another form of sexual assault to be considered is domestic sexual abuse, that is abuse between people who have a relationship with each other, such as partner/partner or husband/wife. Adults may be legally married or in a common-law relationship, or they may be a same-sex couple. Domestic sexual abuse often has a conflict already established, such as money or work problems, and often has alcohol or drugs as the precipitant. The other difference between sexual assault on a stranger vs. that on a partner is that the latter escalates from a quarrel that intensifies into hitting, biting, and throwing things before the assault.

Types of Murderers

Murder means that a person or persons caused a death or deaths that are not justifiable or accidental.

Innately, people do not like to kill. People have become more willing to kill because of desensitization, conditioning, and denial. Desensitization encourages contempt, thereby allowing people to convince themselves that the victim or enemy is different: not human. In World War II, for instance, only 15–25 percent of combat infantry soldiers were willing to fire their guns. By the time soldiers went to Korea, 50 percent were willing to shoot. In Vietnam, the figure was up to 90 percent. Conditioning develops the quick behavioral reflexes of shooting. Repetitive training allows soldiers to shoot and forget that they are hitting real people. The price paid for the ability to kill can be seen in the increase of post-traumatic stress reactions (see page 243). Desensitization has found its way into the general culture.[27]

Murderers are people who have committed a murder. Therefore, no one set of characteristics exists that includes all individuals. Most murderers are *not* career criminals. Many have never been previously arrested. The following are types of murderers where the crime was not accidental, such as a driving accident, or justified, such as self-defense. Each type has distinct traits associated with a particular kind of murder.

ARGUMENTATIVE MURDERER

This murder is born in the personality of the murderer. The murderer uses violence to solve problems and this is an extension of his ordinary behavior. The victim may have insulted the murderer publicly or have a history of assaultive behavior.

TRAITS OF AN ARGUMENTATIVE MURDERER

- Is usually a young adult male with little education
- Does not use sexual assault
- May be using drugs or alcohol
- Has a history of violence (fights, but not murder)
- Knows the victim
- Is sloppy; does not plan

 FIGURES AND STATISTICS In a 2000 study of 600 undergraduates, 60 percent of males said they had a recent fantasy of killing other people; 32 percent of females said the same thing. [28]

DOMESTIC MURDERER

This is a homegrown murder; it can be from different motivations and serve different goals. The murderer may plan the crime, or it may be completely

[27] Grossman (1995). [28] APA Monitor on Psychology (January, 2000).

impulsive; the similarity is that the victim is a relative sharing the home, a parent, child, or spouse.

TRAITS OF A DOMESTIC MURDERER

- Plans murder to look like an accident, suicide, or death by natural causes
- Cannot control internal impulses
- Usually behaves better toward the victim just before the murder
- Demonstrates care and concern toward the victim

EROTOMANIACAL MURDERER

This is a rare type of murderer, often as a culmination of stalking (see pages 135–137). There is a delusional component to this murderer—the killer imagines a relationship has existed with the victim. The victim is sometimes someone well known, especially a person of higher status or a celebrity.

TRAITS OF AN EROTOMANIACAL MURDERER

- Is fixated on someone
- Is preoccupied with and consumed by the victim
- Is often also a stalker
- Does not expect any gain, money, or sex
- Is looking for spiritual union with the victim
- Wants to own the victim
- May be motivated by real or imagined rebuff
- Believes that victim has sent secret messages
- Plans the murder carefully

 WARM UP Write two paragraphs about one of these murderers discovering his or her partner's infidelity.

EXTREMIST MURDERER

This murderer is not a professional hit man but does belong to a group. Murder is committed in the name of a body of ideas; the victim represents opposite beliefs. The ideas can be political (murder of Yitzhak Rabin), religious (Hezbollah extremists), or racist (KKK). Also see Terrorist (page 157). These types of murderers may also kill others because of their association with the intended victim.

TRAITS OF AN EXTREMIST MURDERER

- Looks for a public place; plans escape
- Stalks or watches the victim; usually ambushes the victim
- Has a history of hating a particular group
- Follows the media accounts of the person who is targeted
- Often had a difficult childhood
- Is looking for a purpose in life; the group satisfies that search

FEMALE MURDERER

Murderers are mostly men, but female murderers have some distinct traits that differ from typical male murderers. The average age of a female murderer is thirty-one. Sixty percent are or have been married; 40 percent are unmarried. A third have a past history of violent crimes, and half have an arrest record. When the murderer is female, the crime usually occurs in the victim's home, although over the decades, the room has changed: In the 1950s, it was the kitchen and in the 1990s, the bedroom or den. Occasionally, in especially aggressive murders, the murder does not take place in the home at all, but in the street, alley, or yard. Eighty percent of the victims of female murderers are men who were lovers or friends. Female murderers may also murder in self-defense, in an effort to stop physical abuse before the abuser kills her.

TRAITS OF A FEMALE MURDERER

- Is often unemployed
- Has often been drinking
- Usually uses a gun or knife as a weapon

- Usually murders a person known to her
- Usually murders at night, between 8:00 P.M. and 2:00 A.M.
- Kills children more often than men do, often after a history of abuse and neglect
- Rarely kills strangers (only 7 percent)
- Does not usually commit premeditated murders
- May kill after a fight with the victim
- Often kills out of rage, jealousy, anger, or revenge[29]

INCIDENTAL MURDERER

This person is an accidental murderer; he doesn't have murder as the goal. Unfortunately, the victim was in the way or in the wrong place. The victim is a threat to the success of another crime.

TRAITS OF AN INCIDENTAL MURDERER

- Does not plan to murder.
- Commits murder during panic and confusion or on impulse; may have been startled by an alarm or a scream
- May be either a novice or experienced criminal
- May use alcohol or drugs, which increases volatile nature

INHERITANCE MURDERER

This murderer kills because she will profit from the death of the victim; it has little to do with angry feelings toward the victim.

TRAITS OF AN INHERITANCE MURDERER

- Is motivated by financial profit
- Has a close relationship, business or personal, with the victim
- May plan carefully or be spontaneous depending on personality
- May try to stage murder to look like an accident or natural death

[29] Mann (1996).

- Often chooses suffocation or poison because these methods may escape notice
- Acts as a result of some trigger: money problems, change of circumstances
- Is nervous before and after murder; tries to provide a tight alibi
- May avoid being available for questioning

PASSIONATE MURDERER

The Passionate Murderer is in a state of high emotion, and is not thinking rationally when the murder occurs.

TRAITS OF A PASSIONATE MURDERER
- Responds to a crisis: cheating spouse caught in the act
- Sees murder as the solution to a problem
- Knows the victim well
- Feels provoked
- Does not plan murder; it's reactionary

PROFESSIONAL MURDERER (HIT MAN OR CONTRACT KILLER)

A Professional Murderer is generally married and has a family who is completely unaware of his professional activities.

TRAITS OF A PROFESSIONAL MURDERER
- Kills for material gain: money or favors
- Keeps work separate from all other aspects of life
- Is emotionally distant; can discuss murders matter-of-factly
- May be a member of organized crime
- Takes victim by surprise
- Kills quickly and efficiently; spends little time at crime scene
- Uses sophisticated weapons that indicate a specialist
- Is comfortable with killing
- Leaves weapons at the scene to avoid being found with them
- Rarely has a history of stealing or sexual assault
- Often has a particular style of killing, whether knife, cyanide, or gun

- Has history of violence
- Stalks the victim; murder is often premeditated
- Has no relationship with or emotional attachment to the target[30]

PRODUCT-TAMPERING MURDERER

This is a very specific way to commit a murder. There may be an intended victim or it may be random; in any case, it always appears random. The murderer kills by sabotaging a product such as aspirin, baby food, or soft drinks. The motive is usually to obtain money through a lawsuit on behalf of the victim, or the sabotage of a company or business: a competitor company goes under and stock falls. And often the murderer has more to gain than money; for example, a bad marriage ends, or insurance money is collected.

TRAITS OF A PRODUCT-TAMPERING MURDERER

- Plans the murder carefully
- Does not have a history of violent crime
- Usually only commits this type of murder once

NEW INFORMATION The Psychotic Murderer is an individual who suffers from delusions and is out of touch with reality. Most delusions are harmless to others, and most psychotic individuals are far more likely to suffer themselves than to make anyone else suffer. Usually, the person has a history of hospitalizations. The delusions of a psychotic murderer may involve persecution, relentless voices telling the psychotic individual to kill, or a belief that the psychotic individual is someone else (the Great Avenger), and has a job to do. The psychotic individual may believe that he is being pursued by an evil force or a member of a secret society, and murder is the only way out of danger. They often kill someone they know because a familiar person is more likely to be part of their delusional system. It may be spontaneous or somewhat planned, and there is remorse only if the delusion that motivated the killing is understood to be false. (See the traits of delusions in chapter four under Schizophrenic on page 114.)

---

[30] Douglas and Schlesinger (1980).

SCHOOL SHOOTER

There is no accurate personality "profile" for school shooters. They come from a variety of races, ages, family situations, achievement and popularity levels, and disciplinary history. But these traits have been found in the students (usually male) who have killed people in schools.

TRAITS OF A SCHOOL SHOOTER

- Is rarely impulsive; plans the act
- Does not keep attack secret; others know that something is being planned
- Does not threaten targets prior to shooting
- Beforehand, behaves in ways that concern others, like writing troubled poems or trying to buy guns[31]
- Usually kills himself

SERIAL MURDERER

A Serial Murderer's personality is reflected in his killings. The crimes are not committed for greed, jealousy, profit, or revenge against a close victim. Serial Murderers are severely disturbed, and their compulsion to kill increases over time; it becomes overwhelming.[32]

The urges are driven from inside, not by outside events. Complex motives make finding a serial murderer difficult, but a profile emerges with continued offenses. The killer begins to decompensate and gets sloppy; some want to be caught at this time because they feel out of control.[33]

TRAITS OF A SERIAL MURDERER

- Chooses strangers as victims.
- Is usually a white male between eighteen to thirty-five years old
- Becomes better and more ritualized with each killing; the rituals have meaning for the killer

[31] U.S. Dept of Education and the Secret Service. [32] Douglas and Olshanker (1997). [33] Revich and Schlesinger (1978).

- May be charming, articulate, and glib, but could also be angry and ineffectual
- Wants domination, manipulation, and control over others
- Has a history of bed-wetting, fire-setting, cruelty to animals, solo breaking-and-entering, or sadistic rape; stealing women's underwear during a burglary is a sign in this direction
- May take a trophy from the victim such as a ring or body part
- Rarely expresses hatred toward those close to him
- Lives in a fantasy: fantasy is about killing, and murders are attempts to fulfill fantasy
- Has a history of physical or emotional childhood abuse
- Usually chooses victims of the same race
- Is a loner; generally feels inadequate
- Feels extreme rage
- May commit crimes due to a stressor

SEXUAL MURDERER

There are two types of Sexual Murderers: Planned and Opportunistic. In both, the murderer is usually male and the victim female. Sexual elements are always part of the murder.

TRAITS OF A SEXUAL MURDERER

Planned
- May rape the victim (before or after murder)
- Obsesses over details
- Looks for a certain victim: specific age, appearance, or lifestyle
- Captures victim; often moves her to another place for the murder and the disposal of the body
- May take a trophy from victim: jewelry, driver's license, or body parts
- Behaves aggressively toward victim; for example, biting
- Is socially adept

- May impersonate someone else: a security guard

Opportunistic
- May mutilate victim as part of the murder
- Often uses more violence than is necessary to kill as an enactment of a fantasy
- Acts impulsively; does not plan
- Lives near the scene of the crime
- Feels inadequate
- Is sloppy; random
- Is socially inept and lacks interpersonal skills
- Lives alone or with parents

Experiences of Prisoners

Aside from questions of guilt or innocence, the duration of their sentences, or whether they are in a maximum- or minimum-security prison, all prisoners have some common experiences. Prisoners:

- Are trapped; no physical escape
- Have forced contact with others in prison society
- Lose self-determination; few choices are available
- Lose privacy; everything that happens can be discussed by anyone
- Must follow orders; roles are assigned and maintained
- Are subject to jailhouse public opinion and fast-spreading rumors
- Are exposed
- Learn to display power through physical and status symbols such as dress or visits
- Must behave submissively
- Are at the whim of the inmate social system whose tools are blackmail, threats, social ostracism, death, and mental torture[34]

[34] Korn and McCorkle (1963).

SIMMERING MURDERER

The Simmering Murderer cannot deal with increasing tension. Therefore, the act of murder discharges the tension.[35] Murder is a relief and is seen as restitution for real or imagined wrongs.

TRAITS OF A SIMMERING MURDERER

- Accumulates hostility
- Has history of frustration; becomes obsessed with trivial problems—such as IRS misfiled forms—even after problem is solved
- Is unable to separate trivial problems from real source of tension: self, or relationship change
- Is not experienced in murder but plans well
- Has poor history of working out conflicts in school or relationships
- Usually has long-standing conflict with victim, but may not be close
- Becomes quiet about the injustice that has sparked the killing as the plan takes shape
- Creates an imaginary link between himself and the victim
- May kill because of feeling rebuffed or for revenge for a perceived wrong
- May murder multiple victims

TERRORIST

Terrorism is premeditated, politically motivated violence against noncombatants by subnational groups or agents, usually intended to influence an audience. The focus of "modern" terrorism (since the mid 1980s) has shifted from the Left to the Right ideology.

TRAITS OF A TERRORIST

- Is motivated by political considerations
- Intentionally targets civilians
- Is not a member of a government agency

[35] Schlesinger (1996).

- Makes little distinction between strategies and tactics on one hand and principles on the other
- Is willing to die
- Is usually young, middle class, economically marginal
- Is systematic, not random, in behavior; plans
- Is totally identified with his group
- Wants to send a message[36]

 NEW INFORMATION The goal of counterterrorism is to prevent or decrease terrorism. Useful data in counterterrorism is:

- Data on activities of groups and individuals suspected of terrorism
- Information on false or forged travel documents
- Intelligence on trafficking of explosives, weapons, and nuclear, chemical, or biological materials
- Information on sophisticated communication technology
- Information on links between terrorists and organized crime

---

VISIONARY MURDERER

A Visionary Murderer is psychotic, but in a very specific way. He is on a mission, hearing a voice that commands violence. The voice is from the killer's psyche and provides instruction about the killing or the victim.

TRAITS OF A VISIONARY MURDERER

- Has delusions, and the victim is related to the delusions; has history of violence related to delusions
- Has a history of mental illness
- Feels murder was morally justified; no remorse
- Does not flee
- Can be cult leader or cult member

[36] Henderson (2004).

Organized Crime

Americans tend to think of Organized Crime as being *La Cosa Nostra* (the Mob; the American Mafia). Organized crime flourished in North America as a direct product of Prohibition (1920–1933). When liquor became illegal, organized crime became involved with extortion, gambling, bootlegging, murder, drugs, and prostitution. Today, there are quite a few varieties of criminal gangs (in the U.S. and elsewhere) in addition to the famous Godfather crowd. Outside the U.S., the main organized crime groups are: the Sicilian Mafia (Sicily), the Camorra (Naples), the Russian Mafia, the Albanian Mafia, the Yakuza (Japan), the Triads and the Tongs (Chinese), the Mexican cartels, the Jamaican Yardies and Posses, and the Medellin and Cali cartels (Columbia).

TRAITS OF THE MEMBERS OF ORGANIZED CRIME

- Use force and violence to eliminate the competition
- Supervise activities and lead the associates who work on the street
- Have careers that are almost exclusively in the criminal ring
- Have great allegiance to the leaders
- Follow a code of personal loyalty and behavior
- Discourage any new membership
- Enact clear, violent punishment for transgressions

Today, the opportunities for organized crime are global, and the Mafia has changed specialties. They are engaged in stock market fraud, cybercrime, Internet pornography, banking fraud, and gambling. The drug trade is too large to be controlled by any one organization. There are new opportunities for people-smuggling and white slaving.

There are other organized gangs in the U.S. in addition to the American Mafia. Although they are criminals, these are described in chapter twelve, Group Influences, because of the importance of the group dynamics.

CHAPTER **six**

Sexual Issues

IN THIS CHAPTER

• *Traits of Sexual Behaviors* • *Varieties of Sexual Identification* • *Genetic Sexual Disorders*

People care about being sexually "normal"—preferably sexually superior—and one of the ways individuals evaluate how well they are doing is by comparing themselves to others. In the arena of sexuality, however, comparison becomes difficult. This is because people have no way of knowing what other people are really doing, how they are doing it, or whether or not they are having fun. That may be why external sexiness is so important: It becomes a substitute for genuine information.[1]

The range of normal human sexual activity is broad. Behaviors become sexual problems when they begin to interfere with normal activities or harm others. When behaviors involve children, nonconsensual adults, coercion, or violence, they become the criminal acts that are described in chapter five. This chapter contains sexual issues that are not of a criminal nature.

[1] Tiefer (1995).

NEW INFORMATON When watching films, homosexual men are aroused by male stimuli, and heterosexual men are aroused by heterosexual stimuli. Women have a very different bisexual pattern of arousal on average, no matter whether they are heterosexual or homosexual. This probably means that men's and women's brains are organized quite differently, and furthermore, that sexual arousal does not play as important a role in women's sexual orientation development as it does in men.[2]

Traits of Sexual Behaviors

A survey of more than three thousand men and women ages eighteen to fifty-nine found that 43 percent of women and 31 percent of men regularly suffer from a lack of interest in sex, an inability to reach orgasm, or some other sexual dysfunction.[3] The problems that follow are a mix of behaviors—some have a physical basis and some are exclusively psychological.

SEXUAL ADDICTION OR SEXUAL COMPULSION

A sexual addict is a person, more often male than female, unable to adequately control his sexual behavior. The term "addict" indicates that the behavior has slipped into the disruptive range. The sexual addict has an overwhelming need for sex or is preoccupied with sex or the procurement of it. The term refers to more than excesses in frequency or participation in certain types of sex; it also indicates compulsive sexual behaviors, the most common of which are masturbation and continual affairs (often simultaneously) while married.[4][5]

The threshold for what constitutes hypersexuality is subject to debate, and critics question if a standardized diagnostic threshold even exists. Sex drive varies widely in humans, and what one person would consider a "normal" sex drive might be considered excessive by some, and low by others. The consensus among those who consider this a disorder is that the threshold is met when the behavior causes distress or impaired social functioning. Sexual compulsion can be a symptom of bipolar disorder.

[2] Bailey (2005). [3] The Journal of the American Medical Association (February, 1999). [4] Gold and Heffner (1998). [5] Gold, Steven, and Heffner (1998).

TRAITS OF A SEXUAL ADDICT

Not all of the following traits will be seen in the same person. However, the compulsive aspects are always present.

- Cannot control behavior despite the risk of potential adverse consequences: jobs, marriages or health
- Has frequent sexual encounters
- Masturbates compulsively
- Seeks new sexual encounters out of boredom with the old ones
- Desires to get excesses under control but is unsuccessful in attempts to stop behavior
- Engages in sexual activity without physiological arousal
- Is self-destructive and may jeopardize marriage or career
- Spends excessive time in sexual behaviors, thinking about sex, and sexual encounters
- Desires excitement and may ignore other responsibilities
- Convinces self that sexual behaviors are okay, or rationalizes: "It's not real sex"
- Is guilty, lonely, and angry
- Lacks control in other areas of life
- Believes that sex is the answer to problems
- Has difficulty being emotionally intimate; relies on sex instead as main mode of expression
- May have had a childhood marked by little control and blurred boundaries or abuse

FIGURES AND STATISTICS Six percent of Internet users are compulsive in their online behavior; half of those are sexually compulsive. Fifty percent of people who engage in cybersex move to phone contact; 15–30 percent meet in person.[6]

[6] Greenfield (1999).

SEXUAL AVERSION

A person who has an aversion to sex persistently avoids genital contact. People are vulnerable to this disorder after a trauma, such as rape. It can also be caused by sexual abuse, sexually repressive parenting, or pressure from a partner. There are married people who never have sexual contact with their partners.

TRAITS OF A PERSON WHO IS SEXUALLY AVERSE

- May have sexual desire but is repelled by the idea of sexual contact
- Can become ill at the thought of sex: nausea, diarrhea, vomiting, or sweating
- Deals with sexual anxiety through avoidance
- Has body image or self-esteem problems

BESTIALITY

A person who practices bestiality performs sexual acts with an animal. Animals that are preferred because of size and stability are dogs, sows, mares, heifers, and apes.[7]

TRAITS OF A PERSON WHO PRACTICES BESTIALITY

- May have preferences about male or female animals
- Likes sex with people as well, but is often too anxious; bestiality is usually a diversion or supplemental, rather than an exclusive, sexual interest
- Occasionally occurs because of shame about small penis size
- May believe that one gains supernatural powers or cures disease through sexual encounters with animals

ELIGIBILITY-BASED PARAPHILIA

Eligibility-based paraphilia includes any addictive, repetitious, and compulsive arousal by ineligible (forbidden by some criteria) partner. Eligibility can be based on criteria as simple as hair color, religion, or ethnic group. Or it can be physical only: only a short, a skinny, or a disfigured partner. It may be based on social class

[7] Masters (1966).

or can be as unusual as uniforms, tattoos, or amputees (the turn-on is the stump). An extreme version is necrophilia, sexual arousal or acts with a dead partner[8]

TRAITS OF ALL SEXUAL PARAPHILIAS

- Sexually attracted to and aroused by unusual love objects
- Results from early developmental disturbance that creates a paraphiliac substitute, a very specific nonthreatening object, to transfer normal lust and arousal to; problematic in adulthood
- Is not voluntary
- Does not usually disappear
- Ranges from harmless to dangerous
- Cannot be controlled by willpower
- Are not deterred by punishment; fed by persecution
- May have fantasies accompanying arousal many times a day[9]

Tactics of Sexual Coercion

Sexual coercion means forcing someone to have sex by means of manipulation or threat. It often occurs in situations in which one person has more authority than the other, or when the coercer has a poor understanding of sexual consent. Tactics include:

- Nagging
- Threats to end the relationship or go elsewhere for sex
- Expressions of dissatisfaction with the present sex life
- Verbal aggression such as swearing or put-downs
- Withdrawal, pouting
- Attempts to elicit sympathy
- Positive verbal persuasion, such as compliments or promises

More than any one tactic, coercion is so persistent that it wears resistance down.

---

[8] ibid. [9] Money (1998).

> Why do women comply with sexual coercion?
>
> - To alleviate the pressure from continuing to refuse
> - To avoid the consequences of saying "no" and further aggression
> - To save the relationship
> - Guilt
> - Because they are worn down from the persistence[10]

FETISHISM

A fetishist is an individual who is sexually aroused by urges and fantasies of using nonliving objects (clothing, shoes, toys) instead of a sexual partner.

TRAITS OF A FETISHIST

- Is usually an introverted man who is anxious in sexual situations
- Is excited by nonliving objects that he believes to be sinful
- Prefers objects that are usually female symbols, commonly women's underwear
- Has a compulsive and involuntary attraction to the object

FROTTEURISM

A frotteurist is an individual who is sexually aroused by urges and fantasies of rubbing against a stranger's body (usually buttocks) in a public, crowded place. The victim is often so unbelieving that she does not protest quickly.

TRAITS OF A FROTTEURIST

- Does not want to coerce the other person, only to touch
- Fantasizes that the act is in the context of a relationship
- Is usually a young adult

[10] Livingston (2004).

GUILT

This describes a person who suffers from unusual, overwhelming guilt about sex and usually believes that sex is bad. Guilt about sex can prevent someone from falling in love. It can also result in rejection of one's own sexuality[11]

TRAITS OF A PERSON WITH EXTREME GUILT

- Has impaired ability to have normal adult relationship
- Is influenced by parents' attitudes
- Is influenced by society's values
- Has trouble leaving parents and childhood behind and has trouble becoming independent
- Is most likely introverted
- Sees people as good (nonsexual) or bad (sexual)

NEW INFORMATION Different personality types lead to different kinds of sexual problems. Men who already have difficulty getting and maintaining erections tend to focus on negative outcomes, thereby having more sexual problems. People who are prone to be inhibited are more likely to develop sexual problems, whereas those who are not prone to inhibition are more likely to engage in high-risk sexual behavior.[12]

SEXUAL HYPOACTIVITY

An individual who is sexually hypoactive shows inhibited sexual desire; well below the normal range of sexual interest. Possible causes include low hormone levels, anger with partner, depression, and trouble with sexual orientation.[13]

TRAITS OF A PERSON WHO IS SEXUALLY HYPOACTIVE

- Lacks sexual desire and has no sexual fantasies
- Experiences diminished or non-existent sexual drive because of fear and anxiety
- Does not seek opportunities and refuses chances to have sexual contact
- Has few or poor quality relationships

[11] ibid. [12] APA Monitor on Psychology (April, 2003). [13] Knopf and Seller (1990).

NEW INFORMATION Hypoxyphila, or auto-erotic asphyxia, is a rare sexual problem. This individual is sexually aroused by oxygen deprivation. He achieves oxygen deprivation by a noose, bag, or other device around the head or throat that cuts off the oxygen supply. The individual escapes after achieving orgasm and before being asphyxiated. This disorder is always a problem and is not accepted as a normal variety of sexual choice; it has been known to inadvertently cause injury and death.

SADOMASOCHISM

People practicing sadomasochistic sex are not criminals because these behaviors are consensual. Sadomasochistic sex is usually either heterosexual or between gay men; it is unusual in the lesbian community. It requires careful orchestration of the sexual activity. A sadist and masochist live out a fantasy in which roles, dialogue, costume, and sex are aspects of the ritual. The sadist (dominating partner) is turned on by altering the emotional or physical state of the masochist; the masochist (submissive partner) has a code word to stop the behaviors. Activities may involve pain, so the submissive partner must trust the dominating partner or she cannot enjoy the act. But it is rare that serious injury is caused to either partner[14] (unlike the sadistic rapist, who inflicts unnecessary suffering on victims). [15] Sadomasochism is erotic because of its focus on forbidden acts.

TRAITS OF A SADIST

- Is sexually aroused by inflicting pain on others through games of humiliation, bondage, punishment, and discipline
- Desires to be omnipotent
- Has a strong aggression; wants to render partner helpless
- Often uses prostitutes

TRAITS OF A MASOCHIST

- Is sexually aroused by urges and fantasies of being made to suffer: humiliation, beatings, rape, bondage, whipping, or cutting
- Transforms pain into sensuous ecstasy

[14] Storr (1964). [15] ibid.

- Repeatedly acts on urges and finds others who will perform the range of desired acts
- Often suffers from sexual guilt or inferiority
- Has a strong dependency on others
- Often uses prostitutes

 WARM UP Write a scene in which an inhibited man inadvertently walks into a sadomasochism club thinking he is meeting his brother.

SEXUAL INFERIORITY

An individual who feels sexually inferior sees herself as undesirable as compared to others.

TRAITS OF A PERSON WHO EXPERIENCES SEXUAL INFERIORITY
- Lacks confidence in sexual identity
- Does not identify with society's role for her
- Has a bad role model in same-sex parent
- Is often ambitious in other areas, such as work or sports, as a way to gain love
- Considers fantasy and inner world important
- In the extreme, turns away from any competition to be sexual or attractive

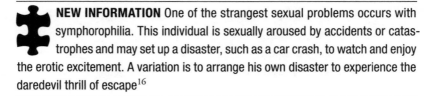 **NEW INFORMATION** One of the strangest sexual problems occurs with symphorophilia. This individual is sexually aroused by accidents or catastrophes and may set up a disaster, such as a car crash, to watch and enjoy the erotic excitement. A variation is to arrange his own disaster to experience the daredevil thrill of escape[16]

VOYEURISM (PEEPING TOM)

This individual is aroused by urges and fantasies of watching others undress or engage in sex. Peeping may be the only sexual activity he engages in.

[16] Money (1998).

TRAITS OF A VOYEUR

- Does not want contact with those he observes
- Is excited by looking
- May masturbate while peeping, or later while thinking about the scene
- Has few personal sexual outlets

Unsafe Sex

What traits encourage people to engage in unsafe sex?

- They may be unrealistically optimistic.
- Their judgment may be impaired by drugs or alcohol.
- They may not recognize the consequences of their behavior.
- They may have certain personality traits, such as sensation seeking or assertiveness; or be in certain mood states, like depression.[17]

Varieties of Sexual Identification

People do not always identify themselves as homosexual, bisexual, or heterosexual. For many, it is more complicated than that, and some individuals do not identity with any of the above labels.

TRANSGENDER

A transgendered person is someone who strongly believes that his or her inner self is incompatible with the outside body gender, for example, a woman who feels she is a man but is trapped in the body of a woman. Most individuals with this disorder choose to "cross live" (live as other gender) or take small steps to change their bodies rather than have surgery to reconstruct or remove breasts and genitals, but some people do have a complete surgical reassignment. This disorder occurs more often in men than in women.

---

[17] APA Monitor on Psychology. (April, 2003).

TRAITS OF A TRANSGENDERED PERSON

- Identifies fully with the other gender
- Dresses in clothing of other gender; enjoys being treated as member of other gender
- Does not act for sexual thrill
- May have two identities and even two names: one male and one female
- Usually has no desire to change anatomy
- Begins in early childhood; believes that he or she has been born into the wrong body
- Believes that he or she is heterosexual, not homosexual
- Is vocal about wanting to be the other gender → insisting that he or she is the other gender

TRANSVESTITE

Transvestites are involved in cross-dressing rather than claiming the opposite sexual identity. Many people occasionally cross-dress and wear clothing of other gender, sometimes to mock societal rules. Today, women can wear trousers and conventional male clothing with little notice, but men cannot wear dresses without attention being called to the deviation. The range of transvestite behavior runs from the occasional use of a piece of underwear to full outfits and makeup worn for extended periods of time: that is, "passing" as a woman. Most transvestites are heterosexual males, cross-dressing for sexual pleasure. Cross-dressing is not associated with any mental disorder.

TRAITS OF A TRANSVESTITE

- Becomes aroused by dressing in the clothes and keeps a woman's wardrobe
- May cross-dress only in private, or sometimes in public: stockings under a business suit
- May be uncertain of masculinity or identify with women

WARM UP Write a scene where your father interacts with one of the types in this chapter.

Genetic Sexual Disorders

ANDROGEN INSENSITIVITY SYNDROME

Androgen insensitivity syndrome is a form of pseudohermaphroditism. A person who suffers from this is externally female and internally male, has testes inside and no uterus, and is therefore sterile. This person is genetically male, but there are no external masculine characteristics. This disorder is discovered at adolescence when the "girl" does not menstruate. The person does grow breasts and has a normal female body (does not respond to male sex hormone), but may lack sexual hair. The disorder does run in families. The person expresses no masculine behavior and carries out ordinary female roles and behaviors.

HERMAPHRODITISM

In this disorder, characteristics of both sexes are present at birth, internally and externally. There is a great variety in the degree of hermaphroditism: Many have external genitalia that are either male or female; some have external genitalia that look ambiguous. If there is going to be sex assignment, it is usually done early, so the child is reared consistently. The sex chosen is based on the predominant external characteristics; when external characteristics are very ambiguous, sex assignment is made on basis of gonads and hormones. Hermaphrodites are often sterile.

KLINEFELTER SYNDROME

Humans have forty-six chromosomes that contain all of their genes and DNA. Two of these chromosomes, the sex chromosomes, determine gender: females have two X chromosomes; males have one X and one Y. In Klinefelter syndrome, which affects males only, there are three sex chromosomes: XXY, giving them a total of forty-seven chromosomes. This extra female sex chromosome causes a man with Klinefelter syndrome to be tall, with long arms and legs after puberty, and small testicles. He is sterile and may develop girl-like breasts, which can be flattened surgically. The men tend to have lower-than-normal IQ.[18]

TURNER SYNDROME

Turner syndrome affects females only. In contrast to the extra sex chromosome of Klinefelter syndrome, a woman with Turner syndrome has only one sex chromosome; the second X chromosome is incomplete or missing, leaving her with forty-five chromosomes instead of forty-six. Her appearance is marked by short stature, low hairline, and webbed neck. They have either no ovaries or underdeveloped ovaries, making them sterile. The expected physical development in teenage years does not occur, but they are mentally normal and often have high verbal intelligence, though they may exhibit space-form perception problems (for example, have difficulty copying a hexagon). They seem to be resilient and stable and cope well.

[18] Money (1998).

CHAPTER seven

Love, Marriage, and Other Arrangements

IN THIS CHAPTER

• Falling in Love • Choosing a Partner • Forming Relationships • Marriage
• Problems in Love and Marriage • Separation and Divorce

There is probably no topic more enduring in literature, and in life, than love. Unfortunately, psychology may understand less about love than about hate and less about long-lasting relationships than about abandonment. In this chapter, I present data on falling in love, as well as information on conflict, on falling out of love, and separation and divorce.

Falling in Love

Although falling in love is uniquely magical to the people involved, there are some common dynamics. All people dream of loving and being loved. They have a desire for wholeness and a wish to merge two people into one. People hope to make up for bad aspects of the past or failed prior relationships by finding new, true love. The desire to fall in love may cause a person to emphasize the similarities in interests and values shared with another, and de-emphasize the differences that may be problematic later on.[1]

After falling in love, the qualities of being in love are more stable and maintain the relationship.

TRAITS OF A PERSON IN LOVE

- Feels a surge of hope
- Exaggerates the loved one's actual characteristics; sees them through rose-colored glasses
- Loves own ideal self as reflected in the other person
- Sees the object of love as holding important values: kindness, success
- Feels attraction, which raises desire or presents a challenge
- Maintains the idealization of falling in love, but sees clearer reality of the other
- Confronts limitations of oneself and partner and survives any disillusionment and disappointment
- Feels compassion for partner
- Tolerates separateness and intimacy
- Experiences the growth of trust and attachment
- Makes a commitment to maintain love
- Replaces envy with admiration
- Enjoys the attitudes of hope and optimism that prevail
- Feels like a big step has been taken on the path out of distress toward enrichment
- Feels less lonely or isolated because of being in love[2]

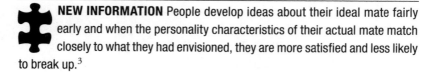 **NEW INFORMATION** People develop ideas about their ideal mate fairly early and when the personality characteristics of their actual mate match closely to what they had envisioned, they are more satisfied and less likely to break up.[3]

---

[1] Troupp (1994). [2] Reik (1949); Troupp (1994). [3] APA Monitor on Psychology (October, 2005).

Choosing a Partner

How do we choose a partner from all the people we meet? The following three theories, Ecology, Similarity, and Complementary Needs, explain mate selection. Then Physical Attraction and Differences begin to explain the push and pull toward certain people.

ECOLOGY

When people are ready to marry, they will meet an eligible partner close at hand.

SIMILARITY

It is easier to be attracted to people who are similar to oneself, particularly in attitudes, personality characteristics, economic characteristics, and race. Also, people are attracted to others who behave as they would in similar situations (for example, laughing at the same joke). The similarity theory also says that individuals prefer people who resemble members of their family of origin and who follow the practices of their own childhood. These people make marriages that are meaningful in terms of their previous experiences with marriage, for example, their parents' marriage.

COMPLEMENTARY NEEDS

Each person is attracted, consciously or unconsciously, to somebody who can help her solve personal problems. The mate completes the partner's personality. Type I occurs when the need, such as achievement, appears in both partners but at different levels of intensity. Type II occurs when different needs are involved; for example, one partner needs to dominate and the other needs to be subordinate. Type III involves needs that are identical and complementary, such as two people with high needs for sex or achievement who can help each other.[4]

PHYSICAL ATTRACTION

Often attractiveness is the initial screening device when people meet. People tend to match each other in terms of attractiveness, which is of course, in the

[4] Benson (1971).

eyes of the beholder. Physical attractiveness becomes less important as the relationship progresses and other traits assume greater importance.

DIFFERENCES

Individuals are attracted to people who are dissimilar from themselves when they widen social networks and leave home; college, travel, military service, and work introduce people who might not ordinarily meet. Away from home, people feel the excitement of new experiences, have the freedom to develop new attitudes, and enjoy the ability to try new behaviors.[5]

Relationships that cross racial, ethnic, and cultural lines are becoming increasingly common in the United States. Diversity makes a relationship exciting, but differences can also cause strain because of lack of understanding. Partners may have been raised with very different expectations as to the roles men and women play, the foods they eat, how to discipline children, or whether the marriage comes before or after family responsibilities. Even simple acts cause people to feel hurt: what to call your mother-in-law, to hug or not to hug, or what is appropriate dinner table conversation.

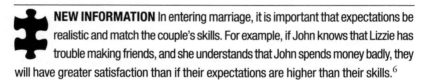

NEW INFORMATION In entering marriage, it is important that expectations be realistic and match the couple's skills. For example, if John knows that Lizzie has trouble making friends, and she understands that John spends money badly, they will have greater satisfaction than if their expectations are higher than their skills.[6]

Forming Relationships

Once people have found each other, they have ways of maintaining levels of closeness and distance that satisfy them, even if they are unaware of doing so.

PATTERNS OF ATTACHMENT

Just as parents and children bond, adults attach to each other in some predictable patterns. The following three types of attachment are major varieties between adults:

[5] Hendrick (1995). [6] McNulty and Karney (2004).

DISMISSING ATTACHMENT

This is a bond marked by extreme self-sufficiency of one or both partners.

Past History

- Was consistently rebuffed by parents; had little affection and little emotional expression
- Associates emotional vulnerability with parental rejection

Present Behaviors

- Expects people to be untrustworthy and unsupportive
- Appears distant, hostile, and irritable
- Is very self-reliant
- Feels misunderstood by others; fears intimacy and high emotions of romantic relationships

PREOCCUPIED ATTACHMENT

This is a bond with anxiety and ambivalence about a relationship with another person.

Past History

- Was insufficiently attended to by parents; they had mixed feelings about being parents
- Received inconsistent parenting and responded by crying and clinging to parents
- Believed in childhood that he was unworthy of love
- Experienced childhood filled with loneliness, doubts, and few friends

Present Behaviors

- Experiences love as an obsession; wants intense closeness
- Displays emotional extremes from ardent attraction to jealousy
- May be a compulsive caregiver
- Chronically worries about being insufficiently loved, rejected, and abandoned

- Discloses too quickly and easily
- Wants approval

SECURE ATTACHMENT

This is a bond in which trust and security are present between two people.

Past History
- Had parents who were respectful, accepting, responsive, and sensitive
- Had happy, friendly, and trusting love experiences

Present Behaviors
- Feels worthy; has high self-esteem
- Expects partner to be responsive and accepting
- Has no serious interpersonal problems[7]

NEW INFORMATION The lavish wedding is again capturing imaginations and incomes. One theory to explain this trend is that fabulous fetes marry "two of the most sacred tenets of American culture: romantic love and excessive consumption." People also desire lavish weddings because they want to escape from everyday life, emulate celebrities, and be stars of their own show. The wedding does not mirror who we are, but instead offers a temporary dream world.

But magic is expensive. From 1984 to 1994, the average cost of a formal U.S. wedding rose from four thousand to sixteen thousand dollars. In 2004, consumers paid twenty-two thousand dollars on average; the average cost of second and third weddings also rose to twelve thousand dollars.

BARRIERS TO GETTING CLOSE

The attachment patterns described previously showed some of the ways that people stay close. The following barriers show the ways that people can maintain distance.

CHECKLIST LOVE
- "I must have this, that, and the other" may be a way of avoiding authentic personal relationships by never straying from the intellectually created list.

[7] Batholomew (1993).

SEX OR LOVE, NOT BOTH

- Some people can get close either physically or emotionally, but not both because it makes them too vulnerable, so sex is good and emotions are shut down, or emotional intimacy is possible and sex disappears.

FIND THE IMPOSSIBLE PARTNER

- One way to never risk intimacy is to become involved with a person who is unavailable because of other commitments: her own marriage or job, she lives elsewhere, or any other factor that could make a real relationship impossible.

FREEZE-DRIED LOVE

- Individuals can get together, but once they are, no change is allowed. They are so terrified of change that they close their lives to any people or situations that are new.

"I GAVE AT THE OFFICE" LOVE

- All intense emotions and commitments have been given to work and nothing is left for another person. The excuse that comes with this fear is often "I'm doing it so I can create a good life when I meet someone." or "I have to provide for my family."[8]

 WARM UP Write a scene in which one newly engaged partner is taken to the family reunion of the other.

COMMON UNHEALTHY RELATIONSHIP PAIRINGS

The previous patterns of relationship attachments and barriers were general; the five types listed next are undesirable relationships with specific unhealthy attractions or choices.

THE CONQUEROR AND DADDY'S GIRL

Growing up, the Conqueror was a mama's boy with a weak father. Both parents were disapproving, and that created in him a strong desire to be in control. The

[8] Callahan and Levine (1982).

result is a "can-do" person: successful, professional, with a good income. But, either married or a bachelor, he is afraid of intimacy. As an accomplished man, he is also sexually proficient, wants his sexual needs met, and is always seeking a woman as a conquest. He may use alcohol or drugs for stimulation and added excitement. His need for control and strong desire for his freedom make the Conqueror a difficult partner.

The woman he attracts, the Daddy's Girl, is young and compliant. She has achieved less than he has in all areas, and wants to be cared for. She waits patiently, goes along sexually, and is generally dependent and undemanding.[9]

THE CHARMER AND THE CHARMED

The Charmer was emotionally or physically abandoned as a child, but has grown up into a good-looking, savvy, and smooth adult. His charm is subtle: He is smart, educated, outgoing, and polished. Passionate and elusive, he shows only the best of himself, which women find appealing. He presents himself as a man who loves women and wants romance. He is looking for his princess, but does not last long in relationships.

The woman he attracts is also good looking, lovely and accomplished, but looks more independent than she really is. She responds to romance and is dazzled by the chemistry between them. The romance depends on illusion and fire rather than substance. She wants to get to know him. She is warm and yearns for love, but is better at longing than at loving. When he leaves, she blames herself and grieves.[10]

THE ADVENTURERS

The Adventurer was very attached to his mother and had an unavailable father. As an adult, he loves fun and freedom. Some of his appeal rests in his willingness to take risks and breaks rules; he rebels against authority. His preference for adventure over intimacy encourages women to compete for him. Some of his risks may be with drugs or money. Adventurers can be very successful or, if they are too volatile and spin out of control, can turn out to be just failed

[9] Carpineto (1989). [10] ibid.

risk-takers. A hallmark of the Adventurer is that he lacks responsibility or a good sense of reality.

He attracts another Adventurer—a woman thrilled by the high-risk game of love and who may also be married. Blatantly sexual, she wants the thrills and risks that he offers. The excitement covers up her feelings of low self-esteem and provides her with a sense of identity.[11]

THE NARCISSIST AND THE HEALER

The Narcissist was raised by unempathic parents so he becomes a needy adult who takes from those around him. He feels dependent but hates to admit it and often turns to sex for comfort. He is addicted to being understood, although he has minimal compassion for others. He is self-centered, self-indulgent, and explosive. Any expressive, analytical, and reflective skills are used to get his own way; ultimately he is always disappointed by his women, who may be forced to leave him because of his demanding behaviors.

The Healer responds to the wounds she senses in the Narcissist. She seems self-sufficient and disguises her dependency; she needs to be needed. He comes to need her, and then hates her because his dependency is intolerable to him. They see their relationship as meaningful and significant. She keeps trying even when the relationship has nothing to offer to her.[12]

THE RESCUING KNIGHT AND THE MAIDEN

He has been brought up to please others, so as an adult he expects to do all the providing for his woman. He feels responsible for making her happy, and is afraid to disappoint her or anyone else. He suppresses his own needs and keeps his aggression under wraps, although anger inevitably seeps out against her.

The woman he attracts is enchanted by the thought that she can be rescued. She is often in a difficult situation when they meet. She is used to being under the power of others and may have been molded by a parent whom she adored but who manipulated her. She is confused when she begins to sense his unspoken anger but afraid to leave.

[11] ibid. [12] ibid.

WARM UP Pick one of the types of men listed in the unhealthy relationship pairings and describe his apartment in detail.

BACHELORS

The men described in the unhealthy relationship pairings are always with women. There are also men who like many partners, want to date, and want to keep their options open. These men are temporarily bachelors.

The Bachelor is another story. Bachelors tend to be mythologized in several distinctive styles: woman-haters, emotionally fixated on their mothers, unattractive to women, pining for a lost love, unacknowledged homosexuals, unlucky, playboys, or workaholics. These types may exist, but research shows that personality traits of bachelors reveal a continuum of qualities from normal to extreme.

TRAITS OF MEN WHO DON'T PLAN TO MARRY

- Fear loss of control over fate if marriage occurs; need autonomy: "I like my freedom"
- Have low need for intimacy: "I don't want a lot of affection"
- Are not very sexual: "Sex is overrated"
- Have trouble making decisions: "I like to keep my options open"
- Are reluctant to get involved in other people's lives or take on responsibility: "I don't want to deal with someone else's problems"
- Are fearful: "What if I make a mistake?"
- Have fears about sex; may not be able to "perform" in a relationship
- Are hesitant to become sexually involved with women
- Find it difficult to feel dependent on other people
- May lack confidence and be unable to assert any needs
- Can become isolated and avoid others
- Lack desire to compromise, and can become angry at women who come too close
- Are emotionally repressed and detached [13]

[13] Waehler (1994).

NEW INFORMATION When time is limited, even people who like novelty gravitate to people and places that are emotionally important and familiar.

PROTECTION AGAINST CLOSENESS

Most people fear romantic involvement to some degree because intimacy involves the risk of getting hurt or rejected. Intimacy also raises the problem of jealousy.

Jealousy attempts to keep a loved one close but winds up creating lies, barriers, and distance. No discussion about relationship traits can be completed without some mention of jealousy. Normal jealousy arises when the fear of losing a loved person or position (job, status of teacher's pet, star athlete, or valedictorian) becomes threatening. Jealousy speaks to a universal desire to preserve anything that is precious.

Jealousy is an aspect of some people's nature and exists in them all the time without relationships, prized possessions, or impending loss. For these people, rivals do not inspire jealousy; jealousy creates imaginary competitors. Jealousy may be kept secret, and others may never be aware of the drama being played out in this person's mind. The worst torment for a jealous person is to be in doubt, and he is always in doubt because he is always suspicious. At its worst, jealousy may slip into paranoia.[14]

One-third of solved murders involve jealousy. Jealousy is linked to family murder/suicides, marital violence, battery, suicide, loss of self-esteem, and divorce. Jealousy is a reaction that ranges from normal → pathological, and feelings are triggered by an event that can range from a simple glance to the discovery of an affair. Typically, men get jealous about sex; women get jealous about deep emotional connections.[15]

GENERAL TRAITS OF A JEALOUS PARTNER

- Perceives a threat, real or imagined; fears partner will leave
- Is predisposed toward jealousy as an emotion; begins early in life with the fear of losing love

[14] Gonzalez-Crussi (1988). [15] Pines (1992).

- May have had a parent who was unfaithful
- May be unaware of own impulses to cheat and attributes own wishes to partner: she wants to go out with other men so she accuses partner of unfaithfulness
- Feels inadequate to hold a mate; feels impotent or unattractive
- Mistakes jealousy for passion and therefore values the feeling
- Needs exclusivity in commitment

Regulating Emotion

"He's so unemotional!" "She doesn't show her feelings!" How do people manage to suppress or regulate emotions?

- They interpret an emotional situation as something less upsetting: an upcoming meeting with the boss is not a threat but a challenge.
- They suppress emotions by distracting themselves with other activities.
- They seek social support for their point of view.
- They conceal their feelings from others by withdrawal, silence, suppression, and repression of emotion.
- They convince themselves that the emotional event is not personally relevant.

WARM UP Men who are "supermasculine"—those who display high hostility and strong conformity to traditional masculine roles—may cause distress to their wives because they are restricted emotionally. These men tend to have lower self-esteem and increased anxiety, depression, fear of intimacy, and hostility toward women. Write a scene describing a supermasculine and his wife at the gay pride parade in San Francisco.[16]

Marriage

Just as individuals grow through a series of developmental stages, marriages proceed through stages, each with tasks to be mastered. The following informa-

[16] APA Monitor on Psychology (October 2004).

tion outlines major tasks and potential problems. More complete descriptions of some stages follow.

STAGES OF MARRIAGE AND FAMILY[17]

STAGE ONE: NEWLY MARRIED

Tasks

- Shift from family of origin to partner
- Develop intimacy; closeness and distance
- Create one's own definitions of *husband* and *wife*
- Clarify expectations about family, work, time, money, and lifestyle
- Accept responsibility for one's own happiness
- Adjust to each other: sex, money, food, solitude, conflicts
- Create a vision for the future[18]

Problems

- Family of origin and in-laws vs. developing family
- Friends and potential lovers who threaten relationship
- Stress about parenthood
- Ambivalence about choices that have been made: work, mate, or home

STAGE TWO: QUESTIONING

Tasks

- Decisions that will affect life for years to come

Problems

- Restlessness and disruptions; fears about permanence of decisions
- Doubts about commitments to work and relationship
- Stress and upheaval as some marriages end, work changes, and new paths are chosen

[17] Solomon (1973). [18] Troupp (1994).

The Relationship Between Mothers- and Daughters-in-Law

When a woman gets married, one relationship she will most likely have to deal with is with her husband's mother. There are many common stereotypes that accompany the mother-in-law, but in many cases, this can actually be a positive relationship.

MYTHS OF THE MOTHER-IN-LAW

- Jealous of son's wife
- Wicked
- Possessive
- Domineering
- Manipulative

TRAITS OF HEALTHY MOTHER- AND DAUGHTER-IN-LAW RELATIONSHIPS

- Shared value of family
- Shared desire to keep connections
- Shared desire to maintain family ties; both are "kinkeepers"

POTENTIAL PROBLEMS IN THE RELATIONSHIP

- Incompatible dreams and expectations of each other
- Disappointment in each other
- Need to constantly strive to be good enough
- Concern about having to make a good impression
- Different generations; different lifestyles, sexual behavior, customs, sense of power, or aggression
- Differing cultures, religions, or economics
- Differing personalities; differing preferences about privacy
- Daughter-in-law's unresolved issues with her own mother
- Mother-in-law may have no experience with a daughter

STAGE THREE: ACTIONS ABOUT CHILDREN

Tasks

- Solidify relationship to each other
- Add new role of mother or father, or decide not to

Problem

- Possibility of giving up the marital role in favor of the parental role
- Possible decision to postpone or abandon parenting plans

STAGE FOUR: SETTLING DOWN/INDIVIDUATION

Tasks

- Settle down
- Deepen commitments
- Pursue long-range goals
- Experience increased productivity at work and competence with parenting, marriage, and friendships
- Modify roles as needed to allow some independence to child and to each other

Problems

- Partners' different styles and individual growth
- Distance may develop

STAGE FIVE: MIDLIFE TRANSITION

Tasks

- Reevaluate life
- Add up successes and failures
- Ponder future goals

Problems

- Conflicts between individual and relationship goals
- Disruptions in established patterns

- Conflicts between adolescent children and changing parents
- Differences between partners can lead to estrangement
- Conflicting desires: stability and drive to change

STAGE SIX: MIDDLE ADULTHOOD

Tasks

- Reestablish and reorder priorities; parental role changes
- Allow children to leave/separate
- Resolve conflicts in marriage/work and stabilize or make changes

Problems

- Concerns about aging
- Conflicts about sex, money, and time
- Different ideas about children, leading to conflict
- Boredom

Traits of Older Spouses

We assume our married characters will deal with different issues as they age, but what are they? Compared to married couples who are newly married, in midlife, or later adulthood, older couples: have fewer disputes about finances and children; derive more pleasure from talking about children and grandchildren, doing things together, and "dreaming"; whine less, and express less anger, disgust, and belligerence.

STAGE SEVEN: OLDER ADULTHOOD

Tasks

- Deal with aging, illness, and death
- Integrate losses
- Relate to grown children in new ways
- Support partner; modify relationship

Problems

- Conflicts rekindled around loneliness, sexual desire, and intimacy
- Losses of health, friends, and work; depletion

Problems in Love and Marriage

Marriage provides endless possibilities for characters and plots. In the January 2, 2005 issue of the *Chicago Tribune,* there were two stories on marriage that prove this point. In a challenge to gay marriages and divorce, evangelical Christian groups are leading a movement to have "covenant marriages," based on biblical teaching, as an alternative to traditional marriage. In the same section of the newspaper, a different story reports on a Saudi man who, over the course of fifty years, has married fifty-eight women. He says that his marital expenses for weddings and divorces have cost more than $1.6 million. "Marriage doesn't bore me," he said.

Couples argue most often about money, sex, and kids. Here are some of those problems and others, including adultery, alcoholism, domestic violence, money, and sex.

ADULTERY

Most couples require fidelity in their marriage to maintain trust and stability. However, some married individuals mutually agree to an "open" marriage in which each is free to pursue other relationships based on a set of agreed-upon rules. Although adultery, by definition, refers to married couples, these dynamics could be applied to any monogamous couple, heterosexual or homosexual.

Infidelity often happens, or is tempting:

- At the beginning of a marriage or in teenage spouses
- Just before the marriage takes place: one last fling
- When romance fades in a marriage
- When beginning a family
- When frequency of sex decreases
- With increased opportunity to have an affair
- At higher incomes levels, which may indicate higher status or ability to travel
- At midlife, because children leave and individuals feel their mortality

Why do affairs happen? Affairs regulate intimacy. Often one partner seeks greater intimacy; the other seeks to move away from intimacy. Some people are "in love with love" and are always searching for some new and exciting relationship. Some people seek out affairs because of a need for acceptance and recognition. Affairs can also happen as a result of depression, sexual frustration, curiosity, boredom, revenge, rebellion, anger, or a low valuation of the marriage. An affair may also be an attempt to hurt the spouse or a misguided attempt to resolve a marital stalemate.

FIVE TYPES OF ADULTERY

The following five types of adultery provide some broad outlines. When the heading says husband- or wife-specific, it means that research has documented these behaviors in either the husband or wife. Perhaps it can be generalized to include either spouse or perhaps not.

Circumstantial Adultery (Husbands and Wives)

- Is not planned; is an impulsive act
- Is not kept a secret; others know
- May be an isolated incident; not a pattern
- May evoke strong feelings of guilt
- Is often the result of the husband or wife falling prey to a "practiced seducer"[19]

Conflicted Adultery (Wife-Specific)

- Is a mistaken attempt to resolve some conflict in the marriage
- May be the result of anger at her husband
- May symbolize a desire to escape
- May reflect boredom
- May be the result of unspoken problems which she acts upon by having an affair
- Has relationship problems

[19] Caprio (1953).

- Occurs in relationships that are sexually unfulfilling, either inadequate or exploitative
- Is an attempt to stabilize the intolerable marital relationship
- Allows her to stay in the relationship; to tolerate the situation by enlisting outside support

Philandering Adultery (Husband-Specific)

- Is deliberate and habitual
- Is not motivated by love of another woman
- Is not motivated by the desire for a divorce from his wife
- Occurs in husbands who are emotionally maladjusted; immature
- Is a compulsive form of adultery
- Occurs in husbands who lack discipline when they have conflicts of desire, although they may be disciplined and successful in other areas of life
- Is an unconscious attempt to boost self-confidence
- Is rationalized: "It wasn't *real* sex"
- Occurs when husband is sexually inadequate[20]

Psychic Adultery (Husbands and Wives)

- Is not an act; spouse *thinks* about the object of his or her affections, but remains sexually monogamous\
- Is very common
- Makes person feel attractive
- Offers fantasies as an outlet for boredom and monotony
- May be an attempt to create jealousy in the partner
- Is characterized by flirtations that evoke a reaction in the spouse
- Satisfies the need to makes oneself feel good
- Stems from deep instinct toward polygamy
- Satisfies rebellious feelings

[20] ibid.

- Is a compromise; fidelity requires self-discipline
- Often makes old friends or former girlfriends/boyfriends/lovers the objects of the fantasy
- May indicate sexual frustration
- May be rehearsal for physical infidelity[21]

Psychopathic Adultery (Wife-Specific)

- Comes from a personality warp that makes her indifferent to ethical considerations
- Is seen in women who are emotionally cold and tend to have an older husband
- Produces no conflict or guilt, so no help is sought
- Is a compulsion[22]

 WARM UP Interestingly, happily married spouses tend to see their relationships in unrealistically positive ways. Write a scene where one spouse is describing his/her idyllic marriage to the (unknown) lover of the other spouse.

ALCOHOLISM

Alcoholism is a major problem in the U.S., affecting not only the individual who drinks, but his or her spouse, family, and work.

TRAITS OF ALCOHOLIC HOMES AND ALCOHOLIC PARENTS, GENERAL

- Households are tense and chaotic
- Home has an atmosphere of conflict and uncertainty
- Adults behave inconsistently, confusing the children
- Fighting is overheard by the children
- Parent who drinks disappears or forgets about the child
- Family becomes isolated from other families; there is low social interaction
- Roles shift; behaviors change; rules change

[21] ibid. [22] ibid.

- Abuse, either verbal or physical, is more common than in households where alcoholism is not present

TRAITS OF AN ALCOHOLIC WIFE

- Is expressive emotionally: happy, guilty, or depressed
- Requires less and less alcohol to have negative interactions
- Causes more disruption in the home than an alcoholic husband
- Is often influenced by the marital relationship: she drinks to alter her mood in response to marital difficulties

TRAITS OF AN ALCOHOLIC HUSBAND

- Feels less guilty than an alcoholic wife
- Blames others; denies the impact that drinking has on the family
- Does not let influence of marriage and family relationships dictate drinking patterns

TRAITS OF A RELATIONSHIP BETWEEN AN ALCOHOLIC HUSBAND AND WIFE

- Frequent instances of negative communication with each other
- Consistently unfriendly toward each other[23]

TRAITS OF THE "CODEPENDENT" SPOUSE

- Behaves in ways that may lessen conflict and ease tension within the family in the short term
- Actually supports ("enables") the spouse's drinking behavior by rescuing him or her
- Has a tendency to get involved in with people who are unreliable, emotionally unavailable, or needy
- Tries to provide and control everything within the relationship
- Ignores his or her own needs or desires

[23] Haber and Jacob (1997).

TRAITS OF CHILDREN OF ALCOHOLICS

Children will have a few or all of the following, depending on their personalities and the specifics of their home life.

- Are anxious and depressed
- Are predisposed to adult alcoholism
- Have difficulty developing identity, therefore have difficulty with relationships
- Carry too much responsibility because of caring for others
- Have school problems
- Feel mistrust of self and others
- May have physical problems: fetal alcohol syndrome or attention deficit disorder

TRAITS OF ADULT CHILDREN OF ALCOHOLICS

- Feel different from others
- Are rigid, serious, distrusting, and in need of control
- Are merciless with self-criticism
- Lie instead of telling the truth
- Have trouble finishing projects that they have begun
- Excessively seek approval
- Behave impulsively
- Adult children tend to fall into one of the following four types:
  - *Super-Responsible:* Leaders; high achieving (all to gain control)
  - *Flexible:* Adjusts to situations; detached socially; follows instead of leads; reactive
  - *Placater:* Sensitive to others; sociable; helpful; eager to please; avoids conflicts
  - *Delinquent:* Disrupts own life and that of family members; feels bad; has false confidence.[24]

[24] Black (1992); Woititz (1983).

DOMESTIC VIOLENCE

(See also Domestic Abuser on page 127)

Physically abusive or violent relationships did not begin that way. Sometime, though, during the course of the relationship, violence erupts. After a milestone such as engagement or marriage, it is harder to break off a committed relationship even if abuse starts. Abuse starts with "minor" acts (pinching, poking, shaking) that do not cause injury and can be dismissed. Many abusers can be charming and also very romantic and caring, behaviors that cause their victim to hope the violent behavior can be eliminated. Many batterers show deep remorse and are full of promises for the future. Batterers can be skilled in blaming their victims, telling her all the things she did or did not do that "made" him behave violently. Shame makes the victim remain silent, depriving her of advice and help. Often, women find prejudice when they do seek legal, social, physical, psychological, or economic aid.[25]

METHODS OF SPOUSAL EMOTIONAL ABUSE

Abusers are both men and women, in both heterosexual and homosexual relationships. Abuse may occur out of fear, as retaliation for a partner's abuse, to coerce a partner, or with the desire to control the other person's behaviors. The following are four methods commonly used to abuse a partner: isolate the partner, degrade the partner, sexually abuse the partner, or damage the partner's personal property.

Whether and when women leave has little to do with the amount of abuse they have endured, and sufferers of emotional abuse leave more quickly than those who undergo physical abuse. The following traits play a greater role in the decision to leave:

TRAITS OF ABUSED WOMEN WHO LEAVE

- Have developed increased assertiveness
- Are capable of defending themselves physically
- Become intolerant of the isolation

[25] Mouradian (Fall/Winter, 2004).

- Realize they have been degraded by their husbands
- Learn to respond to contemptuous comments
- Give up thinking that their husbands will change
- Recognize that their husbands have severe problems that they cannot fix

(See also Stalker on page 135.)

 WARM UP Men are also subject to emotional and physical abuse from their wives, but are less likely to report or admit it. Write a quick scene in which two men are carpooling to work and one notices bruises on the other's face.

TRAITS OF CHILDREN WHO WITNESS DOMESTIC VIOLENCE

The usual scenario is that a child has been exposed to violence between the parents in the home and is then ignored by both parents who refuse to discuss the domestic violence. Children are rarely removed from the violent home. Consequently, they:

- Can begin to believe that violence is normal and acceptable
- Suffer from impaired emotional development
- Desire to escape; may retreat into fantasy; may try to stop the violence
- May turn to brothers or sisters for comfort
- May try to divert parents' attention by either "bad" behavior or "good" behavior
- May become aggressive adults (mostly boys) or marry aggressive people (mostly girls)

 NEW INFORMATION Money has many personal meanings to individuals, most of which remain unconscious. Its significance in the lives of couples is rarely discussed, making it a perfect lightning rod for conflict.

PROBLEMS INVOLVING MONEY

Arguments about money may have any of the following roots:

- Competition: Partners use money in the struggle to determine who is more successful.

- Meeting Needs: Money becomes the means to gain self-esteem, prove something, feel good, or feel important.
- Power: One partner uses money to gain or keep control over the other person or the marriage.
- Distance: Partners keep money separate as a way to maintain distance; they do not get too intimate or have to negotiate spending.
- Old Debts: Present money is needed to pay debts from premarriage days.
- Aging Parents: Taking care of ill or aging parents leads to arguments, especially if parents were difficult during childhood or are unpleasant to the partner.
- "Keeping Up With the Joneses": Money is used for appearances, for competing with others, and to maintain an image that pleases other people
- Reckless Spending: One partner has a problem with out-of-control or addictive spending.
- Miser and Spender: Partners push each other to extremes. When one spends, the other hoards; when one is conservative, the other goes wild.
- Previous Marriages: Money goes to supporting a wife or children from a previous marriage.

 WARM UP Choose a personality type from chapter two and give hima problem with money. Show the character arguing about money with his partner after making a significant purchase.

SEXUAL CONFLICT IN COUPLES

Of all the negotiations between individuals, sex has the potential to be the most difficult because it is the most intimate. Sex, like money, is filled with personal meaning and beliefs that go back to childhood and probably remain unexamined. We are bombarded by sex on the screen and in print, but never educated about the sexual aspects of a relationship.

NORMAL SEXUAL TRAITS IN RELATIONSHIPS

- Sexual attraction is a major component of romantic love, but in long-term relationships, the quantity of sexual activity decreases over time
- Sex can be for procreation: to reproduce (stress increases during pregnancy attempts)
- Sex can be relational: to express affection and increase intimacy
- Sex can be recreational: an enjoyable activity with few strings attached
- Sex can be circumstantial: the effect of a certain situation, like drinking too much

PROBLEMS IN SEXUAL RELATIONSHIPS

- Sex can be coercive: manipulation, pressure, exploitation, aggression, or rape
- Sex becomes a way to communicate anger or power
- Expectations about frequency or infrequency of sex causes conflicts
- Conflict can arise from negotiating birth control or fear about sexually transmitted diseases
- Sexual satisfaction and relationship satisfaction decrease with poor communication[26]

 FIGURES AND STATISTICS Sixty-six percent of married women provide one-half or more of the family income.

SEXUAL PROBLEMS AND TRIANGLES

Triangles are repetitive ways of relating among three people. Triangles often occur when two people cannot talk about or resolve some issue, and bring in a third person.

Here are some examples that create interesting dynamics. Any two angles of the triangle indicate a possible alliance; the remaining angle indicates the relationship that will suffer.

[26] Hendrick (1995).

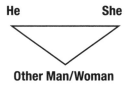

He   She

Other Man/Woman

The well known "other man/woman" who enters an existing relationship, heterosexual, or homosexual, causes a rift in the partnership.

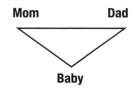

Mom   Dad

Baby

A shift in the marriage occurs when a baby is born and the relationship between husband and wife changes, often putting the dad on the outside. The alliance between one parent and the child can continue indefinitely.

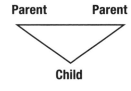

Parent   Parent

Child

Another triangle is the alliance of parents against a difficult child to disguise their own problems.

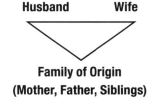

Husband   Wife

**Family of Origin
(Mother, Father, Siblings)**

A strong continuing relationship with the family of origin affects a marriage.

Separation and Divorce

TROUBLED MARRIAGES

WHY MARRIAGES FAIL

Marriages do not fail because of marital dissatisfaction or frequency of disagreements as often as they disintegrate from:

- Disengagement by one partner from the other

- Stonewalling discussions; contempt of the other
- Denial; blaming the partner for difficulties

TYPES OF MARITAL ARGUMENTS
- Loudly argue and fight
- Retreat into silence
- Talk about things that don't matter
- Attribute negative traits to partner
- Emphasize differences rather than similarities

HOW COUPLES ESCALATE AN ARGUMENT
- Show self-righteousness: "I am all right, you are completely wrong!"
- Misunderstand; don't listen, or stop listening
- Go for vulnerabilities
- Raise new issues: "And remember when you *also* did …"
- Counterattack or insult
- Show contempt, or demean
- Make it a personality or character issue rather than behavior

HOW COUPLES DE-ESCALATE AN ARGUMENT
- Listen and show a readiness to understand
- Show tact and concern for other's feelings; avoid "red flags"
- Draw attention to process: "This kind of talk isn't getting us anywhere. Let's calm down."
- Make a goodwill gesture, a small concession
- Accept the other's feelings; recognize that expressing anger can get it off one's chest

PATTERNS OF CONFLICT THAT LEAD TO DIVORCE
- X confronts areas of concern and expresses feelings about these problems → Y avoids, withdraws, whines → X gets resentful and angry

Or:

- X and Y have little overt conflict → X and Y later learn that they have different expectations of marriage, children, and family life

TRAITS OF SPOUSES IN A FAILING MARRIAGE

- Review all that went wrong
- Justify some actions and regret others
- Replay actual events in their minds
- Create alternative scenes in which they could have said or done things differently
- Develop the "story" of the breakup: history and reasons are different for each partner
- Recognize that they may have been mismatched from the start
- Betray, become unfaithful, or act with duplicity
- Dwell on chronic failings in partner
- Suffer from illness, depression, or alcohol
- Lose the ability to talk to one another
- Move in different directions
- Attack each other's confidence
- Feel reluctant to separate
- Often reconcile briefly

TRAITS OF COMMUNICATION IN A DEPRESSED SPOUSE

- Responds better to other people than to spouse
- Communicates with spouse in negative and tense manner; lacks positive statements and congeniality
- Criticizes spouse; disagrees with spouse
- Puts down spouse; intends to hurt, embarrass, or demean
- Speaks in a hostile manner; shows irritation
- Remains preoccupied with self and unsupportive of others
- Disrupts conversational flow; speaks little
- Depressed wives remain in problem-solving conversations; depressed husbands withdraw from problem-solving conversations
- Depressed wives talk more about feelings, including negative emotions, than husbands do[27]

[27] Johnson and Jacob (1997).

STAGES OF MARITAL SEPARATION

EARLY	RELIEF	ADJUSTMENT
• Distress, fear	• Euphoria, confidence	• Loneliness, barren world
• Sadness, vulnerability	• Hopeful about new opportunities	• Acceptance that there is no future with partner
• Inability to concentrate, anxiety	• Realization that partner is now not needed	• In search of respite from feelings
• Shaking, panic		
• Focused on unavailability of partner:	• Relieved there are no more fights	• Ready to begin affairs, work, activity, travel
• Wanting information about each other	• "Best thing I've ever done"	• Wanting information about each other

DIVORCE

Fifty percent of U.S. marriages end in divorce, and 60 percent of divorces involve children. The process of the divorce and the individual and family's adjustment afterward is influenced by:

- Quality of family relationships prior to divorce
- Earlier trauma, such as violence, or earlier stability
- Events after divorce: financial decline, stress of family members, or peace
- Individual personality and methods of coping
- Events surrounding divorce: infidelity, violence, cooperation, or court battles

POSTDIVORCE

Divorce is an event; life continues afterward, but there are customary routine changes: Father is not home for dinner or mother works longer hours. Everyone grapples with:

- Loss of a family member

- Loss of a way of life
- Expectations about one's life change
- Questions about oneself, as uncertainty replaces security
- Routines breaking down
- Overload of tasks for each family member
- More responsibility placed on children; daughters often assume care of younger children
- Plunge in women's income—an average of 40 percent
- Loss of income results in lesser schools, poorer housing, poorer health care, less enrichment
- Less contact with one parent, usually father

ADOLESCENT REACTIONS TO DIVORCE

- Has to figure out how to understand the divorce
- Must manage divided loyalties
- Views world as a less safe and less secure place
- Has confused perception of self, especially if accused, "You're just like your mother/father"
- May move into pseudomaturity, trying to be on her own
- May try to manipulate parents into reconciliation
- May take on parenting responsibilities (especially oldest child for siblings)
- Must face sexuality issues if parents begin to date
- May turn to peers instead of parents
- Has power struggles with teachers and authorities
- Has changing views about marriage depending on parents' behaviors
- Exhibits aggressive behavior
- May feel sadness or anxiety about the future[28]

[28] ibid.

CHILDREN'S REACTIONS TO DIVORCE[29]

AGES 2-3	AGES 3-5	AGES 5-6	AGES 6-10
Regression of toilet training	Regression of other behaviors	Wish to restore family	Wish to restore family
Whining	Self-blame	Appearance of depression	Loneliness
Irritability		Sadness	Sadness Shame
Separation fears	Crying	Anxiety	Anxiety
Sleep problems			
Desire to cling to comfort objects: toys, blanket, bottle	Desire for absent parent	Fantasies about saving hurt parent	Feeling of abandonment
Temper tantrums	Temper	Longing for the parent	Social awkwardness
Aggression	Aggression	Aggression	School/behavior problems

NEGATIVE POST-DIVORCE ADJUSTMENT IN CHILDREN

Most children are remarkably resilient and emerge as competent adults. Some suffer early—for example, with poor school grades—and then recover. Others seem fine, but suffer ill effects later. Possible problems are that they may:

- Have coercive relationships with parents, especially mother
- Fantasize about parents' reconciliation

[29]Wallerstein and Kelly (1980).

- Fear abandonment by one or both parents
- Withdraw socially to avoid disclosing family situation to friends
- Use alcohol and drugs
- Have increased sexual activity
- Have academic problems
- Become depressed (more girls than boys)
- Behave badly (more boys than girls)
- Suffer from lower self-esteem
- Have problems with parents, siblings, and peers[30]
- Get more power; grow up faster

ADJUSTMENT TO DIVORCE: CHILDREN AS ADULTS

Divorce may have an impact on later attitudes toward intimacy and sexuality, so adult children with divorced parents may:

- Marry earlier and choose unstable partners
- Have children before marriage
- Divorce early and often
- Feel less secure in loving and being loved
- Have not been exposed to negotiating and resolving differences
- Possess less effective problem-solving skills
- Use more negative communication during arguments
- Be inept at parenting

[30] Hetherington, Bridges, and Insabella (1998).

CHAPTER **eight**

Creating a Family

IN THIS CHAPTER

• *Parenting* • *Adoption* • *Birth Order* • *Families With a Disabled Child* • *Grown Children's Relationships With Parents* • *Remarriage and Stepfamilies*

The notion of family has wider meaning today than ever before. With international adoptions, assisted reproductive techniques, single parents, gay families, straight families, and stepfamilies, we realize that people are creating families with more diversity than we have seen previously. This chapter highlights some of the traits associated with creating a family.

Parenting

Many couples take becoming parents for granted, but there are changes that occur in their relationship when a child is born.

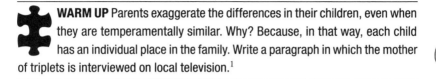

WARM UP Parents exaggerate the differences in their children, even when they are temperamentally similar. Why? Because, in that way, each child has an individual place in the family. Write a paragraph in which the mother of triplets is interviewed on local television.[1]

TRAITS OF THE TRANSITION TO PARENTHOOD

Becoming a parent changes life permanently, and in ways that people never dreamed about. Here are some of the changes that individuals undergo when they become parents.

- Experience heightened self-awareness; changes in self-perception
- Shift roles: partner/lover-self diminishes as parent-self grows
- Become less involved in activities outside the home (usually women)
- Feel increased self-esteem, self-worth, and confidence
- Have new feelings of nurturance, patience, tolerance, anxiety, or anger
- Feel less control over own life, especially mothers
- Feel increased stress
- Have increased sense of responsibility
- Reappraisal of values and beliefs[2]

WARM UP New fathers often revert to gender-stereotyped behaviors after the birth of their first child. Write a scene in which a new father is left alone with his newborn.

TRAITS OF PARENTS AND THEIR FIRSTBORN

- Give child exclusive attention; don't share her for a long time
- Have an intense relationship with the child
- Are in awe of having their own child
- Take nothing for granted; everything is novel
- May be overprotective[3]

[1] Saudine (2004). [2] Michaels and Goldberg (1988). [3] Richardson and Richardson (1990); Leman (1985).

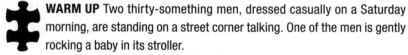

NEW INFORMATION There is no scientific evidence that parenting effectiveness is related to parental sexual orientation. Lesbian and gay parents are as likely as heterosexual parents to provide supportive and healthy environments for their children. In children, sexual identity, personality, and social relationships with peers and adults developed similarly whether parents were straight or gay.[5]

TRAITS OF LESBIAN AND GAY PARENTS

- Have conventional values, careers, and worries about money, power, and responsibility
- Have parental dynamics more similar to those of heterosexual parents than different
- Practice nontraditional gender roles; more egalitarian in relationships
- Worry about discrimination and sexism against selves and children
- May feel the need to hide sexual orientation; strain of secrecy erodes intimacy between the couple and the family's feeling of normalcy
- Are often isolated with few role models
- Receive little, if any, legal or community supports
- Try to create a family unlike the family in which they grew up[4]
- Are likely to be older than the norm for first-time parents

WARM UP Two thirty-something men, dressed casually on a Saturday morning, are standing on a street corner talking. One of the men is gently rocking a baby in its stroller.

Write three paragraphs in which you examine the thoughts and behaviors of several different passersby.

TRAITS OF TEENAGE PARENTS

- Want to become parents to be loved or feel important
- Have family pressures and little support from religion or community
- Lack direction in life

[5] APA Monitor on Psychology (November 2004). [4] Laird (1993).

- Are often poor and unmarried with little education
- Have little time to individuate and grow; little time for dating, school, work
- Have lower levels of marital stability when they do marry
- Obtain less stable employment and have greater welfare use[6]

TRAITS OF MARRIED WOMEN WHO ARE CHILDLESS BY CHOICE

- Feel invisible and stigmatized as selfish or child-hating
- Have concerns about what a child will do to their lives
- May fear pregnancy and childbirth
- View their own parents as limited by birth of children
- Are very aware of sacrifices made by their own mothers
- May have been given a bleak picture of parenting by own parents
- Like freedom
- May have cared for others earlier in life: younger siblings or a sick parent
- Have realistic idea of responsibilities of being a mother
- Like their careers: can take career risks; can be mobile
- Are very involved in marriage[7]

NEW INFORMATION Not every couple decides to have or adopt children. The percentage of couples who remain childless by choice has risen dramatically in the United States, particularly as it becomes acceptable to have a full life without children, and the stigma of being childless is diminished (although not vanished).

SINGLE-PARENT FAMILIES

Individuals become single parents through a variety of means: divorce, widowhood, having a biological child outside the institution of marriage, stepparenting, adopting alone, receiving custody of other people's children, or raising grandchildren. Although there are many, many single-parent families (ten million in the U.S.), it is still a world in which two parents are considered the norm. The

[6] Coley and Chase-Lansdale (1998). [7] Faux (1984).

path to parenting could be your entire story, but here are some traits to think about if you want to create a single-parent family.

TRAITS OF SINGLE PARENTS

- Experience complex emotions (anger, sadness, fear) from handling the responsibilities alone
- May have legal issues to work out
- Experience changes in income, employment, and status after becoming a single parent
- Must set priorities: time management is difficult
- Expect more responsibility from children
- Place great importance on trusted childcare
- Must guard against overinvestment or living vicariously through the child
- Always feel guilty; children learn to trade on it
- Represent the major role model for the child
- Must supply the safety, security, and attention without help from a partner
- Must create family rituals that may not be traditional
- Has to deal with own dating and sexuality[8]

 NEW INFORMATION Teenaged boys whose fathers suffer from depression are seven times more likely to attempt suicide as young adults.[9]

TRAITS OF INFERTILE COUPLES

Couples who are infertile have many issues to deal with beyond the physical problems of infertility. Infertile couples:

- Have difficulty talking about the problem together
- Realize one may not have a choice about whether to produce a child; feel loss of control
- Experience shock and denial
- Feel anger and confusion

[8] Peterson and Warner (2003). [9] APA Monitor on Psychology (October, 2005).

- Harbor negative, secret thoughts: "Should I leave her?"
- Feel less feminine/masculine
- Feel sexual pressures; concentrate on all methods of pregnancy
- Despair when methods fail
- Find it difficult to see other babies or go to baby showers; feel the trauma of deprivation
- Have feelings of inadequacy, guilt, or blame: "If only I had started trying earlier!"
- Deal with the loss of the dream of one's own biological child; feel terrible disappointment
- Get past blaming the infertile partner
- Undergo changed attitudes about family

Adoption

Two to four percent of all families in the United States adopt a child. Many couples must deal with infertility and make decisions about adoption. People who decide to adopt go through a frustrating, expensive, time-consuming process to be able to become parents; they are exposed to the scrutiny of official organizations—something biological parents never have to experience.

TRAITS OF ADOPTIVE PARENTS
- Grieve biological infertility
- Overvalue their adopted child
- Wonder which traits of their child are a product of the environment and which are heredity
- Fear the return of the birth mother
- Have to deal with strange or intrusive questions from other people

EMOTIONS ASSOCIATED WITH THE DECISION TO ADOPT

Adoption is a conscious, emotional decision often including the following:
- Feeling lonely

- Feeling bombarded by other people wanting to solve the problem
- Confronting one's own feelings of inclusion or exclusion
- Grieving the loss of pregnancy
- Adjusting to the loss of biological continuity

EXPERIENCES OF PARENTS DURING THE ADOPTION PROCESS

- Rarely enjoy the full celebration that would have accompanied a pregnancy; for example, a baby shower
- Have either too much or too little time to prepare vs. nine months of pregnancy
- Feel at odds with a society that values biological ties more highly than adoption
- Mourn the idealized, imagined biological child that "looks like me"
- Go public with the decision and hear horror stories
- Reach out into the community in new ways through new organizations
- Must make decisions about public or private adoption
- Open their lives to strangers and public scrutiny: lawyers and adoption personnel in private life
- Must tolerate judgments made about them: age, health, income, and marital stability
- Experience anxiety: "How do we measure up?"
- Sometimes are rejected by birth mother

EXPERIENCES OF PARENTS AFTER ADOPTION TAKES PLACE

- Experience satisfaction at passing all the tests
- Feel relieved; sense of accomplishment
- Feel joyful over becoming parents
- Highly value the child
- Cope with underlying knowledge of grieving birth parents somewhere
- Remain aware of the implied promise made to birth parents to care for this wonderful baby

- Begin to emotionally claim the child
- Must accept the child as she is, just like all parents, even when they don't know what is inherited and what is a result of parenting
- Must exercise caution in interpreting behavior as hereditary[10]

TRAITS OF ADOPTEES

- Wonder why they were given up
- May have no long-term family medical history
- Have no knowledge of biological family; may or may not have physical resemblance to parents
- Tend to search for biological parents after leaving adopted parents' home (more women than men)

 WARM UP Write a scene in which a woman cleaning out her deceased mother's closet finds a letter from a biological mother she never knew existed.

Birth Order

Whether an individual is the first, only, or tenth child, or one child of a multiple birth, the position influences his relationship to parents, other brothers and sisters, and the world: for example, the experiences of being an only child vs. being the girl with six older brothers vs. being a triplet are significantly different. You can create characters whose birth position is influential on your story. Of course, birth order alone doesn't determine a child's personality. Children born at different points in the family life cycle (when parents have more money or when a mother is depressed) often have different traits. In addition to numerical order and the family cycle, there is also a psychological position: a favored child or the only son or daughter. All these differences affect traits.

TRAITS OF THE FIRSTBORN AS AN ADULT

- Identifies with parents; likes to be in authority

[10] Rosenberg (1992).

- Is disciplined
- Has good verbal skills
- Is protective of others
- Wants admiration and respect
- May appear arrogant; seeks reassurance
- Is devastated by failure
- Finds it difficult to delegate: everyone is a little brother or sister
- High achiever → being driven
- Trying hard → pessimism
- Nurturing → being overcommitted
- Responsibility → perfectionism or being a worrier → suicide[11]

TRAITS OF THE ONLY CHILD AS AN ADULT

- Is similar to the oldest child
- May remain childlike into adulthood
- Has high self-esteem
- Is not used to competition, fears, or failure
- Has good verbal skills
- Identifies strongly with parent of same gender
- Is a high achiever; expects a lot from life
- Lacks negotiation skills
- May have trouble with partner when it comes to sharing control
- Wants perfection; has trouble settling for less than excellence
- Is stressed by social situations
- Is good at using her imagination
- May remain single, if male: male only children are most likely of all birth positions to remain single[12]

TRAITS OF THE MIDDLE-BORN AS AN ADULT

- Becomes the family mediator
- May not have developed distinctive traits
- May be confused about identity

[11] ibid. [12] ibid.

- May feel that life is unfair
- Does not feel special like the oldest or the youngest siblings
- Does well in marriage; is loyal
- Can be secretive
- Is social and popular
- Avoids conflict; does well as a friend, knows how to get along, and can share
- May become excessive in peacemaker or mediator role; tries to make everyone happy
- Has a personality that is greatly influenced by siblings
- Desire to be first → competitive or self-destructive[13]

TRAITS OF THE LAST-BORN AS AN ADULT

- Is used to a lot of attention and pampering
- Feels rules have little meaning; may lack discipline in personal life
- May manipulate others to get what he wants
- Is lighthearted; charming
- Looks to others for answers: others have broken the ice
- Is dependent on others; finds it difficult to be self-sufficient
- Is less career oriented than other birth positions
- Is attracted to creative arts
- Is more likely to follow than to lead[14]

MULTIPLE BIRTHS

Multiple births are becoming more common because of new fertility drugs and methods of conception. Order of birth for twins, even by a few minutes, dictates traits of birth order. Fraternal twins may seem more like ordinary siblings than do identical twins.

TRAITS OF TWINS THROUGHOUT LIFE

- Are usually last-born into family
- May develop slower than single-births

[13] ibid. [14] ibid.

- Rely heavily on each other
- Have a great need for closeness and trouble with separations
- May bitterly compete with each other
- Are generally more well rounded as adults if they are raised as individuals
- May have secret language

People born as as twins, triplets, or another multiple birth experience attention from others that they attribute to a strange circumstance of their birth, rather than to any unique quality in themselves. Entering restaurants, going to parties, or walking down the street with the rest of the family draws attention that other people do not experience. They are referred to as "the triplets," and others, who try to see them as separate individuals, prematurely assign identities to them ("the smart one and the sweet one") making them feel locked in. Children with many brothers and sisters may also feel labeled ("the boys"), but do not have to deal with the "freaky" experience of multiples.

 WARM UP A family is on vacation to celebrate their parents' fiftieth anniversary. Create at least three adult children from the lists given and have them work together to prepare the celebratory dinner.

Families With a Disabled Child

All members of the family have to cope with the disability of one of its members, but everyone has different reactions and different psychological work to do.

TRAITS OF THE FAMILY WITH A DISABLED CHILD
- Suffers increased stress
- Experiences disruption of family ways; old ways must be changed
- Goes through stages: each member individually experiences denial, anger, depression, and adjustment
- Experiences emotions dependent upon extent and type of disability
- Rides an emotional roller-coaster depending on present state of disabled member
- May find previously unknown resilience

- May expect less from disabled child
- May become enmeshed, overprotective, or rigid
- May be unable to resolve conflicts
- May involve disabled child in their disagreements

TRAITS OF SIBLINGS OF A DISABLED CHILD
- May feel guilt for being normal
- Try not to cause trouble
- May feel resentful over lack of attention; then guilty
- May overcompensate and try to achieve for two

TRAITS OF THE DISABLED CHILD
- May feel the need to please the parents
- May experience emotional or behavioral problems (about 20–30 percent)
- Has to determine when she can be independent and when to depend on others

Grown Children's Relationships With Parents

In creating characters, it may be helpful to remember that parents are powerful not only when individuals are children: Parental influence, good and bad, permeates the lives of their children. Many strong stories have been constructed around parental influence that existed long after the parent's death. Throughout this book there are many traits of people with problems, whether alcoholism or mental illness or something else, and many of these people have children who will spend a good portion of their lives coping with the effects of their troubled parent.

For many individuals, the twenties are marked by making peace with parents and finding new ways to stay connected. Adults in their early twenties still lean on parents; when they reach their late twenties, they do more on their own.

All people in their twenties are not alike, however. Their levels of maturity can create sharp differences in character traits. Contrast the traits of immature twenty year olds with those of their more mature counterparts.

TRAITS OF IMMATURE TWENTY YEAR OLDS

- Have intense emotional bond with parents
- Are overwhelmed by intense feelings of rage or dependency
- Lash out at parents
- Seek to avoid disapproval or anger[15]
- See parents in black-and-white terms
- Cannot see parents as individuals
- Involve parents in the minute details of their lives

Or:

- Are estranged from parents
- Have little interest in parents

TRAITS OF MATURE TWENTY YEAR OLDS

- Have an emotional bond with parents
- Can discuss feelings
- Have strong confidence in own abilities to make decisions
- Feel in control of emotional responses to parents
- See themselves as best judges
- Can risk parents' disapproval
- See complexities of parents' lives
- Can draw a clear line between own lives and lives of parents
- Feel proud of parents as role models[16]

Four Patterns of Relating to Parents

COMPETENT AND CONNECTED (MORE WOMEN THAN MEN)

- Have independent views
- Feel empathy
- Understand shortcomings

---

[15] Frank, Avery, and Laman (1988); White, Speisman, and Costas (1983). [16] ibid.

DEPENDENT (MORE WOMEN THAN MEN)

- Feel emotionally trapped by parents
- Engage in power struggles

INDIVIDUATED (MORE MEN THAN WOMEN)

- Feel respected
- Enjoy company but maintain distance
- Have clear boundaries

FALSE AUTONOMY (MORE MEN THAN WOMEN)

- Pretend indifference
- Avoid parents
- Feel resentful and contemptuous[17]

Remarriage and Stepfamilies

Sixty-six percent of divorced adults (more men than women) eventually remarry. Fifty percent of divorced individuals remarry within five years. Divorce in second marriages occurs at a rate 10 percent higher than in first marriages. Remarried wives divorce at significantly higher rates than remarried husbands. Thirty-three percent of the U.S. population is in a "step" situation, and the numbers are increasing. Discomfort with the mix leads to words such as *blended* and *reconstituted*. An important thing to remember is that there is no legal relationship between stepparent and stepchild.

STEPFAMILY ISSUES

TRAITS OF CHILDREN IN STEPFAMILIES

- Boys respond more favorably than girls to a stepfather
- Girls have more conflict with stepmother than with stepfather

[17] Frank, Avery, and Laman (1988).

- One-half of stepfamilies have a joint or "our" child
- Families feel conflicting loyalties; for example, hearing one parent talk against other
- Families may divide along roles of insiders vs. outsiders: kids living all year round vs. visiting
- Kids have "dual citizenship" in two households: two cultures and two sets of rules

TRAITS OF STEPFAMILY HOUSEHOLDS

- Households may have different foods, languages, and ways of doing things
- Family members feel tension around comings and goings, packing and unpacking, and other transitions
- Boundaries are less clear in terms of privacy and property: "Who sleeps where?"
- Households are formed by losses in another family, and need to mourn

TRAITS OF STEPPARENT/STEPCHILD RELATIONSHIPS

- Power issues must be dealt with: "If you aren't nice to me, I'll go live with my father!" or "If you don't behave, I'll send you to your father!"
- Parents and children alike must confront coercive tactics: "Mom lets me stay up until eleven!" or "I'll buy you a car if you stay with me."
- Recognition that emotional attachments take time; there is no instant love
- Dreams have shattered and need to be altered
- Different traditions must be developed
- Changing priorities: adult-adult relationship now comes before the parent-child relationships

 WARM UP Write a scene in which a teenaged stepdaughter overhears her stepmother on the telephone and becomes convinced that she is having an affair.

TRAITS OF THE STEPPARENT

- Stepparents try to ingratiate themselves
- Stepparents may disengage, especially if rejected by stepchild
- Stepfathers bond better with stepchildren if they have no biological children
- Stepfathers tend to behave like "polite strangers," monitoring children less and showing less closeness and control
- Stepfathers tend to be more abusive than biological fathers
- Stepmothers have difficulty integrating themselves into reconstituted family
- Stepmothers are expected to participate more actively in parenting; therefore, they are forced into more confrontations[18]

FIGURES AND STATISTICS In 1960, 32 percent of married women were employed, compared to 89 percent of married men.

In 1995, 61 percent of married women were employed compared to 78 percent of married men.[19]

[18] Visher and Visher (1993). [19] U.S. Bureau of the Census.

nine

CHAPTER

Ordinary and Extraordinary Events

IN THIS CHAPTER

• *Creating Friendships* • *Adolescence* • *Transitions* • *Aging* • *Bereavement and Trauma*

A thirty-year-old client came into my office for her weekly session and plopped down on the couch. She looked very satisfied—not her recent frame of mind. For months, she had been struggling with making decisions, the meaning of her life, and never having enough control over events: all serious but not unusual dilemmas. "I figured it out," she said proudly. "Life happens along the way." I've always liked her explanation.

Individuals may make deliberate, elaborate plans, but life happens. This chapter offers characteristics of many life events—both the everyday and the unusual, the normal developmental stages and unforeseen trauma—and the ways individuals cope with them. Many traits are associated with age, development, and decisions that we all must make in life, rather than exclusively with personality.

We cannot know the day of a toddler's first steps, or what precise physical and emotional changes she will encounter when reaching puberty, adulthood, or old age—but we can make general guesses. These are normal stages of human development, events and transitions we expect to take place, and we also expect to be able to cope with the changes as they present themselves.

Trauma is the opposite. Trauma is an event such as rape, assault, war, or a natural disaster that overwhelms the individual or community and sorely taxes the ability to cope. This chapter details some of life's stages—both predictable occurrences and traumatic events.

Creating Friendships

Friendships are an important aspect of life from childhood through old age. There are benefits to having friends that are different from those associated with family.

TRAITS OF FRIENDSHIP IN YOUNG CHILDREN

- Focus is on common activities: "We play"
- Concrete reciprocities: "I give him candy, he gives me gum"
- Similarities in social skills are often a basis for early friendship
- Similarity in physical activity is a basis for boys' friendship
- Similarity in attractiveness of personality and social network is a basis of girls' friendship[1]

TRAITS OF FRIENDSHIP MIDDLE CHILDHOOD

- Focus is on understanding: "A friend is someone who likes you and doesn't hit you"
- Loyal and trustworthy
- Shared interests; shared secrets
- Similarity in social behaviors is a basis for friendship
- Friends spend time together; friendships are very important and occupy much time[2]

[1] Hartup and Stevens (1997). [2] ibid.

TRAITS OF FRIENDSHIP ADOLESCENCE

- Focus is on support, dependability, understanding, and acceptance
- Reciprocity in intimacy, confidence, and trust
- Shared interests, experiences, activities, and communication
- Similarity in aspirations, school-related attitudes, and achievement
- Shared adventures; Socializing together
- Mutual support in transition to school, puberty, and dating
- Adolescents spend 29 percent of waking hours with friends[3]

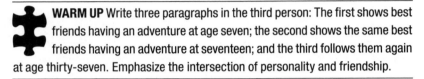 **WARM UP** Write three paragraphs in the third person: The first shows best friends having an adventure at age seven; the second shows the same best friends having an adventure at seventeen; and the third follows them again at age thirty-seven. Emphasize the intersection of personality and friendship.

TRAITS OF FRIENDSHIP IN ADULTHOOD

- Reciprocity in intimacy, confidence, and trust
- Ease of communication; similarities in experiences and interests
- Blend of social and work relationships
- Shared friendships between husbands and wives
- Friendships closely tied to family activities
- Mutual support in transitions of marriage, work, childbearing, and family concerns[4]

TRAITS OF FRIENDSHIP IN OLD AGE

- Reciprocity in intimacy, confidence, and trust
- Less activity; more letters, favors, phone calls, gifts, and expressions of respect
- Mutual support in transitions of retirement, illness, aging, and death[5]

NEGATIVE TRAITS IN FRIENDSHIPS OF ALL AGES

- Encouragement of negative behaviors

[3] ibid. [4] ibid. [5] ibid.

- Involvement of friends in destructive activities
- Power struggles: can outstrip negotiation
- Competition: can outweigh cooperation
- Inequality: if influence is out of balance, one is always the follower
- No allowance for growth beyond the confines of friendship
- Conflicts: can overshadow support[6]

Adolescence

ADOLESCENT TASKS OF DEVELOPMENT

Specific traits of children and adolescents at different ages are listed in chapter three. The general tasks of adolescence are outlined below.

GENERAL TASKS OF AN ADOLESCENT

- Adjusts to the physical and emotional changes of puberty
- Establishes effective social relationships
- Establishes working relationships with peers
- Achieves independence from parents
- Prepares for a vocation (see chapter eleven for stages of career choice)
- Moves toward a sense of values
- Develops a secure identity, including a sexual identity and a positive sense of self

DIFFICULTIES FOR AN ADOLESCENT WHO IS GAY

Adolescence can be made even more difficult by issues that complicate the work of growing up. Some gay adolescents have none of the following problems; others have many of them.

- Needs to distance self from peers because they fear that closeness will be misunderstood

[6] ibid.

- Makes sexual contacts without any accompanying social interaction (more likely for males than for females)
- Fears rejection from family
- Withdraws emotionally from family to minimize possible rejection
- Is threatened with abandonment by parents
- Is persuaded by parents to recant his sexual orientation
- Is forced into therapy to "fix" the sexual preference
- Feels guilty or sinful
- Sees few role models of lifelong gay relationships
- Has few opportunities to learn how to manage sexuality in a positive manner
- Feels depressed or hopeless as a result of the barrage of others' negative attitudes
- Becomes truant or drops out of school
- Uses alcohol and drugs to numb anxiety and depression[7]

Coping Strategies of Gay Adolescents

- Denial: denies sexual orientation
- Repair: tries to abolish homosexual feelings and behaviors
- Redefinition: sees behaviors as "just a stage"
- Avoidance: stops behaviors; limits exposure to individuals of the same sex; avoids information that might confirm homosexual fears; tries heterosexual relationships; becomes antigay avoids facing knowledge through substance abuse
- Acceptance: Comes to terms with sexual orientation[8]

 WARM UP People tend to make the same New Year's resolution year after year. Write a quick scene of a couple discussing their New Year's resolutions on January 20.

---

[7] ibid. [8] Radowsky and Siegel (1997).

Transitions

Transitions are periods of discontinuity when people move from one time of life to another. Some transitions are smooth (high school graduation); most have bumps (marriage). Occasionally, the transition erupts into a full-blown crisis or positive transformation (midlife). The following types of transitions can provide rich material for short stories, novels, or historical analysis.

Types of Transitions

AREA OF LIFE	TRANSITION EXPERIENCE (EXAMPLES OF LIFE EVENTS)
Personal/Self	Identity crisis; periods of personal development; pursuit of solitary hobbies; times of loneliness, times of freedom; relocating
Personal/Family	Decisions about marrying and children; worries about performance as a spouse; empty nest
Personal/Health	Personal illness or injury; adjustment to a physical handicap or recovery from illness such as heart attack or mastectomy
Personal/Work	Career decisions; retirement; career changes such as an athlete or homemaker might make; career plateaus or shifts
Personal/Economics	Financial problems; gambling losses; lottery winnings; inheritance
Interpersonal/Self	Disagreements with friends; breakup of love affair or friendship; meeting new people; travel

Interpersonal/Family	Marriage or marital problems; joys and troubles being a parent; blended families; aging parents; siblings with problems
Interpersonal/Health	Sickness or death of family member
Interpersonal/Work	Relationships with boss and subordinates; concerns about a friend or family member's work
Interpersonal/Economics	Financial problems of friend or family
Community/Self	Public award or recognition; public disgrace; arrest or conviction of self or family member for a crime
Community/Family	School and plant closings; changes in local laws
Community/Health	Epidemics; contamination of water supply; disaster, hazardous wastes
Community/Work	Public recognition of work; public business failure; running for office
Community/Economics	Concern about economic policies; taxes, housing[9]

 WARM UP Choose one of the transitions mentioned in the chart and write the dream/nightmare a character has after being confronted with that particular change.

[9] Schlossberg (1984).

IMMIGRATION

One major life transition is immigration. Have any of your characters come from other lands? In general, immigration entails changes in social networks, socioeconomic status, and culture. Here are some broad issues to consider in character and plot development.

- Being young and male fosters faster acculturation than older and female.

- Women who migrate to the U.S. involuntarily (for example, because their husbands say so) suffer high levels of depression as compared with their voluntary counterparts.

- Extrafamilial supports redress the loss of family and provide intimate, supportive contacts.

- Grief and mourning are expected ingredients of culture shock.

- People remain in stressful positions because of deep-seated obligations to send money to family members in their own country; for example, Filipina domestic workers.

- There are a great many trade-offs, even for the young. For example, Chinese students at U.S. universities attain academic success while disproportionately experiencing problems of personal adjustment.

- Some immigrants must take work that is significantly different from their careers in their original countries with mixed results. For example, Indian professionals in Australia became "reluctant entrepreneurs." Downgraded from professions of medicine, accounting, or teaching, they were forced to try new work, which for some provided a freedom they had not previously known. Not surprisingly, others found the downgrade humiliating and frustrating.

- Individuals who are integrated into society through marriage or high-status occupations (such as English-speaking Westerners in Japan) gain social relationships that create a satisfying adaptation.

- When migration works well for the individual, the feeling is often described as a sense of renewal or rebirth.[10]

[10] Rogler (1994).

- Children adjust to values and styles of host country faster than parents, because parents often cling to styles and norms of original culture; these different adjustment rates cause family clashes.

THREE TYPES OF FAMILY ADJUSTMENT TO IMMIGRATION

"Kangaroo"

The Kangaroo type of adjustment works best when new country is undesirable.

- Parents keep offspring in a "pouch," protective of the children.
- Parents preserve original culture in food, dress, language, and customs.
- Parents see new culture as a threat to children.
- Parents maintain confidence and consistency.
- Family remains segregated.
- Family experiences low stress because there is little involvement with outside.
- Family is supported by a community that agrees with and encourages kangaroo style.
- Children who stray into new culture are guilty of betrayal.
- Children who identify with new culture risk estrangement and scape-goating.

"Cuckoo"

Cuckoo adjustment works best when new country is seen as better than old.

- Parents raise offspring in the nests of other birds.
- Parents maintain old ways.
- Parents often come to resent new influences.
- Family relinquishes its power.
- Family risks cohesion, continuity of generations, and cultural past.
- Children are entrusted to formal and informal socialization such as boarding school.
- Children rapidly assimilate into new country.

- Children later search for lost connections between present and past.
- Children may feel neglected by both parents and society.

"Chameleon"

Chameleon adjustment works best when new country has positive advantages and differences are minor.[11]

- Parents encourage children to live peacefully in both cultures.
- Parents allow children to explore values and behaviors of new country.
- Parents do not expect to change very much.
- Family risks opening up cultural/belief/value/behavior gaps that cannot be bridged.
- Family desires to understand new country in order to adjust.
- Family maintains contact with old ways.
- Family maintains cohesion and continuity.
- Children behave and dress like others outside the home.
- Children may speak original language, or behave differently in home.
- Children learn to negotiate between two worlds.
- Children do not have to choose.

Does Your Character Want to Change?

It isn't easy. Why do people try again and again after they have failed at a task? Here is the cycle of false hope:

People commit to make the change: diet, stop drinking, gambling, smoking. → They have unrealistic expectations about the speed, ease, amount and rewards of change. → They have feelings of control for having made the decision. → They experience success in the early stages. → As time goes by, the task becomes more difficult to sustain. → Progress slows or stops. → Relapse!!!! → They abandon the "failed" project. → They eventually soften the failure and they try again, remembering their small successes and positive expectations for the future.[12]

---

[11] Strier (1996). [12] Polivy (2002).

POSTPARTUM BLUES

Another major transition is that of becoming a parent. Postpartum blues is the name for a mother's depression that occurs after giving birth to (or adopting) a child. Seventy-five percent of new mothers feel let down in the early weeks after giving birth, but 10–20 percent suffer severe symptoms. It occurs in the months following the birth and symptoms can last as long as a year. It may result from emotional problems, hormones, role changes, marital problems, or stress.

TRAITS OF A WOMAN WITH POSTPARTUM BLUES
- Experiences magnification of previously existing problems
- Experiences fear, panic, and dizziness
- Becomes depressed
- Feels guilt because she thinks she ought to be happy
- Blue → psychotic with delusions and hallucinations
- Blue → murderous[13]

The Process of Change

Here are the stages of change, using getting over a drug addiction as an example:
- Precontemplation is the stage at which there is no intention to change and might reflect unawareness or underawareness of a problem. John is convinced that smoking dope daily is not a problem, although his wife thinks otherwise.
- Contemplation is the time when people are aware of a problem and think about it, but have not made a commitment to action. John realizes that dope smoking interferes with his activities.
- Preparation involves the intention to take action. John has the phone number of Narcotics Anonymous.
- Action means that people have begun to modify their behavior and committed time and energy to the task. John has stopped smoking marijuana.

---

[13] DeAngelis (1997).

> - Maintenance is the time when people work to prevent relapse and consolidate their gains. John stays away from his druggie friends; he attends NA and has support from his wife.
> - Termination is the stage at which people have completed the change process and no longer have to work to prevent relapse. Two years later, John is not yet certain whether he achieved in termination.[14]
> - Success is often defined as not giving in to temptation so each breach is considered a failure.

AGING

Adulthood is not a stable plateau. There are developmental changes throughout life, changes and crises involving the workplace, relationships with family and friends, and the state of one's health. Listed below are some of the situations commonly faced by men and women of each age group; how they react to these challenges can have a significant impact on the remainder of their lives.

STAGES OF MEN'S ADULT DEVELOPMENT[15]

MIDLIFE TRANSITION (AGES 40–45)

This stage is the termination of early adulthood: a crucial developmental change unmarked by any one particular event. Contributions to midlife transition or crisis are subtle changes in both biology and psychology; declines in quickness, strength, and endurance; loss of youth; alienation; stagnation; confrontation with personal mortality (the knowledge that life ends); being seen by others as older; asking profound questions ("What have I accomplished?"); examining fulfilled and frustrated dreams; and reappraising life. Often, an event that would have, in another time, passed unnoticed changes a man's life course.

[14] Prochaska (2001). [15] Levinson. et al. (1978).

MIDDLE ADULTHOOD (AGES 45–60)

The positive outcome to the midlife transition is stability with increased qualities of wisdom, maturity, and reflection. The negative outcome is an impossible and desperate desire to turn back the clock.

LATE ADULT TRANSITION (AGES 60–65)

This transition may be precipitated by retirement; there is a noticeable bodily decline. Old ways must end; the task is to modify earlier life structure.

LATER ADULTHOOD (AGES 65–80)

Later adulthood brings more frequent illness and death of contemporaries. Men at this stage may be pushed out at work by a younger generation and seen as obsolete. The tasks of these years are to find new balance of self with society, enhance integrity of life as a whole, and make peace with self and the world.

OLD AGE (AGES 80+)

At this point, the territory of life shrinks in size; the ultimate involvement is with self. Often dealing with chronic illness, the task of this age is to make peace with dying.

Pathological Traits in the Elderly

Pathological traits can appear at any age. New pathological traits can emerge in the elderly when:

- Bad, damaging childhoods that were covered over lose the cover.
- Earlier protections are gone.
- Carefully constructed life patterns that promoted security in earlier days are dismantled.
- Adult skills that allow change and growth were never learned, so they become stuck.
- Adaptation to change was never learned.
- Choices made in earlier adulthood were limiting and defeating, so in later years they have little to rest on.

- Chances were missed: Opportunities for intimacy, parenting, learning work skills, or engagement with social/political/religious organizations passed them by.
- Early traumas, conflicts, or psychological injuries were never resolved.
- Strengths and internal resources were not built.
- Losses cannot be replaced with satisfying substitutions.
- Changes in self-image based on having to adapt to the environment rather than changing the environment.

There are gender differences in aging problems. Problems for the older woman arise from her balance, or imbalance, of autonomy and dependency. Problems for the older man arise from the need to be caring vs. the need to assert himself without destroying others.

STAGES OF WOMEN'S ADULT DEVELOPMENT

MIDLIFE TRANSITION (AGES 40–45)

Midlife transition is a period that terminates early adulthood. It is a crucial developmental change, begun less by age than by time of life and what events have transpired (early childbearing vs. late; early career vs. late). Contributions to midlife transition or crisis include: biological change, including menopause; facing personal mortality (the knowledge that life ends); acceptance of the passing of youth; and asking the question, "What have I accomplished?" Women at this stage examine fulfilled and frustrated dreams and reappraise their lives. Many simplify their lives and work to return to an authentic self too often obscured in lives filled with attention to others.[16]

MIDDLE ADULTHOOD (AGES 45–60)

Women in middle adulthood go in one of two directions: They either feel stuck and continue the path of life that has been followed, or they use the transition to redirect their lives in ways that make more sense. They accept changing

[16] Edelstein (1999).

relationships with children and increasingly attend to their own interests. Still occupying a good deal of time may be the need to care for aging parents.

LATER ADULTHOOD (AGES 65–80)

This period is marked by increased frequency of illness and death of contemporaries. Like their male counterparts, they may be seen as outmoded and pushed aside at work by the younger generation. On the positive side, they find a new balance of self with society. The primary task of these years is to enhance integrity of life as a whole and make peace with oneself and with the world.

OLD AGE (AGES 80+)

For women in old age, as for men, the ultimate involvement is with self. The territory of life shrinks in size; there is decreasing social contact and women often are dealing with chronic illness. The task of old age is to make peace with dying.

 NEW INRORMATION Adversity encountered in adult life affected individuals' adult health more than the adversity they encountered in childhood[17]

LATER LIFE

Traits in later life can be viewed as a mix of character (personality, traits, internal structure), social context (life events), and the changes over time of both character and context. There is less personality change than most people imagine, and what people image to be significant change is often people becoming "more of" whatever they have always been: for example, more of an inflexible personality. In later life, personality traits are less hidden by youthful activities, but it is complicated by physical declines and the necessity of dealing with a variety of losses. Those who have made a successful transition through middle adulthood are better able to withstand the losses and declines of aging.

[17] Kraus, Shaw, and Cairney (2004).

NEW INFORMATION Anorexia, a disorder we generally associate with young women, has been documented in the elderly. A report from Great Britain describes six cases, all individuals over sixty-five years old, men and women, who suffered from self-inflicted low body weight. Some of them had episodes of anorexia beginning in youth; others suffered only in their later years. The symptoms were food avoidance, conviction that they were fat, fear of weight gain, and, for some, laxative abuse.[18]

GRANDPARENTS

Grandparents in the 1880s were always old, with "silver hair" and "dimming eyes," but today, as more people live long enough to become grandparents, we see a vast age range and a variety of roles. The average person becomes a grandparent at midlife, and may spend as much as four decades in the role. And, with increased divorce, there are also stepgrandparents.

BECOMING A GRANDPARENT

Grandparents come in all ages: a young (twenty-eight- to forty-year-old) grandparent provides different character material than an older one. The role also depends on the grandparents' health, financial status, and their relationship with their child, as well as their personalities.

Some traits, however, are similar in all grandparents, because of the nature of the role.

Traits Common to Grandmothers and Grandfathers

- Often stick to safe topics of conversation: they provide a "demilitarized zone"
- Provide stabilizing force in lives of children and grandchildren
- Provide buffer against mortality for own children
- Act as catalysts for family cohesion: the "excuse" for people to get together
- Interpret their child to their grandchild

[18] Wills and Olivieri (1998).

- Mediate for family members
- Symbolize connection across lifetimes
- Have time to listen to children and grandchildren
- Provide link to known and unknown past
- Are always in reserve if help is needed[19]

Traits That Differ Between Grandmother and Grandfather

GRANDMOTHER	GRANDFATHER
Attends to interpersonal relations	Attends to tasks
Talks about friendships and family	Talks about education, job, and money
Treats granddaughter and grandson similarly	Concentrates attention on grandsons
Organizes family gatherings	Acts as an advisor, particularly to grandsons
Is most involved with daughter's daughter	Is most involved with son's son

SIX TYPES OF GRANDPARENTS

Formal

- Follow what they regard as proper role
- Maintain clearly defined roles
- Babysit; indulge grandchildren occasionally
- Do not offer advice on parenting to children
- Maintain constant interest in child and grandchild
- Want grandchildren to have good manners, to be neat and clean, and to be self-controlled

[19] Hagestad (1985).

Hedonistic

- Want freedom from family responsibilities
- Are no longer interested in being of service to family
- See grandchildren as nuisances
- Lifestyle marks a breakdown of the family[20]

Fun Seeker

- Have an informal and fun relationship with grandchildren
- Join grandchildren in activities for pleasure
- Think of grandchildren as a source of leisure activity
- Do not act as strong authority figures
- Want grandchildren to also have fun
- Want grandchildren to be happy and get along with others

Distant

- Emerge for holidays
- Make fleeting and infrequent contact with grandchildren
- Are benevolent but remote

Surrogate Parent

- Are usually grandmothers
- Take care of the grandchild in absence of parents
- Want grandchildren to try hard, to be obedient, and to be good students

Wise

- Are usually grandfathers
- Have an authoritarian relationship with grandchildren in which skill and wisdom are dispensed
- Clearly delineate positions between generations; both children and grandparents are respected
- Command respect; children and grandchildren are deferential to older generation
- Want grandchildren to be honest, have good common sense, and be responsible[21]

[20] Gutmann (1985). [21] McCready (1985).

WARM UP Write a scene in which a young grandmother fears looking old to others, refuses to engage in the traditional grandmother role, and complains that she wants to have her own active life.

Bereavement and Trauma

One of the certainties of life is that, sooner or later, we will deal with loss. It is ironic that the most predictable aspect of life is also one of the most tragic. Losses are not only in the physical world. Some of the most devastating losses are those that occur emotionally, such as betrayal or loss of love. There are many types of losses: illness or injury to the body; loss of material possessions such as a home, jewelry, or money; the separation from or death of a loved one; developmental losses such as aging; the loss of an abstraction that has meaning, such as one's homeland; and even an aspect of oneself, such as when we turn into people we did not expect to become.

BEREAVEMENT

The following chart illustrates the stages of bereavement and the adaptation to the death of a loved one.

IMPACT (BRIEF)	DISORGANIZATION	REORGANIZATION
• Hears the news	• Struggles with changes in roles	• Finds loss is less consuming
• Is numb; in shock	• Experiences family disruptions	• Returns to normal activities
• Feels disbelief	• Undergoes social and economic change	• Begins new activities
	• Experiences strong waves of emotion	• Becomes increasingly emotionally stable
	• Is angry, sad, confused	• Experiences return of well-being

People always wonder, "When will I get over the loss?" The answer is, never. We go through losses and come out somewhat changed on the other side. We are formed by all our experiences, good and bad, and losses become integrated into our personalities and into our lives. Many creative people integrate their losses into their work; for example, writers, artists, and sculptors. Creative works are healthy channels through which one can deal with loss. Less artistic people often create memorials, such as charities or scholarships, to commemorate loved ones.[22]

WARM UP A young parent dies, leaving a spouse and small child. The dead spouse's mother comes into town to help. Write two paragraphs about the mother's advice and behavior; in the first paragraph, make it the wife who dies and her husband survives to care for their child; in the second, make it the wife who survives.

STAGES OF PARENTS' REACTIONS TO THE DEATH OF A CHILD

Technology and health care have increased women's ability to have healthy children, and today we expect all our newborns to live. But it was only at the beginning of the 1900s that the highest mortality rates were for women of childbearing age and infants. Reactions to the death of a child are among the most painful and severe of family tragedies.

- Early Reactions → Shock; numbness; physical pain
- Disorganization → Disbelief; inability to concentrate; poor functioning; strong emotions such as anger, sadness, despair, hopelessness
- Holding On/Letting Go → Many memories; reality sets in; daily thoughts; high emotions
- Reorganization → Integration of loss into ongoing life; memorials; return of good days

Mourning may never completely end for parents who have suffered the death of a child.

[22] Edelstein (1984).

Children's Reactions to Death

How children react to death depends on age, mental development, life stage, and family influences. The following chart lists reactions by age and mental development; below are the effects of life stage and family influences.

LIFE STAGE

Children express emotions differently at different ages. Whereas an adult who hears about the death of a loved one is likely to cry, it is rare for a child under the age of five to weep. Children may seem to lose interest in the death, even the death of a parent. Don't be deceived by the behavior: The impact is profound and long lasting.

FAMILY INFLUENCES

Values and behavior of family members influence adult, child, and adolescent behavior. Families often unknowingly dictate behavior during a crisis. If a child gets the message that everyone is being stoic, she will attempt to be silently brave. If Mother faints when a question is asked, the questions will stop. If an individual must make plans and care for other people's feelings, personal emotions may be intense but behavior will have to appear normal.

AGE	MENTAL DEVELOPMENT
0–2	Infants have no concept of death; therefore, an infant's responses are to loss of care, attention, and attachment. Infants can respond to parent's grief and feel the isolation, withdrawal, self-absorption, and intense emotion of the adult.
3–5	Children conceptualize death as similar to sleep. They can remember the image of the person but think of death as temporary: "I know Papa is dead, but when is he coming to visit?" Children blur fantasy and fact: "Mom is watching over you" results in the child looking at the clouds for a glimpse of Mom.

5–6	Children begin to understand death with loss of a pet. They still believe that death can be escaped if you are quick. Life is attributed to organic things; for example, trees or rocks.
7 and up	Children understand finality of death
9 and up	Children understand that functions cease. They may be less emotional and less responsive than nine to eleven year olds.
12 and up	Preteens and adolescents have an understanding similar to that of adults: All things die, life ends. They understand that one's own life eventually ends. They grieve and show emotions more like an adult than like a child.

POST-TRAUMATIC STRESS DISORDER

The term *shell shock* used first during World War I was a forerunner of understanding post-traumatic stress disorder. In this disorder, individuals develop characteristic symptoms after a severe trauma, usually an experience in which the individual was involved or witnessed an event that included actual death, the threat of death, or severe harm to himself or to another person. (A variation of the trauma is learning about the event rather than witnessing it firsthand.) Almost always, the person reacts with terrific fear, horror, and helplessness. The most common events that induce this disorder are war and military action, violent personal assault, natural or manmade disasters, accidents, and contracting a life-threatening illness. Fifty to sixty percent of the U.S. population is exposed to traumatic stress but only 5–10 percent develop PTSD.[23]

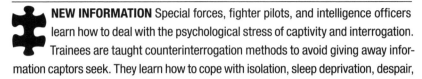

NEW INFORMATION Special forces, fighter pilots, and intelligence officers learn how to deal with the psychological stress of captivity and interrogation. Trainees are taught counterinterrogation methods to avoid giving away information captors seek. They learn how to cope with isolation, sleep deprivation, despair,

[23] Ozer, (2003).

and ambiguity and how to deal with the anticipatory anxiety of what may come next. Trainees are taught to think about their colleagues and crew because it reminds them they are not alone; it encourages them to resist in order to protect others.

TRAITS OF POST-TRAUMATIC STRESS DISORDER

- Flashbacks or reexperiencing of the trauma: reliving a rape
- Terrible dreams
- Memories: visions of war or torture
- Triggers (sights, sounds, or smells) that symbolize or jog a memory of the trauma
- Avoidance of anything associated with the trauma: the building, street, activity, or people
- Memory loss around specifics of the event
- Isolated feelings and behaviors; detached: company of others is painful
- Diminished feelings and emotions: flat speech, little happiness or sadness, or numbness
- Preoccupation with death
- Hypervigilance: always watching and alert
- Trouble sleeping
- Difficulty concentrating: mind wanders so work suffers
- Jumpiness
- Anger, irritability, and frustration
- Refusal to acknowledge or discuss event, making it difficult to get help
- Impaired personal relationships because of these symptoms

 FIGURES AND STATISTICS Thousands return from most military actions suffering from PTSD. In Iraq, 90 percent of troops have seen dead bodies, or been shot at. About half have killed an enemy combatant.[24]

PREDICTORS OF PTSD (POST-TRAUMATIC STRESS DISORDER)

- Lack of social support
- Lack of education

[24] APA Monitor on Psychology (April. 2005).

- Prior psychiatric history
- Difficult family background[25]

COLLECTIVE TRAUMA

Trauma is not always an experience of only one person. When a flood, tornado, or other disaster strikes an entire community, the process of trauma and recovery is shared: Collective trauma refers to those events shared by a group or community, such as 9/11 or Hurricane Katrina's devastation in Louisiana and Mississippi.

TRAITS OF COLLECTIVE TRAUMA

- Loss of community
- Loss of ordinary life, such as seeing your neighbor or shopping at the neighborhood store
- Desire to leave town afterward
- Feelings of sympathy and helplessness
- Difficulty expressing the sense of loss
- Euphoria at surviving right after the disaster, then shock and numbness, then depression
- Disorientation (confusion, distraction, perplexity) for months or even years
- Feeling of apathy
- Insomnia and nightmares
- Loneliness
- Disruption of marriages; sexual desire may decrease
- Idealization of old community or times
- Feelings of vulnerability
- Healing found through sharing with others who suffered same experience
- Few long-term problems[26]

[25] Brewin (2000). [26] Erikson (1976).

WARM UP People who work with, or are close to, victims of trauma may also experience symptoms. This is called "vicarious trauma."[27] Write a scene of a worker returning home to a privileged family gathering after a day with victims.

TERRORISM

Terrorism is premeditated, politically motivated violence against noncombatants by subnational groups or agents, usually intended to influence an audience. The focus of "modern" terrorism (from mid 1980s to the present) has shifted from the far left ideology to the far right ideology. See traits of collective trauma, post-traumatic stress disorder, and bereavement for an understanding of traits of terrorism victims.

Why Don't People Evacuate a Building During an Emergency?

The myth is that people rush out when they hear the alarm. Not true. Psychologists have been studying reactions for twenty-five years and find slow responses because:

- People want to define a situation before they respond, so they wait for more information, such as a smoke or a co-worker urging them to leave
- People know that the probability of a genuine, threatening fire is low
- People do not initially panic at the sound of an alarm
- People stay to help others even if they put themselves at risk
- People are inertial creatures; they don't like to stop what they are doing
- People are reluctant to use exits that are unfamiliar [28]

GENOCIDE

Genocides induce collective trauma of massive proportions. There have been slaughters in Europe during the Holocaust, and more recently in Central America, Africa, and Bosnia.

[27] Astin (1997). [28] APA Monitor on Psychology (September, 2004).

POSITIVE TRAITS OF SURVIVORS OF HOLOCAUSTS

- Able to rally and go on
- Are willing to work and flexible about types of work
- Adjust quickly; astoundingly resilient
- Have deep connections to family and relatives
- Are sensitive toward others; concerned and altruistic
- Possess strong feelings of self-worth
- Are tenacious

NEGATIVE TRAITS OF SURVIVORS OF HOLOCAUSTS

- Suffer from post-traumatic stress disorder
- Are pessimistic
- Feel guilt for surviving; anxiety
- Suffer physical ailments
- Fear new persecutions
- Keep silent about events
- Are depressed; feel continuous sorrow[29]

Protection Against Stress

Hardiness seems to buffer individuals against extreme stress. Traits of hardiness include: the commitment to find meaningful purpose in life, the belief that one can influence the outcome of events, and the belief that one can grow from positive and negative experiences.

"People hang on to anger to distance themselves from those responsible for their pain," writes an African psychologist. If victims see their perpetrators as real people rather than evil monsters, they fear that they will compromise their moral strength. When a perpetrator offers a sincere apology, however, he shows his human side; then both sides are able to find an emotional connection. Victims can see the remorse of those who wronged them and hatred can collapse, allowing forgiveness. A sincere apology reaches out and invites the victim to engage.[30]

[29] Whiteman (1993). [30] Gobodo-Madikizela (2003).

CHAPTER **ten**

Physical and Mind/Body Disorders

IN THIS CHAPTER

> • *Remembering and Forgetting* • *Pseudophysical Disorders* • *Sleep Problems* • *Substance Abuse* • *Eating Disorders* • *Communication Disorders* • *Sexual Disorders*

The strong and influential relationship between mind and body has become increasingly appreciated, even trendy. Physical problems shape personality, influence behavior, and may have grave psychological consequences. The reverse is also true: Psychological or emotional problems affect and are often displayed through the body.

This chapter includes: neurological disorders, such as amnesia; other disorders that blend psychological and physical difficulties, such as substance abuse; and problems that are psychological in origin but have physical consequences, such as eating disorders, sexual disorders, malingering, and psychogenic amnesia.

Remembering and Forgetting

Remembering and forgetting is taken for granted, like breathing. Only when there are problems in these areas do we recognize the power of memory. Memory means that I recognize my children and remember our muddy hike in the rain forest; I can recount the family stories served along with our traditional Thanksgiving foods (which I remember to cook). Memory for someone else may also include trauma and abuse. Which moments are remembered and which forgotten create the stories of our lives. To forget is to lose our own experiences; to be disbelieved is to shatter our confidence.

AMNESIA

Amnesia is a memory disorder, usually long-term, whose cause can be either physical or psychological. Though it is usually the result of a physical disorder (for example, brain damage caused by a virus, injury, alcohol, or a tumor) it can also be a mind/body disorder, meaning that the mind has influenced the body (see Psychogenic Amnesia for psychologically based amnesia).

TRAITS OF GENERAL AMNESIA

- Intact I.Q.
- Selective memory loss: not all areas of memory are damaged
- Intact short-term memory storage; for example, individual can have conversations and remember the present
- Loss of past events
- Impaired logical memory
- Possible impaired recognition
- Temporary or permanent state[1]

TRAITS OF PHYSICAL AMNESIA

Transient Global Amnesia

- Sudden memory loss over a recent period: the previous month or year
- Short duration: the attack lasts five minutes to several days

[1] Parkin (1997).

- Inability to retain new information; individual asks same questions over and over
- Disorientation about time
- No loss of identity; no other impairment
- Physical triggers: change in temperature (for example, a cold shower); physical stress; eating a large meal; or intercourse[2]

Korsakoff's syndrome

- Physical cause: severe thiamine deficiency, usually brought on by long-term alcohol abuse (diet-induced syndrome seen in prisoners of war); less common causes include thalamic ischemic attack and brain aneurysm
- Ataxia: jerking or irregular movements
- Gross confusion
- Visual abnormalities
- Profound memory disorder: incapable of learning anything new because new information cannot be retained[3]

Confabulation

- Made-up, fantastic recollections to fill in gaps of memory
- Result of brain damage in frontal lobe
- Stories are disbelieved except by the person telling them

TRAITS OF PSYCHOLOGICAL AMNESIA

Dissociative Amnesia

- Breakdown in identity
- Psychological cause: no physical trauma to the brain; however, the body can be affected
- Specific sets of forgotten events; everything else is remembered
- Forgotten events that tend to be traumatic or painful: sexual assault, combat
- Reversible nature rather than permanent[4]

2 Parkin (1997). 3 Talland (1965); Parkin (1997). 4 Grinker and Spiegel (1945); Janet (1904) was the first to document cases.

Fugue

- Loss of old personal identity; a new identity is adopted
- Individual often turns up in a new location away from home, usually engaged in purposeful activity
- Psychological cause: person is unaware anything is wrong
- Reversal of fugue state when the person "comes to" and remembers his past identity
- Resumption of original identity after fugue passes, and the fugue period is lost
- Short-term or long-term: can last days or years

Psychogenic Amnesia (psychologically induced amnesia)

- No brain damage or physical pathology
- Psychological cause rather than physical; for example, witness to brutality

DEMENTIA

Dementia, a disorder that causes cognitive deficits and memory impairment, is another cause of memory loss, but is often progressive and irreversible. Types of dementia include: aphasia (impaired language; cannot name objects), apraxia (impaired motor abilities; difficulty eating, dressing, cooking), and agnosia (inability to recognize and identify familiar objects and people).

TRAITS OF DEMENTIA

- Difficulty planning and initiating activity
- Inability to recall previous events
- Difficulty acquiring new information
- Poor judgment
- Lack of awareness of impairment

There are different causes of dementia and many have distinguishing traits. The following lists include the types and specific characteristics that can be added to the previous list.

HIV-INDUCED DEMENTIA

This dementia is specific to the progression of HIV.

Traits of HIV-Induced Dementia

- Forgetfulness
- Slowness and apathy
- Social withdrawal
- Tremors and loss of balance

ALZHEIMER'S DISEASE

This is the most common cause of dementia in the United States. There is a genetic component to early-onset Alzheimer's, but no foolproof tests exist for diagnosing any form of the disease; it is diagnosed by ruling out other causes.

Traits of Alzheimer's disease

- Gradual onset
- Slow, predictable progression
- Personality changes
- Forgetfulness
- Memory loss

HUNTINGTON'S DISEASE

This is an inherited, progressive, degenerative disease of cognition, emotion, and movement.

Traits of Huntington's disease

- Twitching and tremors
- Lurching gait
- Explosive speech
- Depression

OTHER CAUSES OF DEMENTIA

- Dissociation

- Head trauma
- Multiple personality disorder
- Pick's Complex
- Parkinson's disease
- Vitamin deficiency

 WARM UP People wonder, "What would I do if I had only one year left to live? Write a scene with an older character who has just found out that she has an added twenty years of life.

RECOVERED MEMORIES

The topic of recovered memories is an excellent place to explore the mind/body connection. Memories are encoded in the brain, a physical process, during and after an event; but what happens when those details never really happened? Or, another debate: Can memories really be repressed and remain unavailable for years? There have been bitter debates in psychology about the validity of recovered memories. News stories have carried accounts, and the courts are processing lawsuits based on later recall of childhood events. Memories are rarely entirely, massively repressed; most horrible incidents of childhood are remembered at least in part. Memory plays a vital role in stories. Here are some facts.

FALSE MEMORIES

False memories are events that never occurred. Specifically, an individual has a belief about the past that is experienced as a memory, but it never happened. Therapists, books, movies, or other individuals may unwittingly induce memories in susceptible people. Recall of false memories can, under the right conditions with easily influenced people, spread like a contagious disease.

How false memories are created is a way not only to enhance a character, but also a novel method of manipulating readers.

HOW TO PLANT FALSE MEMORIES
- Association: When people are presented with a list of happenings, characters, or words, they may incorrectly recall something not on the list; for

example, if given a list including nurse, sick person, ambulance, lawyer, medicine bottles, but not doctor, their recall may include doctor because it is natural to associate doctor with the other words on the list.

- Mixing: When people are given unknown, made-up names mixed in with well-known names, they may assume the unknown name is a credible person: "I enjoy women writers, especially Jane Austen, Virginia Woolf, Abigail Bronk, and Lillian Hellman."

- Retelling: People retell stories, omitting certain details they were given and adding others that are more consistent with their own experiences. This is idiosyncratic, based on the content of someone's experience; for example, a four-year-old city boy hearing the story "The Boy Who Cried Wolf" might repeat the tale with a lion and a child calling "Mom!"

- Post-Event Information: After a genuine event occurs, another person can introduce elements into the remembering which will be recalled as fact. For example, Ben and Tom see an auto accident. The police officer asks Ben, "Did the car stop at the stop sign?" (There was no stop sign.) Later, Ben will have more difficulty and less accuracy than Tom in recalling whether there was a stop sign. In this way, reports can be distorted by false information introduced post-event.[5]

- Implantation: A psychology experiment convinced a fourteen-year-old boy that he had been lost in the mall at a young age. His older brother, a researcher, told him a series of stories about his childhood, all of which were correct except for getting lost in the mall. Asked to recall the stories, the fourteen year old initially did not remember the fictitious event, but after five days, began to generate memories of the event. Weeks later, asked to recall and rate his memories on vividness and accuracy, the mall story came out ranked very high.

People can construct memory reports for entire events that never occurred, and these reports can be very convincing.[6] Some individuals who reported recovered memories have since retracted the accusations; some have even sued

[5] Lampinen, Neuschatz, and Payne (1998). [6] Loftus and Ketcham (1991); Loftus (1993).

their therapists for planting false memories. Planted false memories seem to have several characteristics in common: Abuse described in recovered memories was reported to have started at a much earlier age than abuse that was never forgotten, accusations were usually nonspecific, and accusations arose in the context of therapy.[7]

MEMORIES OF CHILDHOOD ABUSE

Abuse of children has probably taken place in all times, social groups, and cultures. In the 1980s, at first in the United States and then spreading to other countries, adults reported apparent "recovery" of previously unknown abuse, usually sexual. A recovered memory is the emergence of a recollection of abuse of which the individual had no previous knowledge. Recovery is different from the normal, everyday memory retrieval we all experience through active recall or simple remembering. For example, a thirty-five-year-old client had always known that he had been brutally beaten as a child, although he rarely talked about it and avoided thinking about it. However, talking about it in therapy where he felt safe, he even recalled the color of his pajamas on the day he had stayed home and been beaten badly enough to require hospitalization. He was recalling and retrieving memories, not recovering them. He remembered more than he had ever before remembered, but some basic awareness had existed. By contrast, and very rarely seen, is the kind of situation in which someone watches Oprah talk about child abuse, and, out of nowhere, up come personal memories of a similar situation that had been completely out of awareness.

NEW INFORMATION The type of emotion felt influences what an individual recalls about an event. For example, if an event is happy, memories tend to be a broad scene without details. When anger is the emotion associated with the memory, people tend to focus on the details of the obstacle that made them angry. Both are equally accurate and inaccurate. As people recount their memories, for example, what they were doing on 9/11, they begin to fill in details which may or may not be accurate.[8]

[7] Brandon et al (1998). [8] APA Monitor on Psychology (September 2005).

Pseudophysical Disorders

Pseudophysical problems are a collection of disorders that are physical problems with emotional causes or consequences. These disorders are not based in any known physical problem, yet the individual's body tells her that pain exists. An individual feels pain, so she is convinced that some medical condition is undetected.

There are people who suffer one or more physical disorders that have no basis in the physical body; that is, no known medical condition. While some of them could certainly have conditions that have not yet been diagnosed, or even discovered, many are dealing with problems that seem to originate in mental or emotional disturbances rather than bodily upsets. The following types represent the different possibilities. Medically, these disorders are referred to under the rubric of *somatoform* (soma is from the Greek word for body, "somatos") disorders.

People who suffer from somatoform disorders have a very difficult time because family and professionals say, outright or through implication, "It is all in your head," adding anger and distress to the situation. Some psychologists believe that the brain has produced, for that person, some transformation of psychological pain into bodily pain. The body carries emotion in the way that it knows best: physical symptoms. The body pays the price for some internal disturbance. It is easy for a person to say, "I had a lousy day and it gave me a headache," but it stretches the ability of most of us to imagine, "I hate my job and feel so trapped that I have gone blind." or "I am in such grief over my husband's death that I faint several times a day." But these things do happen.

SOMATOFORM DISORDERS

Sufferers of somatoform disorders can be found to have no medical explanation for their physical symptoms; however, the problems are not intentionally faked. Psychological factors can be established as important in the beginning or maintenance of the disorder. The individual may be unable to function well in life, work, or love. People suffering from these disorders run up huge medical bills with visits to doctors and repeated tests. The following are types of somatoform disorders.

NEW INFORMATION Beliefs influence our reactions. That is the basis for the "placebo effect." When touched with harmless leaves they believed to be poisonous, thirteen out of thirteen Japanese students developed a skin reaction. When the same students were touched by poisonous leaves that they believed to be harmless, only two reacted.[9] Other dramatic responses based on expectations can be seen in hypnosis. People show involuntary movements, partial paralysis, selective amnesia, and positive and negative hallucinations in all senses.[10]

HYPOCHONDRIASIS

Hypochondriasis is the unreasonable fear of having diseases. Unfortunately, severe disorders like multiple sclerosis, brain tumors, syphilis, and lupus may appear at their outset, because of vague symptoms, to be hypochondriacal concerns.

Traits of Hypochondriasis

- Preoccupation with self
- Excessive attention on one's body
- Overestimation of physical symptoms
- Frequent visits to doctors and enjoyment of the relationship with them
- Avoidance of psychotherapy in favor of medical attention

FLAMBOYANT COMPLAINING

This disorder is similar to the Flamboyant personality type in chapter two, but is dominated by physical problems. The disorder is usually seen in women and begins in early adulthood before reaching thirty years of age. The woman may have suffered physical problems as a child.

Traits of Flamboyant Complaining

- Continuous complaints about various problems: stomach pain, sexual symptoms, vomiting, diarrhea, or loss of sensation in a part of the body

[9] Ikemi (1962). [10] Kirsch (1995).

- Symptoms that may be severe; for example, blindness or paralysis
- Complaints that are always dramatic and overstated
- Frequent treatment with many practitioners
- Anxiety and depression

CONVERSION DISORDER

Conversion disorder is so named because symptoms are converted from psychological turbulence to physical. This disorder mimics known pathology (such as stroke, heart attack, or hearing or speech problems) but has no underlying damage—for example, after a great deal of testing and worry, the heart checks out fine.

Freud wrote about hysterical blindness and paralysis, a condition in which an individual (he said women only) becomes incapacitated, blind, or paralyzed without a physical basis. By treating people with hypnosis, he was temporarily able to relieve the symptoms.

Traits of Conversion

- Unusual and dramatic symptoms: blindness, paralysis, or loss of sensations in the body
- Traumatic event that precipitates symptoms: financial loss or abandonment
- Symptoms suggestive of brain lesions
- Symptoms that may allow avoidance of an unpleasant event; for example, the individual can no longer work
- Short-lived symptoms, usually lasting only hours or days; although some have been known to linger
- Lack of concern displayed by the individual over symptoms, which may aid in diagnosis
- Infrequency in the United States; strangely, the disorder is more common in Iceland
- Difficulty in diagnosis; errors are very common

FACTITIOUS DISORDER

A factitious disorder is an illness whose symptoms are either self-induced or falsified by the patient. The role of a sick person serves to satisfy needs for care.

Traits of Factitious Disorder

- Symptoms that are consciously and intentionally produced
- Creation of illness to obtain sympathy, lenience, and nurturance; not motivated by external gains such as drugs or disability payments
- Use of illness as a substitute for receiving help in normal ways
- Dramatic, vague, and inconsistent symptoms
- History of surgeries, procedures, or medical evaluations

Variations of Factitious Disorders

- Munchausen syndrome is a variation in which the individual actually does some harm to his own body to get treatment.
- Munchausen syndrome by proxy is child abuse in which the adult intentionally creates symptoms in a child. There is a rapid onset, symptoms disappear when adult is not around, and the illness cannot be explained.
- Faking is also intentional but with a clear goal of avoiding work or prison or getting a reward of money.

BODY DYSMORPHIC DISORDER

A person with a body dysmorphic disorder actually sees her body differently than an objective observer would see it.

Traits of Body Dysmorphic Disorder

- Imagined defect in appearance, which can range from wrinkles to the shape of a body part
- Possible existence of actual defect, usually very slight: a wrinkle or an oddly shaped finger
- Exaggerated attention to and preoccupation with the defect; can become delusional in proportions
- Onset in adolescence
- Ineffectiveness of talk or reassurance
- Time taken up by the disorder to the exclusion of social events, work, or relationships

- Flare-ups when stress runs high and confidence is low; may be worse for people who tend to be obsessive or compulsive
- The extreme version of a body dysmorphic disorder can result in *Appearance Addict* who is willing to go to extremes to "fix" the problem and often uses plastic surgery to correct their appearance.

Sleep Problems

We take sleep for granted, but there are estimates of staggering numbers of individuals with different forms of sleep disorders. Most people have occasional sleep problems that are annoying and produce fatigue or a bad mood the next day. Severe disorders can have a much greater impact on personality, mood, and the ability to function. Some serious sleep disorders are detailed below.

SLEEP APNEA

- Relaxation during sleep of muscles in the airway until the brain senses a build-up of carbon dioxide and reactivates the muscles
- Interruption of deep sleep
- Occurrence in people who snore, are obese, drink alcohol, or have abnormalities of the jaw or soft palate
- Excessive sleepiness during the day

INSOMNIA

- Inability to sleep or to remain asleep for a reasonable period
- Disturbance in feeling of being rested
- Possible causes: fear, stress, and anxiety

NARCOLEPSY

- Inability of brain to regulate sleep-wake cycles normally, disturbing night-time deep (REM) sleep and resulting in excessive daytime sleepiness
- Urge to sleep periodically throughout the day without warning; may be overwhelming

- Other characteristics of the disorder: sudden episodes of loss of muscle function, hallucinations during sleep onset or upon awakening, or brief episodes of total paralysis at the beginning or end of sleep
- Possible triggers: sudden emotional reactions such as anger, fear, or laughter

NIGHTMARE DISORDER

- Repeated nightmares
- Detailed recollection of long, frightening dreams, usually occurring in the second half of sleep period
- Immediate alertness and orientation upon awakening
- Results in clinically important distress or impairment of occupational, social, or personal functioning
- Nightmares do not occur solely during another mental disorder
- Symptoms are not caused by general medical condition or by use of substances, such as medications

SLEEP TERROR

- Sudden, extreme terror accompanied by appearance of wakefulness, but individual is confused, disoriented, and unresponsive
- Screams or cries during sleep, usually during initial hours of sleep
- Difficulty in awakening the individual: unlike nightmares, sleep terror disables full wakefulness
- Difficulty in comforting the individual: she may appear to be terrified of family members
- Little or no memory of the episode the next day
- Precipitating factors of emotional stress, fever, and sleep deprivation
- Genetic predisposition
- Occurrence in children ages four to twelve and adults ages twenty to thirty; is very transitory

SLEEPWALKING

- Participation of the sleeping person in activities normally associated with wakefulness: the sleeper can eat, dress, smoke or drive, but most often they walk
- Occurrence in the early portion of the night
- Blank stare; activities are conducted with open eyes and sleeper responds to questions, albeit slowly
- Can be a danger to self; for example, if the sleeper falls or uses tools
- Difficulty awakening sleeper
- Occurrence in people of any age: 1–17 percent of the U.S. population is affected

 WARM UP Write a scene about the "morning after" a character suffers from one of the sleep disorders previously described.

Substance Abuse

Substance abuse refers to an overuse, dependency, or addiction to one or more legal or illegal substances. Abuse means that the person cannot easily stop and usually results in impaired functioning, often in physical or emotional deterioration. Intoxication from alcohol, cocaine, hallucinogens, and marijuana heightens anxiety; withdrawal from alcohol, cocaine, and sedatives may also cause anxiety.

The following substances are among the most commonly abused in the United States: cocaine, hallucinogens, marijuana, and alcohol.

COCAINE

Cocaine comes from a plant probably native to Peru, but now grown widely in the mountains of South America. It had been cultivated by the Peruvian Indians and was regarded as sacred. By 1885, cases of cocaine addiction were being reported around the world.

Cocaine is extracted from the coca shrub with kerosene and evaporated into a paste where it exists as a free basic substance. Hydrochloric acid is added, which converts the substance to a salt that is then recrystallized into powder.

Cocaine stimulates the central nervous system; its effects last for forty-five to sixty minutes. When snorted, coke reaches the brain in three to five minutes. When made liquid and injected, it reaches the brain in fourteen seconds. When converted into its freebase and inhaled from a pipe, it reaches the brain in six seconds. "Street" coke (*blow*, *toot*, *lady*, and *snow*) varies in purity from 90 percent in the kilograms down to 10 percent in grams.

PSYCHOLOGICAL SYMPTOMS OF COCAINE USE

- Euphoria, followed by coming down: the fatigue and depression
- Irritability
- Anxiety
- Restlessness

PHYSICAL SYMPTOMS OF COCAINE USE

- Brain is stimulated; a "high" is produced by increased action of the brain's alerting system
- Anesthetic effects are achieved by blocked transmission of impulses in the sensory nerves
- Blood pressure and heart rate are elevated; blood vessels are constricted, causing sweating, decreased skin temperature, diarrhea, and decreased ability to gain and maintain an erection but increased ejaculation when it is achieved
- Body temperature is elevated; respiration rate is increased; pupils may be dilated
- Euphoria is produced, activity is increased, and feelings are dulled
- Physical dependence is produced; can cause paranoid psychosis.

COMMON PROGRESSION OF COCAINE USE

Introduced to "snorting" at a party → Uses when others provide drug → First purchase → Keeps a gram for weeks → Uses until cocaine is gone → Buys more than originally intended → Self-medicates side effects with other drugs → Tries new ways to administer (intravenous, freebase) → Finds occasions for use → Uses at work → Irritable or depressed when cocaine is not readily available → Needs more to reproduce original high → Attempts to control use → Attempts to stop for varying lengths of time → Uses consistently for several days and then crashes.

HALLUCINOGENS (PSYCHEDELICS)

LSD is one of the most common hallucinogens. It is manufactured from lysergic acid found in ergot, a fungus. It is colorless, odorless, and tasteless. LSD is used in tablets, capsules, as a liquid, and intravenously. Mescaline is made from the peyote cactus and is similar to LSD but not as strong. Mescaline is smoked or swallowed as capsules or tablets.

PHYSICAL SYMPTOMS OF HALLUCINOGEN USE

- Body temperature is elevated; pupils are dilated
- Blood pressure and heart rate increase
- Sweating, loss of appetite, dry mouth, sleeplessness, and tremors occur
- Dependency on drug is felt
- Heavy use results in brain damage, impaired memory, mental confusion, and difficulty with abstract thinking

PSYCHOLOGICAL SYMPTOMS OF HALLUCINOGEN USE

- Mood swings; may have several different emotions at once
- Altered perceptions, self-awareness, and sense of time
- Abnormal sensations: *hearing* colors and *seeing* sounds
- Impaired thinking

MARIJUANA (CANNABIS SATIVA)

Marijuana, a green, gray, or brown mixture of dried shredded flowers and leaves of the hemp plant, is the illegal drug most used in the U.S. Hashish (hash) is the stronger drug made from same plant, but all forms of cannabis are mind-altering. Also known as pot, grass, weed, Mary Jane, reefer, joint, or newer terms like Aunt Mary, skunk, boom, gangster, kif, and ganja, marijuana is stronger today than it was in the 1960s. Street names denote different strains—"Texas tea" or "Maui Wowie"—and the names change from city to city.

Most marijuana is rolled into cigarette paper and called a joint or nail, but it can be smoked in a pipe or a water pipe called a bong, mixed into food, brewed into tea, or mixed with tobacco in a cigar, called a blunt.[11]

PHYSICAL SYMPTOMS OF MARIJUANA USE

- Heart rate and pulse are increased
- Eyes are red and bloodshot
- Mouth and throat are dry; lungs are irritated
- Coordination is impaired; dizziness occurs
- Reproductive systems are impaired; loss of fertility
- Hunger occurs
- Sleepiness occurs as the effects fade

PSYCHOLOGICAL SYMPTOMS OF MARIJUANA USE

- Silliness; giggly for no reason
- Difficulty remembering events that just happened
- Loss of motivation
- Decreased concentration
- Paranoia[12]

 WARM UP Marijuana is now found in grade schools and more than five million Americans smoke it at least once a week. Write a scene in which a twelve-year-old boy catches his father smoking pot and confronts him.

TRAITS OF A USER OVER TIME

Disputes are ongoing about whether prolonged use increases likelihood of the following disorders.

- Is withdrawn; fatigued

[11] U.S. Department of Health and Human Services (1995). [12] ibid.

- Appears disheveled; shows careless grooming
- Is psychologically dependent
- Changes habits; for example, loss of interest in sports; changes in sleeping and eating patterns
- Has impaired memory for recent events
- Shows impaired timing and coordination, poor reaction time and bad judgment of distances, which may lead to car crashes
- Has poor judgment; may result in unsafe sex and other risky behaviors
- May be prone to depression or mental illness;[13]

TRAITS OF AN INDIVIDUAL LIKELY TO USE

- Belongs to a family in which other members use drugs and alcohol
- Hangs out with others who use
- Needs to cope with anxiety, anger, stress, or boredom[14]

ALCOHOL ABUSE

Alcoholism is a dependency on alcohol characterized by craving, inability to control or stop drinking, physical dependence and withdrawal symptoms, and tolerance (increasing difficulty becoming drunk). Alcoholism is often progressive and fatal. Of the two-thirds of the North American population who consume alcohol, 10 percent are alcoholics.

TRAITS OF A HEAVY DRINKER

- Frequently and excessively uses alcohol
- Takes quantities sufficient to cause intoxication
- Binges at parties or on weekends
- May continue for life or may cut back with age

PHYSICAL TRAITS OF AN ALCOHOLIC

- Drinks excessively; relies on alcohol

[13] ibid. [14] ibid.

- Suffers the consequences as drinking interferes with social life and economic functioning
- Has no consistent control over the start or end of drinking
- Is a chronic and repetitive behavior
- Suffers ill effects on health, contributing factor for head injuries, accidents, violence, and assaults
- May drink alone and may begin first thing in the morning
- Experiences blackouts or amnesia
- Has regular hangovers or nausea
- Chooses activities according to the availability of alcohol
- May spend extravagantly[15]

PSYCHOLOGICAL TRAITS OF AN ALCOHOLIC

- Feels self-disgust
- Lies about drinking
- Has irrational fears and resentments
- Is in denial; does what he says he will not; denies what has been done
- Manipulates others to protect continued drinking
- Deflects criticism of the drinking and resultant behavior
- Blames others for failures of responsibility
- Blames someone or something for out-of-control drinking
- Tries to control levels of drinking by manipulating environment and people
- Wants help on own terms
- Puts others on the defensive
- Plays on sympathies of others
- Is ashamed and fearful so he covers up and hides addiction
- Experiences downward spiral of problems and crises
- Coerces others into covering up and protecting[16]

[15] Clinard (1963). [16] Reddy (1984).

- Is preoccupied with alcohol
- Knows adverse consequences but uses anyway

People in the Alcoholic's World

In the alcoholic's environment, we find people who take the following unhealthy roles.

ENABLER

Traits of the Enabler (usually a helping professional who does not recognize alcoholism: clergy, doctors, lawyers, or social workers):

- Is helpful; is compelled to be a rescuer
- May suffer from guilt or anxiety
- Wants to relieve friend of unbearable tension
- May be meeting own needs without realizing it
- Can be as compulsive to rescue as alcoholic is about drinking[17]
- Never carries out threat to stop

VICTIM

Traits of the Victim (usually co-worker or person at work)[18]

- Takes responsibility for getting the alcoholic's work done
- Protects alcoholic from consequences by covering up
- Never carries out threat to reveal problems

PROVOKER

Traits of the Provoker (usually spouse or partner)[19]

- Is a veteran player who endures and accepts broken promises
- Is hurt and upset by repeated episodes
- Is always outwitted and undermined
- Keeps life going but displays bitterness, resentment, hurt, and fear

[17] ibid. [18] ibid. [19] ibid.

- Controls, forces, sacrifices, and adjusts, but never gives up
- Does not want to fail the alcoholic
- Adjusts to all the crises
- Is always upset; never knows what to say without adding guilt and bitterness
- Never carries out threat to leave

Eating Disorders

Eating disorders are epidemic in the U.S. and rapidly spreading throughout the world. Eating disorders have a major distinction from alcohol and drug problems in that people can stay away from alcohol and drugs, but everyone must have some relationship with food—and that relationship is often very troubled. Even if one of your characters does not have a fullblown eating disorder, she can have a strange or difficult time with food or weight. Eating disorders used to be primarily a woman's disease, but both anorexia and bulimia are increasingly being diagnosed in boys and men.

TRAITS OF FAMILIES IN WHICH EATING DISORDERS ARE OFTEN FOUND

- Little expression of feelings except high conflict, anger, and marital discord
- Low cohesion
- Dampening of independent and assertive behavior
- Competitive one-upmanship
- High achievement expectations, but low emphasis on intellectual, recreational, and cultural activities
- Similarity to healthy families regarding rules and control, but have more relatives with alcohol problems

- Unrealistic expectations of the young person, but no encouragement of the independence, free expression, and intellectual pursuits necessary to achieve results, causing the individual to feel trapped

ANOREXIA

The essential nature of anorexia is a refusal to maintain minimally normal weight, fear of gaining weight, and a distorted image of the body. Anorexia usually begins in adolescence. Some people recover completely, while others struggle with the disorder for years. Hospitalizations are common to help stabilize weight. There are a surprising number of deaths each year. Some theories about anorexia suggest that young girls are afraid of increasing sexuality and want to remain children. The American culture is also preoccupied with weight and thinness, adding to the strain for girls and women.

TRAITS OF A PERSON WITH ANOREXIA

- Achieves weight loss by starving
- Exercises excessively
- Induces vomiting or uses laxatives
- Is preoccupied with food and always feels fat
- Cannot see accurate reflection of body image
- Is always thinking about eating or not eating
- Is very concerned with approval of others
- Feels good, or not good, depending on weight at the moment
- Considers losing pounds and not eating an accomplishment
- Is very restrained emotionally
- Tries to control her surroundings beyond food intake

BULIMIA

Bulimia can be harder to recognize than anorexia because the excessive thinness is not usually present. Bulimia is marked by binge eating and purging, either by vomiting or using laxatives. More women than men suffer from bulimia and many college age women show some of the following traits even if they do not have the fullblown disorder.

TRAITS OF A PERSON WITH BULIMIA

- Binges (eats uncontrolled, large quantities of food) typically followed by induced vomiting, laxative use, starvation, or excessive exercise
- Feels helpless; behaves nonassertively
- Has low self-esteem
- Fears growing up
- Has not learned to manage tension; does not know how she feels
- Desires to be perfect; wants to please
- Feels ashamed of body; shame is hidden behind masks of independence, smiles, or lies
- May have been traumatized: some bulimic women were raped or molested when they were younger; many blame themselves
- Is concerned with appearances
- Seems unemotional; emotions, such as anger, are hidden
- Typically has a normal weight and above average intelligence, is middle class, ambitious, and motivated, and appears to function well
- May have begun with a diet but actions are out of control
- May show physical effects of bulimia, including swollen glands, broken blood vessels in the eyes, abrasions, and bruises on the backs of hands and fingers[20]

Communication Disorders

A communication disorder is a condition that partially or totally prevents a person from communicating with others. The problem can be in producing communication, receiving communication, or understanding. Most are problems

[20] Johnson and Flach (1985).

that exist from birth. The examples listed below are some of the most common communication disorders.

DYSLEXIA

Dyslexia is a defect of the systems used in reading. Since reading is so basic, individuals show anger from frustration, and may develop other behavioral problems.

- Onset in childhood, but may go undetected until later; can range from unnoticed to severe
- Reading aloud is distorted with sounds and words omitted or substituted
- Reading is slow
- Problems understanding material that has been read
- May also result in writing problems
- May be part of a larger problem of delayed language development

LANGUAGE DISORDER

Language disorder can be expressive, meaning that it affects speaking and understanding, or receptive, meaning that it affects speaking, understanding, reading, and writing.

- Onset in early childhood; may be remediated with help
- Child with language disorder cannot properly express himself
- Non-verbal intelligence is not delayed or affected
- Speech and vocabulary are limited; child speaks in a simplistic fashion
- Strange word order

STUTTERING

Stuttering is a speech disorder that is not present at birth.

- Onset early in life between two and seven years old
- Speech is not fluent; sounds are repeated
- Usually ends by age sixteen
- Anxiety exacerbates the problem

NEW INFORMATION Those who have suffered from a traumatic brain injury may fail to accurately assess others' emotions and incorrectly understand the subtleties of communication: This is particularly true after an injury to the frontal lobe area of the brain. The person may not notice anger and not be able to infer sarcasm, taking all comments literally. This certainly can interfere with social competence.[21]

Sexual Disorders

Although the majority of sexual dysfunction probably has some physical basis, much has a psychological or emotional cause. Sexual disorders, whether mainly physical or psychological in nature, can result in distress. For example, the individual with a sexual disorder may suffer related anxiety and sexual frustration, which in turn leads to other complications that may affect self-esteem and close relationships. The following are some of the most common sexual problems.

ORDINARY, TEMPORARY AROUSAL INHIBITIONS

Temporary arousal inhibitions include diminished or absent sexual arousal that occurs in most men and women at various times. They may be caused by:

- Alcohol use
- Fatigue, stress, boredom, illness, or anger with the partner
- Anxiety about impressing a partner
- Fear of inability to please partner
- Fear of sexual dysfunction
- Lack of self-esteem
- Poor body image
- Self-consciousness: becoming a spectator
- Competitiveness: monitoring, grading, or comparing own performance to imagined others

[21] McDonald (2004).

SEXUAL DYSFUNCTION IN WOMEN

The first two sexual dysfunctions listed below are physical in nature but may have a psychological component; the third is emotionally based.

VAGINISMUS

- May have painful intercourse or it may be impossible because of muscle contractions
- May be result of fear
- May occur after trauma

DYSPAREUNIA

- Causes pain during penetration in intercourse
- May be caused by hormone imbalance
- May result from attempts at intercourse before arousal

ORGASMIC DYSFUNCTION

Orgasmic dysfunction is the inability to reach sexual orgasm, which can occur for a variety of reasons:

- Partner is of non-preferred sex
- Influence of cultural taboos
- Lack of sexual knowledge; inexperience
- Past trauma
- Fear of one's own performance or partner's performance
- Strict religious upbringing
- Disappointment or dislike of partner; dissatisfaction with any or all aspects of the relationship
- Anger or anxiety
- Guilt about sex or pleasure; learned to hide sexuality
- Lack of mutuality with partner
- Unmet requirements of sexual needs
- Poor psychological adjustment

- Negative body image; feeling of inferiority
- Is romantic but not sexual[22]

SEXUAL DYSFUNCTION IN MEN

Sexual virility is virtually a requirement of the male role, so erectile disorder, impotence, and premature ejaculation are not simply problems of the penis—they become negative descriptions of the man.

CAUSES OF SEXUAL DYSFUNCTION IN MEN

- Existing physical problems
- Lack of sexual drive; lack of sexual interest
- Psychosis
- Disturbed relationships
- Means of withdrawing from relationships or intimacy
- Depression or anxiety
- Phobic response to women (for straight men)
- Phobic response to sex
- Underlying homosexuality (for straight men)

 WARM UP Your character is attracted (for the first time) to a co-worker of the same sex. They have a project together. Write a scene showing them working closely on this job.

PREMATURE EJACULATION

Premature ejaculation is common; 15–30 percent of men experience it at some period.

Traits of Premature Ejaculation

- Inability to control response to stimulation
- Guilt and anxiety
- Worry about not pleasing partner

[22] Masters and Johnson (1970).

- Age, frequency of sex, and newness of partner are contributing factors
- Heightened sensitivity in penis
- Premature ejaculation may cause men to avoid sex[23]

IMPOTENCE

Impotence occurs when a man previously able to have erections presently cannot achieve and sustain an erection to permit intercourse with his partner; however, he may be able to achieve an erection during masturbation. Impotence occurs increasingly after age sixty. Impotence can lead men to fear rejection by their partner, and therefore, they may avoid sex.

Urologists estimate that thirty million American men suffer from erectile dysfunction and the number is increasing.[24]

POSSIBLE CAUSES OF IMPOTENCE:

- Physical: malfunctioning valves in penis; smoking
- Mental: Lack of pleasure and lack of excitement during sex
- General anxiety or performance anxiety
- Fear of making partner pregnant (straight men)
- Guilt or shame

CONTINUOUS IMPOTENCE

Most men experience occasional impotence because of the previous reasons listed. However, there are some men who are never able to achieve or sustain an erection during intercourse. This is rare, estimated at approximately 2 percent.

Causes of Continuous Impotence

- Maternal issues: sleeping in mother's bed until adolescence; washing or touching by mother; inappropriate sexual display from mother
- Sexual abuse
- Strict religious upbringing

[23] Doleys, Meredith, and Ciminero (1982). [24] Sleek (1998).

- Misinformation or lack of knowledge; equally uniformed/inexperienced wife/partner
- Sexual taboos
- No prior sexual activity; lack of confidence
- Drugs or alcohol
- Homosexuality during the teen years
- Denial of homosexual desire
- Traumatic experience with prostitute

INTERMITTENT IMPOTENCE

Intermittent impotence is common and is a temporary inability to experience sexual feelings or arousal and to perform sexual activities.

Causes of Intermittent Impotence

- High or exaggerated expectations about own performance
- Increased life expectancy: dysfunction triples between the ages of forty and seventy
- Prior problems with premature ejaculation
- Fatigue, anger, stress
- Humiliation
- Performance anxiety
- Excessively dominant father in childhood destroyed confidence in masculinity
- Strict religious upbringing
- Sexual failures that were psychologically damaging
- Immaturity
- Early homosexuality (for straight men)
- Medication for other problems: drugs for diabetes and hypertension
- Physical disorder: diabetes, vascular problems, or hypertension[25]

---

[25] Masters and Johnson (1970).

What Can Go Wrong in a Hospital

In a hospital with one hundred patients, who take four different drugs four times daily, with ten possible places in the system where things can go wrong, there are 480,000 opportunities each month for a mistake in the medication chain. Common mistakes include:

1. Doctors prescribing the wrong drug
2. Doctors prescribing the wrong amount of a drug
3. Pharmacists misreading the doctor's handwriting
4. Pharmacists selecting the wrong drug
5. Pharmacists mislabeling the drug
6. Pharmacists mixing the drug under unsanitary conditions
7. Nurses administering the wrong drug
8. Nurses giving the drug to the wrong patient
9. Patient neglecting to mention all the drugs he was taking, leading to problematic drug combinations
10. Patient failing to take the drug[26]

---

[26] APA Monitor on Psychology (April, 2003).

WRITER'S GUIDE TO CHARACTER TRAITS

eleven

Career Traits

IN THIS CHAPTER

• Career Choice • Career Problems • Traits of People in 42 Careers

Work is an important element in people's lives and, when things are going well, generally enhances their self-esteem. For many individuals, the choice of a career represents an extension of personality. Career also represents a preferred lifestyle.

Career Choice

Identification with adults in childhood often influences career directions, if not specific jobs. I am certain that as a psychologist, I am following in my mother's footsteps—she did her informal counseling at the kitchen table and everyone consulted her. I'm probably not as skilled as she was, but I have turned her way of life into my well-paying occupation. Admiration for a parent or another adult can be, knowingly or unknowingly, very formative. The favorite English teacher at school has launched many avid readers and fine writers.

Identification works in reverse as well. Years ago I treated a young man who wanted to become a police officer. Why? Because as a child he had been tied up and physically abused. He wanted to be in a position in which no one would hurt him and he could protect others.

Psychoanalytic theory has ascribed unconscious motives to career choice, but, although it makes sense intuitively, the theory has not stood up well to research. Still, it is fun to think about unconscious motivations for our character's choice of work. For example, psychoanalytic theory would suggest that aggressive impulses might be gratified by a career choice such as a butcher, hit man, or a surgeon. In two out of three choices, the aggression is sublimated or channeled appropriately into socially acceptable work. Stretch this idea further and we have a little boy fascinated by his stream of urine becoming an engineer who builds waterways or canals.

 NEW INFORMATION Do you want a character with fascinating career possibilities? How about a member of the EIS, Epidemic Intelligence Service, formed in 1951. These people scour the country looking for clues to dangerous epidemics.

Career Problems

When you imagine career problems, you may first think about workaholics, those people whose problem is working too much to the detriment of their health or family relationships. Perhaps they are driven by a desire for success, fame, and money or maybe it's a fear of failure that motivates overworking. Another problem is an inability to keep a job. Is it laziness? Perhaps—but depression or a self-defeating personality could also be to blame.

Certainly, we can see how motives and problems that come from childhood, whether conscious or unconscious, are influential in careers. The student who is driven to succeed in order to compete with a successful father is one example. The other side of that same equation could be the student who is afraid to succeed because success would feel like the destruction of a mother who had not achieved her goals. Avoidance of success could also come from the fear that a parent's love would be lost or that the child would suffer real or imagined retaliation from the parent who has been surpassed.

Traits that are successful on the job may fail miserably at home. The aggressive, powerful cop may be intimidating at home, much to the dismay of his wife and children. The exceptional dealmaker in business may drive her family crazy with activities. The meticulous conference planner may ruin friendships with his overattention to the details of everyone's lives.

Given the importance of work in people's lives, and the amount of hours invested in work, we don't see it very often as a central component of many novels—unless your character is a spy or a cop.

Stages of Career Development

PERIOD	AGE	DYNAMICS OF CAREER DEVELOPMENT
FANTASY	CHILDHOOD	Plays with no realities of ability or time; tries on roles such as cowgirl, police officer, parent, or movie star
TENTATIVE		
Interest	11–12	Recognizes need for work direction; sees/identifies with parents' work; concentrates on enjoyment
Capacity	12–14	Begins to evaluate her ability and looks around at others
Value	15–16	Thinks about her role in society; notes differing lifestyles, perspective broadens; wonders how to use her talents
Transition	17–18	Has some independence; feels the need to make some realistic moves about direction; thinks about financial rewards; may seek new surroundings to try out ideas

REALISTIC		
Exploration	18–24	Has narrower interests but is fearful of making wrong choice
Crystallization	18–24	Is involved; knows what she likes and does not like; commitment grows
Specification	18–24	Selects path: some never arrive here[1]

Traits of People in 42 Careers

The many diverse traits listed in the following sections have been shown to be associated with people in these fields. No one person possesses all the traits, and people may possess many traits that are not listed here. Also listed are the ways that people in certain careers tend to run into trouble, either with personality disturbance, mental illness, or substance abuse.

ACCOUNTANT

- Self-controlled, practical
- Introverted, introspective, and serious
- Judgmental, demanding, and reserved
- Responsible; makes a good impression
- Wary of impulse; plans ahead; organized
- Willing to give advice
- Conservative; conventional; a conformist[2]

ACTOR

- Eager to exhibit herself; exhibitionism is satisfied in a healthy way
- Expressive

[1] Roe (1956). [2] Granleese and Barrett (1990).

- Vulnerable to stress
- Self-critical: self-observation leads to self-criticism and overidentification with roles; some lack identity
- Dependent on admiration: gains self-esteem from applause and narcissistic satisfaction from entrancing audience
- Able to concentrate
- Observant
- Able to draw on remembered emotion
- Able to copy or mimic characters
- Able to recognize specific talent fairly early in life
- Prone to possible problems with alcohol and drugs and emotional problems of mania or anxiety
- At higher risk of suicide rate than people in other fields[3]

ARTIST, GENERAL

- Unconventional, nonconforming
- In need of some isolation; but also needs others for stimulation and sharing of ideas
- Inwardly driven
- Emotionally connected with art productions; they are his "babies"
- Creative, imaginative
- Emotionally expressive
- Indirect in relation to other people; relates to them though art
- Not always self-controlled; dislikes structure
- Asocial[4]

ARCHITECT

- Attentive to civic duties
- Very creative and sensitive to beauty

[3] Roe (1956). [4] ibid.

- Self-reliant; follows own ethics and values
- Talented into old age
- Flexible
- Independent of social constraints; unworried about making a good impression
- Aggressive
- Goal oriented
- Reliable, outgoing, and resourceful
- Able to delegate
- Possibly subjected to early adjustment problems
- Possibly depressed or anxious[5]

ASTRONAUT

- Agreeable; willing to cooperate with others on a team
- Patient; rarely irritable
- Gullible
- Not egotistical or arrogant; modest
- Able to share concern for others; effective interpersonally
- Not very open to new ideas; sticks with accepted ways of doing things
- Not fussy or whiny
- Perfectionistic[6]

WARM UP Randomly select any two careers from this chapter. Have a character of your creation go through a day of work in one of these careers (emphasizing the traits of that particular career); then have the character go through a day in the other career.

ATHLETE, NONPROFESSIONAL

- Extroverted
- Able to tolerate pain

[5] Dudek and Hall (1991). [6] Rose et al (1994).

- Sensation seeking
- Assertive and competitive
- Agile; fast reactions
- Secure; has low anxiety
- Naturally athletic; benefits from strong genetics
- Tough minded and self-confident[7]

ATHLETE, GENERAL TRAITS OF PROFESSIONAL/CHAMPION

(Specific athletic categories follow)

- Focused on the physical body rather than emotions
- Independent
- Used to doing battle with other men or women
- Competitive
- Highly aggressive
- Uncontrolled emotionally
- Very anxious
- Ambitious; has high aspirations
- Self-assured
- Able to concentrate on desired objectives
- Very concerned about physical power and physical perfection

Traits of Top Players in Individual Sports (riding, swimming, fencing, or track and field)

- Dominant and aggressive
- Adventurous and self-sufficient
- Stable and normal
- Unsophisticated
- Introverted

Traits of Top players in Team Sports

- Neurotic

[7] Furnham (1990).

- Sophisticated

- Extroverted

- Prone to guilt

NEW INFORMATION "Roid rage" is a steriod-induced aggression seen in people who take large doses of steroids for an extended period of time. The parts of the brain responsible for impulse control are affected. Steroids are especially damaging during the teenage years when hormones are in flux and the brain is developing rapidly. One reason teenagers use steroids is to emulate their athletic heroes.

INDIVIDUAL ATHLETIC TRAITS

Boxer

- Often from lower socioeconomic classes: rage is the way out
- Willing to adhere to rigorous training
- Willing to fast or exercise vigorously to make weight
- Disciplined; with notable exceptions such as Mike Tyson
- Able to control pain
- Aggressive; likes to inflict pain
- Physical and direct; the world is a physical place
- Able to transform primitive rage into art; anger is ennobled[8]

Dancer

- Unhappy; anxious
- Graceful
- Willing to follow directions
- Hypochondriacal
- Obsessive; dependent
- Motivated by achievement
- Subject to feelings of inferiority and self-contempt[9]

[8] Oates (1987). [9] Marchant-Haycox and Wilson (1992).

Fencer

- Reserved
- Aggressive
- Autonomous
- Experimental
- Creative

 NEW INFORMATION One way to inoculate athletes from "choking" under pressure is to expose them to observation and criticism. They learn to deal with feeling self-conscious and perform better when the stakes are high.

Football Player (American)

- Less depressed than general population but more fatigued
- Submissive to authoritarian rules; accepts standards of harsh discipline
- Controlled; likes rigid control of life off the field
- Willing to be obedient
- Narrow-minded
- Conventional and conservative
- Focused on mental aspects of the sport
- Vigorous; bold[10]

Golfer

- Solitary and individualistic
- Similar to tennis players
- Dependent solely on himself for success
- Intuitive
- Confident
- Able to concentrate
- Focused on his own rhythm
- Calm; not nervous or jumpy, tolerates slow pace

[10] Freudenberger and Bergandi (1994).

- Content with more sedate life than other sports: pro players travel with families; little nightlife
- Able to deal with nearby audience[11]

High-Risk Athletes (Mountain climbers, snow skiers, snowboarders, etc.)

- Stable
- Thrill-seeking, sensation-seeking; desire stimulation
- Inclined to underestimate risk
- Impulsive
- Extroverted and adventurous
- Highly sensitive to reward; low sensitivity to punishment: [12]

Martial Artist, Woman

- In search of self-development
- Empowered by martial arts; may use career as a road back to bodily comfort
- Willing to face challenges
- Highly aware of body
- Physically and mentally disciplined
- Earnest; takes self seriously [13]

Tennis Player, Female

- Task oriented more than people oriented
- Competitive; deliberate
- Uncomplicated and unpretentious in approach to others
- Technically very well trained
- Emotionally stable; high ego strength; high confidence
- Low anxiety and low depression
- Domineering
- Intelligent

[11] Feinstein (1995). [12] Goma (1991). [13] McRay and Schwarz (1990).

- Tendency to be conservative when young; older players are more radical[14]

Sports and Personality.

Certain personalities gravitate to certain sports. For example, men seeking high-sensation sports play raquetball, pool, and water ski. Low-sensation-seeking males prefer jogging, weightlifting, or hiking. High-sensation-seeking women try whitewater rafting, windsurfing, or kayaking. Low-sensation-seeking women prefer sailing, handball, or ballet. [15]

BOOKKEEPER OR BANK TELLER

- Conventional
- Structured and orderly; likes rules
- Self-controlled
- Deferential toward those with power and status[16]

COACH

- Simplistic, conservative, and dictatorial
- Thick-skinned; cannot be hypersensitive or shy
- Able to tolerate public nature of work: failures and successes equally visible
- Able to work under pressure
- Aggressive; highly organized; a leader
- Persistent, inflexible, and dogmatic

COMIC

- Willing to sacrifice dignity
- Willing to use self-degradation in work
- Given to masochistic or sadistic tendencies
- Observant
- Able to channel critical nature into work

[14] Gondola and Wughalter (1991). [15] Furnham (1990). [16] Roe (1956).

CORPORATE BUSINESSPERSON, ENTRY-LEVEL

- Loyal
- Accepting of authority
- Willing to conform to prescribed behaviors; knows that "fitting in" and being like the others is important: there is no room for eccentrics
- Trustworthy
- Dedicated[17]

CORPORATE BUSINESSPERSON, TOP ECHELON

- Circumscribed; lives in a closed circle
- Hardworking
- Conventional; little room for novelty
- Often consumed by career: every activity is tinged with corporate position; no distance between work and play
- Good at fitting in and organizational politics
- Often charismatic
- Attuned to image and importance of appearances[18]

 NEW INFORMATION When smart people behave stupidly, they tend to possess (or believe they possess) the following traits:

- **Egocentrism**: It is all about them; only their own interests are taken into account

- **Omniscience**: Because they know a lot about some things, they think they know about everything

- **Omnipotence**: They believe they are all-powerful and can do whatever they want

- **Invulnerability**: They believe they can get away with whatever they do: they will never get caught; and even if they were to be caught, they would find a way to get out of the mess[19]

CORPORATE WIFE

- Valued for her adaptability, attractiveness, discretion, and social graces

[17] Kanter and Stein (1979). [18] Kanter and Stein (1979). [19] Sternberg (2002).

- Confined; has little freedom to refuse role
- In the public eye: no private acts; all behaviors reflect on husband's position
- Protective: makes sure nothing comes between husband and work
- Expected to have beautiful, well-mannered children
- Gracious; maintains well-appointed home; entertains with ease, and sometimes with little notice, either informally or extravagantly
- Publicly benevolent: works in charity
- Charming; smiles and pretends to enjoy all meetings and trips
- Aware of the importance of image; looks, talks, and dresses tastefully: no extremes
- Diplomatic; prevents scandal
- Articulate and well informed: stays up-to-date on current events and business and is occasionally her husband's instrument of communication
- Content to remain in the shadow of her husband: confirms husband's image and message; hides her own opinions and plays down her own ability[20]

 WARM UP Without naming the career, have a character clearly act out one of these jobs in two paragraphs.

CORPORATE WOMAN
- Conflicted between values of work and family
- Aware that big corporations are still men's arena
- Ambitious; tries to balance values and family with corporate work culture
- Unsure whether the success is worth the cost
- Determined to find a way to fit in
- Trained to show little emotion[21]

[20] Kanter and Stein (1979); Morris (1998). [21] Sampson (1995).

- Willing to leave corporate work when it demands more than she is prepared to sacrifice

CHEMIST/BIOLOGIST
- Inquisitive; an investigator
- Thinker, not a doer
- Orderly; likes organizing
- Asocial; no strong need for close contact[22]

DEALMAKER
- Shrewd; able to read others well
- Polished; smooth
- Calculating; always thinking of an angle
- Secretive, guarded; stays removed from people and situations
- Knows how to get things done
- Ambitious
- Able to manage groups well

ENGINEER
- Objective, realistic
- Inclined toward technical hobbies such as chess
- Intelligent
- Ineloquent
- Mechanically gifted[23]
- Procedural, action oriented and concrete

WARM UP Women in traditionally male-dominated fields, such as engineering and finance, are seen by their co-workers as unsociable and difficult to work with. However, if women excel in stereotypically female positions, such as employee-assistance managers and educators, they do not face similar disapproval.[24] Write a paragraph in which two sisters, a secretary and a chemist, compare their day.

[22] Roe (1956). [23] Roe (1956). [24] Heilman (2004).

FARMER

- Realistic; likes dealing with concrete problems
- Hard-working
- Skilled; strong
- Masculine
- Stoic; inclined to hid emotion[25]

FLIGHT DECK OFFICER (IN-AIR POLICE)

(This is a new job for pilots since the 9/11 tragedy with requirements similar to law enforcement officers)

- Emotionally stable
- Able to comply with rules
- In control of own aggression
- Able to use deadly force[26]

FUNERAL DIRECTOR

- Social
- Caring; likes to be helpful
- Ordered; likes systematic activities
- Composed; tactful

KEPT WOMAN

- Young and good-looking
- Able to fill the fantasies of the men who keep them
- Insecure; hides it with exaggerated expressions of self-worth
- Fearful of rejection
- In need of male approval
- Possibly employed in good, respectable job

[25] Roe (1956). [26] APA Monitor on Psychology (2004).

- Seduced by a lifestyle better than anything she could pay for; has time to be free and alone; feels important through gifts and being desired (especially by married men); limited time makes activities more exciting
- Confined: must make herself available and on call; nature of relationship prevents commitment
- Possibly angry, self-centered, or manipulative
- Previously unresolved difficulties in relationships
- Unwilling to let others know her beyond her beauty
- Manipulative; uses sex to get what she wants
- Able to convince herself that she has power
- Possibly a past victim of sexual abuse
- Able to rationalize: "I'm special." "He prefers me to his wife." Or: "We are always on a honeymoon."[27]

NEW INFORMATION Does your character want an advanced degree with no superior knowledge? Use an organization that sells specialty credentials to anyone. There are many of them out there now; mail order organizations that provide certificates for cash with no training, no exams, no credentialing of their own.

MUSICIAN

- Cynical and resigned
- Introverted and unadventurous
- Reserved and sober
- Apprehensive and tense
- Imaginative
- Emotionally sensitive
- Persistent
- Good manual skills

[27] McKay and Schwartz (1990).

PAINTER

- Wounded; creates in order to heal own wounds, or old family wounds
- Abstract thinker; creative thinker
- Fearful of mediocrity
- Not adaptable
- Driven toward achievement
- Sensitive
- Not aggressive[29]

POET

- Abstract thinker
- Creative
- Sensitive
- Not aggressive
- At higher risk for suicide than other fields
- Prone to problems with mania, psychosis, and depression
- Prone to drug and alcohol use

POOL/BILLIARDS HUSTLER

- Able to manipulate impressions to create false images
- Able to deceive opponent ("sucker" or "fish") about level of skill to get a game

[28] Roe (1956). [29] National Institute for Occupational Safety and Health.

- Skillful in assessing people
- Disciplined; can refuse tempting shots
- Courageous
- Energetic; has stamina
- Not easily rattled or upset
- Flexible

 WARM UP The following characters attract trouble. Write a scene using one of the following and a randomly selected criminal from chapter five.

Taxicab drivers and chauffeurs (attract most crimes or criminals)

- Sheriffs and bailiffs
- Police officers and detectives
- Gas station and garage workers
- Security guards[30]

POLICE OFFICER

- Observant of behavior
- Investigative
- Motivated by desire for excitement and desire for respect from others
- Healthy, strong, and agile
- Unflappable; not excitable
- Idealistic (at beginning of career)
- Willing to make decisions and take action
- Comfortable with physical force and firearms
- Used to directing and controlling: demonstrations and emergencies
- Community-minded; wants to serve

POLITICIAN

- Enterprising
- Articulate; good verbal skills

[30] Roe (1956).

- Manipulative, assertive
- Outgoing; likes to dominate,
- Driven by desires for power and status[31]

Importance of Personality Characteristics of Politicians

Personality has become prominent. Politicians must project images that match the desires and expectations of the voters. Voters want energy (activity, assertiveness) and openness (broad interests and exposure to people and ideas; seen in friendliness conscientiousness emotional stability). The more voters see apparent similarity to themselves, the more they like the candidate. In a complex world, voters take mental shortcuts to organize information. These days, centrist/right voters value power, security, and self-enhancement. Centrist/left voters value universalism and benevolence. When the candidate seems to share these values, he is chosen.

NEW INFORMATION What made some presidents great? In examining traits of all U.S. presidents, it was found that the most successful tended to be hard-working and achievement-minded, willing and able to speak up for their interests and valuing of the emotional side of life. They "set ambitious goals for themselves and move heaven and earth to meet them." The great presidents tended to be open-minded to new ways of doing things, stubborn, imaginative, extroverted, and assertive.[32]

REAL ESTATE SALES/INVESTMENTS/AUCTIONEER/INSURANCE SALES

- Sociable; likes face-to-face contact
- Personally persuasive
- Mildly exploitative in relationships
- Likes work
- Resourceful
- Energetic

[31] Rubenzer (2000). [32] ibid.

- Not interested in routine selling
- May be insincere: interest in people not genuine, but a means to an end[33]

SALESPERSON

- Able to see through the eyes of the other person
- Able to find out what others care about: money, happiness, or family
- Able to apply information to making a sale; persuasive
- Willing to ask questions; does not make assumptions
- Interested in others; curious
- Knowledgeable about his product and competition
- Independent; likes being own boss and making own hours
- Gregarious: likes meeting new people
- Energetic
- Involved in the community
- May be deceptive

 WARM UP Write a scene in which your character uses the following sales approach:

Prospects: Everyone is a possible sale; likes people who make things happen

Sets the stage: Enjoys and perfects the performance

Closes the deal: Asks for the order

SCIENTISTS, SOCIAL

- Investigative
- Abstract, original, and independent
- Likely to have grown up in an overprotective home
- Oriented toward people
- Close with family[34]

[33] ibid. [34] ibid.

SCIENTISTS, PHYSICAL/BIOLOGICAL

- Investigative
- Abstract, original and independent
- Likely to have grown up in cool, demanding home
- Achievement oriented, not people oriented

Traits of Eminent Scientists

Well-known scientists are more likely to have had a childhood disturbed by divorce or death, be distant from family, have psychosexual problems, and be dedicated to work.[35]

SOCIAL WORKER

- Protective
- Supportive; encouraging
- May be provocative
- Skilled interpersonally; more concerned with people than with ideas
- Seeks situations with other people
- Altruistic; attends to others
- Intelligent; shies away from physical skills
- Generally outgoing
- Satisfied with career; likes work; likes to exert influence
- Practical
- Slightly inhibited
- Slightly compulsive[36]

TEACHER

- Comfortable with and enjoys children
- Stable; likes security
- Socially at ease, friendly, idealistic

[35] Roe (1956). [36] Roe (1956).

- Sensitive to the opinions of others
- Curious
- Cooperative, patient, good disposition
- Responsible and efficient[37]

 NEW INFORMATION After the first thirty seconds of a first class, the evaluations of the teacher are similar to those evaluations given after the entire semester.

THERAPIST/GUIDANCE COUNSELOR

- Service oriented
- Attentive to needs of others
- Interested in connecting with people rather than ideas: prizes personal relationships
- Slightly compulsive
- Verbal and intelligent
- Mildly extroverted

Women in the Trades

Skilled trade careers include auto repair mechanics, carpenters, plumbers, electricians, computer technicians, and heating and air conditioning technicians. Federal legislation in the early 1970s opened the door for women to work in skilled trades and in organized labor shops.

TRAITS OF WOMEN IN TRADES

- Comfortable working against traditional sex roles
- Part of a supportive inner circle; often has a strong role model
- Independent; enjoys autonomy
- Subject to ridicule from men

[37] Greene and Stitt-Gohdes (1997); Galligani, Renck, and Hansen (1996); Moss, Panzak, and Tarter (1992).

- Overwhelmed at times
- Individualistic: "I don't care what anyone else says!"
- Iconoclastic; has a history of pattern-breaking experiences
- Confident that she has the ability to do the job
- Interested in earning good money
- Physically fit; enjoys physical activity
- Satisfied with who she is and what she does; has a strong sense of herself
- Enjoys being successful in a man's world[38]

TRUCK DRIVER

- Realistic; likes dealing with concrete problems
- Reliable; responsible
- Skilled; strong
- Able to follow instructions
- Masculine
- Tough; able to be alone for long stretches of time[39]

WRITER

- Wounded; creates in order to heal own wounds, or old family wounds
- Sensitive, imaginative; abstract and creative thinker
- Driven toward achievement; fearful of mediocrity
- Dismissive of ordinary problems
- Not adaptable
- Not aggressive[40]
- Prone to alcohol use, especially after forty; younger writers have increased risk of depression
- Prone to problems with anxiety and drug use

[38] Roe (1956). [39] Roe (1956). [40] Ludwig (1992).

- Unconventional, nonconformist
- Isolated at times; has to tolerate periods of being alone
- Required to let go of work after completion
- Likely to have come from families with both mental illness and creativity
- More likely to be bisexual or homosexual[41]

NEW INFORMATION Many professions (police officers, dentists, psychologists) grimly claim the highest suicide rate, but which is truly the deadliest profession is unclear. Why? One may have a higher suicide rate in a certain geographical area but not nationally; death certificates do not always list the occupation correctly; and doctors do not always list cause of death correctly. Three groups have elevated suicide rates: white male physicians, black male guards (including crossing guards, police, protective services and supervisors), and white female painters, sculptors, craft-artists and artist printmakers. Many, however, say that occupation is irrelevant: Mental illness, substance abuse, loss of social support, and availability of a firearm are the top predictors for suicide.[42]

---

[41] APA Monitor on Psychology (2001). [42] APA Monitor on Psychology (2001).

twelve

Group Influences

IN THIS CHAPTER

• Families • Group Development • Traits of Leaders in Groups • Roles of Group Members • Traits of Specific Groups, Gangs, and Cults

"I don't care to belong to a club that accepts people like me as members." In spite of this curmudgeonly assertion attributed to Groucho Marx, humans are sociable. We belong to groups all our lives, beginning with family. Some groups—such as tall people—are groups we can see; others are carried around inside, such as religious affiliation or being a writer. From birth to death, we live and work in groups: families, schools, sports teams, work, religious institutions, classes, and political or social organizations.

Family is perhaps the most powerful group, the one that creates us and travels along in our heads: We are rarely alone. The values, tastes, and rituals developed in our families of origin remain strong. Family influence can be seen easily: Almost any woman, when taken to a dress department, could tell you what outfit her mother would have picked out for her even if her mother is long dead; almost any man can repeat his father's instructions about how to take care of a car.

Other groups exert influence also. Professional allegiances are obvious: Writers always listen for material; skaters choreograph moves in their heads whenever they hear a good piece of music. Tragedy, too, creates group membership, which soldiers or survivors of disaster can testify. Groups create some traits and also evoke traits in people. Only in group settings do certain traits emerge because it is necessary to have a gathering of people for the traits to be displayed and observed (for example, mobs or hazing practices).

Whether individuals choose membership in a group (the Democratic Party or the KKK) or individuals are born into a group (being Puerto Rican, male, or poor) belonging carries ways of thinking and behaving. At their best, groups give us a sense of belonging, direction, and enrichment and provide a climate for innovative thinking. At their worst, groups reduce intellectual richness, critical judgment, and rational decision-making. (Irving Janis, in his book *Victims of Groupthink: A Psychological Study of Foreign-Policy Decisions and Fiascoes* analyzes the best and worst of these processes in several examinations of political decisions.)

This section explains general characteristics of groups, of group membership, and of specifics associated with selected groups.

Families

The group with which we are most familiar is our family, an often strange, tightly bound collection of individuals. Even if your character's family does not appear on the page, they have done their work influencing your character's personality and behaviors. The following family types can be used for background, or may inspire you to create certain dynamics for your plot development.

THREE BASIC FAMILY TYPES

I describe three basic family types: closed, random, and open. The traits are based on how these families try to achieve their goals. The following dimensions allow you to construct families or family members based on how they conduct themselves in the course of everyday affairs, as well as in unusual situations. Families are neither entirely closed to outside influences, nor entirely open. Families can be constructed and examined with regard to the following variables: space, authority, goals, emotional tone, time, energy, crises, and flaws.

Closed families do not tolerate strain or deviation because the closed family cannot tolerate a change to its equilibrium. The closed family believes that family interests come before individual goals.	**Random** families encourage change because the random family thrives on disequilibrium.	**Open** families mix change and constancy: they permit strain and deviation, but restrain excess through negotiation and management of closeness and distance.
Space is fixed: traffic (locked doors, supervised trips, privacy, secrecy, parental control of media, unlisted phone numbers) coming in and going out is regulated. The family remains distinct and apart from the larger community.	**Space** is dispersed: each person develops his own patterns. Entering and leaving family space is not regulated. The family members sometimes feel invaded. Members choose voluntarily whom and what to mix with.	**Space** is moveable: traffic is regulated by consensus, so the family is brought into the larger community, and outside culture comes into the home. Space may include varieties of activities, people, and pets.
Authority is tightly maintained by the parents ("We run a tight ship.") who are the main links or bridges to the world and regulate friends, requests, or interactions.	**Authority** is dispersed; individual freedom can be maintained at the expense of others. Authority is relinquished on the justification of "do your own thing."	**Authority** is shared; individuals bring in guests and information as long as others are not caused discomfort. All members serve as links or bridges to the world. Individuals can have freedom as long as family guidelines are not violated.

Values are tradition, fairness, propriety, family unity, responsibility, discipline, thrift, strength, perseverance, and self-sufficiency.	**Values** are freedom, genuineness, voluntary action with no coercion, individual decision-making, spontaneity, creativity, and discovering potential.	**Values** are change, variation, fairness, freedom with limits, family cohesion, limited experimentation, personal responsibility, openness, developing talent, and autonomy.
Goal is stability.	**Goal** is adaptation to individual's and family's needs.	**Goal** is free exploration.
Emotional tone is stable intimacy and nurturance and staying composed.	**Emotional tone** is exploratory intimacy and nurturance and being original.	**Emotional tone** is adaptive intimacy and nurturance; share and do, don't withhold.
Time that is valued is the past; newness is not accepted. Schedules are important, whether they provide for waking, dinner, chores, or the age to marry.	**Time** that is valued is equally the past, present, and future, depending on interest. There is little in the way of a family schedule; for example, no fixed mealtimes or bedtimes. Schedules are fixed by individuals, and plans may be discarded without completion.	**Time** that is valued is past, present, and future, but especially the present. Variations are accepted within a range of family comfort. Schedules are guidelines rather than blueprints. The family tries to synchronize members in order to pursue goals, but the plan is open to modification.

WRITER'S GUIDE TO CHARACTER TRAITS

Energy is steady, and activities are well planned with little deviation. Energy is directed toward clear goals, and excessive emotion is discouraged.	**Energy** fluctuates as individuals pick up and put down activities. Tomorrow can be very different from today; energy can be high, and tasks are attended to, but not for long.	**Energy** is flexible; members demand variation and are allowed to tap new sources, such as different music. Too much variety can lead to members spreading themselves too thin and activities becoming inefficient.
Crises are met primarily by suppressing the individual. When suppression fails, sometimes a severe schism may erupt. Less often, a successful rebellion occurs.	**Crises** occur often because members tend to fly in different directions. Crises are often unresolved and effects often unchecked. Resolution, albeit temporary, may come from one family member imposing leadership on the others.	**Crises** that are minor become frequent occurrences and are preferred over constraint. Energy runs high and low. Open discussion is the route to crisis resolution.
Flaws of this family are lack of escape or relief, insularity, lack of preparation for members to live in a big, heterogeneous world, or individuals' violent departure.	**Flaws** are seen when unconnected members dissolve in chaos, no vital connections exist, and individualistic members compete, making family irrelevant.	**Flaws** are obvious as members detach; there is no resolution of conflict, no standards, and members withdraw, so the family fails.[1]

[1] Kantor and Lehr (1975)

Like any group or organization, the family is a system that interacts with the outside world: Members go to school, work, meet outsiders, and reproduce. A family is not permanent; people are born or brought in, and they leave. A family grows and matures, sustains challenges to its structure, is torn down, and is rebuilt throughout the lifetimes of its members.

Group Development

These traits exist on a continuum, and are neither good nor bad. They simply help to define the behavior of any group.

GROUP TRAITS	CONTINUUM OF BEHAVIOR	
Autonomy	Independence from other groups →	Dependence on other groups
Cohesiveness	Strong unity within group →	Autonomy; distance between members
Control	High regulation of behavior of members →	Low regulation of members
Flexibility	Rigidly structured procedures →	Informal procedures
Tone	Predominantly pleasant tone →	Unpleasant-feeling tone
Homogeneity	Similarity among members →	Diversity among members
Intimacy	High level of familiarity with each others' lives →	Little detailed knowledge of each others' lives

Participation	Much time and effort given to group →	Little effort given to group
Permeability	Easy access; anyone can join →	Difficulty in joining; others cannot be members
Polarization	Unity; one goal for all members →	Individual goals predominate
Potency	Power over members held by group →	Little power over members held by group
Size	Many members →	Few members
Stability	Constancy; group stays the same over time →	Flux; group changes over time
Stratification	Clear hierarchy of status →	No differentiation in status[2]

WARM UP Social projection means that people exaggerate the similarity between themselves and members of their own "group."[3]

Write a quick scene using a sorority girl, minister, or young mother on the phone with a friend describing their similarities with the other members of their "group."

CONFLICTS ENGENDERED BY GROUP MEMBERSHIP

The basic conflict on entering any group is "How much of myself do I surrender in order to belong?" Whether it is a young bride trying to fit in with her husband's family, a police officer wanting to be accepted by the other cops, or

[2] Borgatta, Cottrell, and Meyer (1971). [3] Krueger (2004).

an immigrant moving to the United States, the basic conflict is the same, and the solution depends on the individual. If a person surrenders all, then she belongs wholeheartedly but gives up individuality (for example, Nazi soldiers). If a person gives up little of herself, she retains individuality, but never fully belongs to the group or take on the group's norms, values, and beliefs (for example, the family black sheep).

Members want to participate and belong but preserve their own identities. The conflict of self vs. other is not static; it shifts over time, depending on many factors, including personal needs, time of life, other commitments, and interest. For example, a young woman might be a devoted sorority sister during college, but remain group-free for years afterward.

GROUP DEVELOPMENT

Groups grow and develop. Like individuals, groups in their infancy have much to learn and work ineffectively. Groups in adolescent stages rebel, trying to find an identity. In maturity, groups settle down and get some work done before they die.

Members also have reactions to the authority figure in any group, whether boss, parent, or teacher. Common negative reactions to authority are submissiveness, rebelliousness, or withdrawal. Common negative reactions to peers in groups are destructive competitiveness, emotional exploitation, or withdrawal.[4] The following information provides some ideas about phases of groups, the dynamics, and the members' personal crises.

STAGES OF GROUP DEVELOPMENT

Phase One: Coming Together

- Members take on the same roles in the group as they usually do outside: someone eagerly makes introductions; someone else tries to assume leadership
- Individuals rely on existing leadership, are dependent on a leader, and are preoccupied more with the leader than with peers
- People look for orientation, rules, and how to do the task

[4] Bennis and Shepard (1965).

- Members must decide whether they want to join and give up some individuality in favor of a group cohesiveness—if they give up too much individuality, they feel like sheep; if they give up too little, they remain outside
- Group mood is anxious; wanting security

Phase Two: Defining the Task

- Members create or are given a task and determine how the job is to be accomplished
- Group mood is temporary relief

Phase Three: Unrest

- Members do not feel as agreeable as previously as newness wears off
- Group members struggle with individual rights and want to take back some of their personal autonomy
- Members are disenchanted with leader and with each other
- Members try to figure out where they belong in the hierarchy; control takes on importance
- Group task continues, although emotions are higher
- Group mood is hostile

Phase Four: Cohesion

- Members begin to feel like a team
- Members look for commonalities among themselves; are less preoccupied with leader and more interested in each other
- Mutual involvement helps sense of "we-ness"
- Group norms are established
- People discuss the task or work; they give and receive opinions
- Group mood is upbeat

Phase Five: Interdependence

- Members operate together, take responsibility, and believe in the subculture they have created: emotions and task come together

- Group works together as a team to handle tasks
- Group mood is cooperative

GROUP AS A WHOLE

Each group takes on a life of its own, has a group mentality, and creates a culture that is different from the sum of the individual members.

Group mentality is the collective and unanimous opinion, willpower, and desire of the group at a particular moment; it develops as the group functions as a unit. Group mentality may never be in the awareness of the members, and it may be in conflict with opinions, willpower, or desires of individual members, producing anger or discomfort in them.[5]

Group culture develops from an interplay of group mentality and individual desires. It includes group structure, leadership, task, and organization.

When groups are good, they are creative, and can generate more ideas than an individual. When groups are bad, people may behave less competently, make strange alliances (often unconsciously), allow projections to take over, and practice scapegoating.

GROUP TRANSFORMATION

Group transformation can be seen in a classroom during the school year: the students meet, find friends, assume certain roles, bond or not, have conflict, and part. More complex groups can be observed in families over the years, as infants are born into the family, everyone grows and ages, some leave, and others enter. Certain persons lead and others follow; some are central and others are peripheral. Those who marry in are treated in certain ways. Holidays and rituals are observed and, over the years, as membership changes and the family grows, the group is transformed, whether they like it or not, peacefully or through conflict.

For example, a small mom-and-pop restaurant starts with a cook/boss, waitress/wife, part-time hired help, and ten tables, and they are in business. If they succeed, others are brought in (cashier, accountant, waitstaff); still more are hired as

[5] Bion (1959).

work becomes more specialized (pastry chef); the physical setup changes (they add the storefront next door or redecorate); and conflict results because change is rarely accomplished smoothly. So the mom-and-pop atmosphere, in which the boss knew and guided everything, is now divided among different people with diverse agendas.

CAUSES OF INTERGROUP OR INTRAGROUP CONFLICT

Groups interact with other groups—one football team with another, or one software company with its competitor—and that can lead to *intergroup conflict*. When the conflict is among members of one group (for example, siblings) it is *intragroup conflict*. The following are causes of conflict.

- Change: Some members or groups believe they are worse off and others better off than before the change occurred. A common example these days is restructuring a company or blending a stepfamily.
- Unfair Trading: Someone or some group gives up more than they get.
- Reactions: Members or groups react to each other's behavior in ways that create a continuing negative spiral, heightening hostility.
- Stalemate: A group or group members cannot make a decision because of being pushed or pulled in two directions at the same time, producing disorganization and self-hatred.

TRAITS OF GROUP EVOLUTION

Some reasons that groups evolve over time include:

- Change of acceptable behaviors: for example, fraternity hazing is less tolerated
- Change of economic needs
- Culture and psychological forces affecting the group; for example, discrimination, harassment, or increased women in positions of authority
- Unwillingness to abide by old decisions made using rules of thumb or what a manager remembers from times past
- Emergence of new technology

- Competition from other groups
- Failure of outdated routines
- End of cycle of stability; beginning of a period of upheaval

Traits of Leaders in Groups

People in groups take on roles for which they have some attraction: a meek, shy woman is not likely to emerge as the leader. The following leaders exemplify roles that emerge in groups.

CHARISMATIC LEADER

- Visionary, inspirational, and influential
- Inspiring; articulates a vision
- Focused on distant rather than proximate goals
- Demanding; has high expectations of followers' performance
- Confident; self-aggrandizing
- Adaptable; adjusts easily to new social situations
- Willing to exploit others; aggressive
- Insensitive to the rights and feelings of others
- Narcissistic; inflated self-importance
- Intolerant of criticism; seeks admiration
- Articulate; speaks with words that convey basic emotions, sensations, and visions
- Dominant; likes control over others or control over the environment
- Able to transform needs and values of followers from self-interest to collective interest[6]

CREATIVE LEADER

Creative leaders can be broken into eight types:
- Replicator: maintains the status quo; c ontinue the work of predecessor
- Redefiner: puts a new spin on existing leadership; for example, entering new markets

[6] House and Howell (1992).

- Forward incrementor: takes the field or organization to the next step in the same direction
- Advanced forward incrementor: tries to take the field further than others are ready for
- Redirector: points the field in a new direction, one not attempted previously
- Regressive redirector: reintroduces an old, successful idea, such as Classic Coke
- Reinitiator: initiates a fresh start, an innovative product, or new program
- Synthesizer: integrates the best ideas from previous work[7]

 NEW INFORMATION Women are more harshly evaluated as leaders because they are stereotypically seen as softer and more nurturing; therefore, when they assume authority, people have strong, often negative, reactions.

FEMALE LEADER
- Likes going into a "man's world"
- Expresses feelings more freely than male counterparts
- Uses intuition in problem-solving
- Emphasizes personal relationships
- Stresses collaboration, teamwork, and empathy
- Is usually willing to share power
- Supports, confirms, and participates
- Had close relationships with parents and had mother who worked
- Understands competition, winning, and losing
- Had male role models[8]

WARM UP Women are less likely to emerge as leaders when the expectations for the role are incongruent with prevailing gender stereotypes; for example, when men and women work together on a task that is traditionally masculine, the women will probably not lead. Write a scene in which the opposite happens: a leaderless humanitarian rescue mission in which a woman assumes authority.

[7] Sternberg (2003). [8] Parker and Ogilvie (1996); Sachs, Chrysler, and Devlin (1992).

MALE LEADER

- Is autonomous
- Is strong and self-confident
- Uses rational and confrontational strategies; is directive
- Competes rather than collaborates

DYSFUNCTIONAL LEADER

- Is incompetent, inexperienced, or naïve in work skills
- Has poor personal skills: minimal self-awareness, low interest, malignant personality characteristics, or mental health problems
- Neglects protégés
- Violates boundaries: steps over the line with regard to ethics, sexuality, privacy, or responsibility
- Poorly manages the personal/professional role; has impaired objectivity, mixes personal with business
- Is exploitative: uses power to manipulate, bully, intimidate, harass, or coerce subordinates[9]

Traits That Cause Leaders to Fail

As the headlines tell us, leaders regularly fail. If one of your characters is going to self-destruct, here are some guidelines. For other ideas, look through the traits of white-collar criminals (see chapter five) and adult personality types in chapter two.

- Lacks adaptability or resourcefulness: skills suited to one job are insufficient for the next set of responsibilities
- Is a primadonna; unable to work with others or build teams
- Has character flaws: moodiness, dishonesty, insensitivity, arrogance, contempt, and vindictiveness
- Alienates others with office behavior: is overly ambitious or lazy, aloof or overly talkative/a gossip, domineering/unable to delegate tasks or indecisive[10]

---

[9] Johnson (2002). [10] Hogan (1994).

ROLES OF GROUP MEMBERS

Roles are scripts unconsciously followed by different members of any group. The group uses roles to isolate an emotion in one person, who then plays it out. The rest of the group then feels at ease because each of them is spared having to express feelings contained in the one individual. For example, during a meeting of the hospital staff, a young nurse begins crying because of a death on the unit. Others comfort her, but are secretly glad that they did not break down. Similarly, expression of emotion can alleviate tensions for others. High school boys crack jokes during an anxiety-filled discussion on birth control, easing the embarrassment for everyone. This also translates into behavior. An individual takes over leadership in a chaotic hiking team, relieving others. Or a cop crosses the line when he is interrogating an attractive female prisoner; and other cops know that they have thought about doing the same thing but stopped themselves.

The following are some of the roles assumed by group members.

- Hero: wants to lead and be noticed; a champion; high energy; filled with ideas and prepared to take action; ready to go out front
- Seducer: wants to bewitch others; seduction can be with sex, power, or money; he knows which key works and uses it to his own ends
- Silent One: keeps opinions to himself; has long periods of silence, often deliberate; wants to be courted to participate
- Taskmaster: reminds the group to get back to work; appreciates the task and wants to reach solutions; not usually distracted by conflicting demands or emotions
- Clown: jokes, relieving tension through silliness and often taking the group away from more serious matters; good at breaking tension but also good at moving off-task
- Victim: tries hard, but sees everyone else as getting the rewards; everyone else looks stronger; theme is "poor me," even if those words are never said aloud

- Oppressor: likes to dominate; wants her own way; not interested in democratic action; treats high-status people with much more respect than low-status individuals
- Conciliator: tries to manage a compromise; doesn't take a position except to bring people together and avoid disagreement; is distressed by overt conflict, inserts himself in the middle as the peacemaker
- Combatant: is easily angered; sees a fight as the answer; likes action; finds it hard to sit still
- Nurse: is usually a woman who tends to everyone's needs; concerned about others; often gets resentful that she is not highly valued; hides feelings of anger, jealousy, or competitiveness
- Young Turk: desires to compete for leadership; just like Macbeth, in which the soldier kills the king
- Innocent: is usually a young person; can ask questions and be naïve; may not be taken seriously by the others and has a hard time exercising any power
- Scapegoat: represents and repents for the weaknesses of the group; is isolated by the group as the source of conflict or bad feelings and, consciously or unconsciously, is kept in that role; usually the group has deposited unwanted feelings (guilt, incompetence, or rage) into that individual rather than share responsibility; scapegoating is the most dramatic behavior of group exploitation

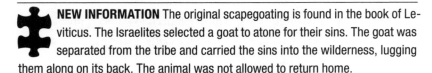 **NEW INFORMATION** The original scapegoating is found in the book of Leviticus. The Israelites selected a goat to atone for their sins. The goat was separated from the tribe and carried the sins into the wilderness, lugging them along on its back. The animal was not allowed to return home.

Traits of Specific Groups, Cults, and Gangs

Characters are not the only personalities in books and stories: Groups also have distinctive personalities and traits that make them ring true to your readers. Groups created to perform certain tasks have specific traits; for example, juries and outlaw motorcycle gangs are both groups held together by specific goals, but they differ dramatically in membership, group traits, and aims. The following examples of diverse groups, gangs, and cults can provide cultural, social, and psychological settings for your characters.

GROUPS

TRAITS OF JURIES

The jury is a small group and therefore subject to small-group processes as well as some dynamics unique to the judicial system.

- Usually reaches a decision that agrees with that of the judge (80 percent of the time)
- Usually votes the same on the first ballot, guilty or not guilty, as on their final ballot (90 percent of the time)
- Often selects the first person who was nominated for foreperson; people seldom seek the position
- Often has other leaders emerge; jury forepersons are not necessarily the most influential people
- Is not always conducive to free speech; minority members are reluctant to speak up without an ally; male jurors talk more than female jurors; less confident members "go along" rather than argue
- Has intractable members, who get a lot of attention at first, and then are ignored
- Is more lenient with defendants who are physically attractive because they are seen as "better" people than those who are unattractive (unless attractiveness facilitated the crime)
- Is more lenient with older people than young people and with thin people than obese people

---

 FIGURES AND STATISTICS In assessing monetary damages in court, injured male genitals were valued about three times as highly as female genitals.[11]

---

[11] ibid.

TRAITS OF A SORORITY OR FRATERNITY

- Is exclusive; has set roles and behaviors
- Has lifelong membership
- Provides a ready-made social life
- Has secret practices and traditions
- Provides an identity
- Provides safety of a homogeneous group

Traits of Fraternity Hazing

Hazing includes any activity that intimidates, exhausts, or distresses participants. The activities have a possibility of injury or even death, and certainly of humiliation. In doing these rituals, fraternity brothers:

- Do to others what was done to them; payback
- Show manliness; they want to impress each other
- Want to conform through ritual of belonging, joining, and bonding
- Demand submission and obedience from pledges
- Suspend norms of behavior
- Do not tolerate dissenters; brothers seem unified, all in agreement
- Lose individual responsibility to the group
- May allow sadistic brothers the opportunity to rule; weak president may allow cruelty to get out of control
- See behaviors as tradition, not out-of-control impulses[12]

TRAITS OF A SPORTS TEAM

- Cooperates and competes simultaneously
- Has interdependent relationships among members
- Values conflict resolution for success of team
- Usually feels a strong allegiance to the coach, his rules, and his ideas
- Looks for support and feedback from coach
- Unifies to defeat competitors

[12] Nuwer (1990).

- Follows rules and instructions
- May be insular because players train, eat, travel, and compete together
- Has assigned roles; each member plays and perfects one position

TRAITS OF SPORTS FANS
- Become vicarious players
- May enjoy channeled aggression of sport
- May become aggressive after a game
- Identify with the team; are loyal
- Identify a clear opponent and a clear ally
- Collect team memorabilia
- Follow and charts team statistics
- May participate in fantasy leagues: fantasy baseball or football
- Read the sports section in the daily paper first (and maybe skip the other sections)
- Watch *SportsCenter* on ESPN religiously
- Feel jubilant when their team wins; feel despair when they lose
- Gather with other fans to watch games
- Own (or long for) season tickets
- Bond to team and other fans
- Accumulate knowledge of the team and the sport

TRAITS OF SELF-HELP GROUPS

Self-help groups form based on a common problem/situation/experience; for example, depression, grief, or alcoholism. The members help each other rather than relying on a professional leader or therapist.
- Receive and give emotional and social support
- Identify with each other
- Take responsibility to facilitate the group's progress
- Mix expectations of family with aspects of formal professional help
- Have varied goals: behavior change, adaptation, and coping
- Have open communication among members and links with others
- Model themselves after others who had similar experiences

- May be a discussion group or based on the twelve-step principles of Alcoholics Anonymous

TRAITS OF SECRET SOCIETIES
- Can be positive, negative, or neutral: Masons, KKK, etc.
- Are voluntary, not coercive or deceptive like a cult
- Have special dress, language, ritual, and structure
- Are an opportunity for safe bonding
- May be created to defend a way of life
- Are predictable, stable, and satisfying
- Provide a place to be gregarious
- Minimize or disguise weaknesses of members
- Create a culture within the larger society, often differing from majority
- Stimulate aggression against outside culture
- Create boundary between inside and outside[13]

How Groups Can Promote Bad Behavior

What makes people do bad things? What allows abuses such as those that occurred in Abu Ghraib prison in Iraq? Classic experiments in psychology showed that the line between good and evil is permeable; anyone can cross it depending on the situation.

Situations can foster evil if they:

- Provide people with an ideology and beliefs to justify their actions
- Make people take a small, bad, first step, and then increase those behaviors
- Make those in charge seem like a "just" authority
- Transform a once-compassionate leader into a dictatorial figure
- Provide people with vague and ever-changing rules; keep their living situation difficult
- Rename actions to legitimize them

---

[13] Tiger (1969).

- Tell participants that they must follow the orders
- Surround reluctant people with others who willingly comply
- Allow people to voice dissent as long as they follow orders
- Dehumanize the enemy, reducing social responsibility
- Maintain the cohesiveness of the group; behaviors in groups reduce the feelings of individual responsibility; individuals can hide in groups[14]

THE ROAD TO PRISONER ABUSE

How can a leader shape reactions to the "enemy"?

- Use derogatory labels, drawings, and descriptions to create hostile images
- Hold prisoners under conditions that exclude them from the Geneva Conventions, sending the message that prisoners are less than human and of no value
- Create dehumanizing prison rules—such as prisoners having to ask permission each time they want to go to the bathroom—encouraging the guards to degrade them and see them as people to whom general values need not be applied
- Have little or no supervision by a higher authority who could create a culture of humanity

TRAITS OF A MOB

- Relinquish personal responsibility
- Act without thinking
- Will follow a leader blindly
- Are volatile; changeable
- Take action that can lead to violence

[14] APA Monitor on Psychology (October 2004).

CULTS

A cult is a group of individuals who follow a living, usually male, leader. Cults and the intense sense of belonging that characterizes them fill a vacuum for people who want answers. Individuals need to belong, to replace chaos with tranquility, and flee from a frightening, complex world that requires unwanted responsibility and choices.

The group leader makes extreme claims about his person or abilities; for example, he is God's agent, all-knowing, or has the absolute truth. Membership in the cult requires complete acceptance of the leader's claims, complete obedience to the rules, and complete loyalty to the leader.

FIGURES AND STATISTICS The Power of The Group: In the 1960s, psychologist Stanley Milgram and colleagues found that if one person stopped on a busy New York street and gazed at the sky, only 4 percent of those passing by joined him. When five people looked up at nothing, 18 percent of those passing by joined them. But when a group of fifteen gazed upward, 40 percent of others then joined, nearly stopping traffic in one minute.

TRAITS OF CULTS

- Exist in an encapsulated environment
- Exclude outside or contradictory information; cult offers comfort and answers to life's questions
- Make decisions for members
- Restrict communication
- Seduce the spirit; misuse faith
- Subject members to repetitive lectures, chants, and rituals
- Apply psychological pressure for conformity
- Discourage inquiries by making the questioner feel guilty
- Create a new identity for members
- Require submission to authority; repeated key phrases stop doubts from entering members' minds.
- Give rules from a charismatic, not democratically elected, leader
- Encourage fear and hatred of nonmembers: "us vs. them" mentality

NEW INFORMATION On November 18, 1978, in the jungles of Guyana, South America, Peoples Temple cult leader Jim Jones called on followers to drink Kool-aid laced with cyanide. 913 people died at Jonestown. There are lessons to be learned about the power of situational and social influences. Influence is like fire—it can be used for good or evil.

WHO ARE CULT MEMBERS?

Who joins cults? Recruits are similar to other people; no particular factors predispose certain individuals to cult membership. However, some people who may be initially attracted to cults are:

- Idealistic students who want to believe in something
- People who are lonely, alienated, disenchanted, or depressed
- Individuals in need of an authoritative figure (may have weak relationship with father)
- People who need direction and discipline, are uncertain, or have trouble making decisions
- People searching for the answer to their own problems and those of society
- Individuals who relinquish individual reason in favor of group thought
- People who want acceptance
- Individuals who may have a fragile internal world and who, at an extreme, can border on psychotic
- People who are amenable to being recruited [15]

WARM UP Phobia indoctrination is a technique through which the cult plays on a person's fears with threats, such as the person will develop cancer or go insane if he or she leaves; food or sleep deprivation can also be used.[16]
Write a paragraph in which a new recruit attempts to leave and is confronted by the charismatic leader.

HOW A CULT LEADER MANAGES COMPLIANCE AND OBEDIENCE

- Encourages followers to spy on one another
- Blasts voice over the loudspeakers; is present while they eat, work, or sleep

[15] Kaslow and Sussman (1982). [16] APA Monitor on Psychology (November, 2002).

- Requires followers to give him written statements about their fears and mistakes; later, if they disobey, this information is used to humiliate them during public meetings or to subject them to their fears
- Has them practice suicide drills
- Blurs the relationship between reality and words: for example, workers give their leader daily thanks for their food and work even though they may be starving and working six-and-a-half days a week
- Moves them from urban to remote regions to generate uncertainty; when uncertain, people look to others for cues on how to behave[17]

What is Mind Control?

Mind control is the process by which individual or collective freedom of choice and action is compromised by agents who distort perception, motivation, affect, cognition, or behavior. It is accomplished through the basic principles of:

- Conformity: all people being the same
- Compliance: submission
- Persuasion: influence to comply
- Guilt and fear arousal: creating a state of mind in which it is difficult to disagree
- Modeling: showing the behaviors
- Identification: unconscious desire to be the same as another person

These principles are most successful when combined with a charismatic authoritarian leader, social isolation, physical discomfort, threats, promised rewards, and a compelling ideology, all working over time.[18]

GANGS

Gangs originally tended to be exclusively one race, religion, or ethnicity (although the Mafia was organized by both Jews and Italians). This has continued to be the case with exclusively African-American, Chinese, or Mexican gangs, but

[17] APA Monitor on Psychology (November, 2003). [18] Zimbardo (2002).

it is changing. The predictions for the future are that some of these gangs will join forces, become increasingly diverse, and proliferate.

There is little systematic national data on the numbers of gangs and their locations. It is estimated that 1–5 percent of arrests for violence involve young people—either street gang members or non-gang youth.

Street gangs are an organized urban phenomena born out of poverty. In the U.S., there are African-American, Cuban, Mexican, Chinese, and Dominican gangs.

TRAITS OF URBAN STREET GANGS
- May be composed of all men or all women
- Have a "turf" that they protect but they rarely control much turf; are subservient in connections with larger organizations
- Show very visible signs of membership, which may be clothing or tattoos
- Have strong hierarchy and leadership; may recruit through fear tactics
- Derive income mainly from drugs
- Recruit people from dysfunctional homes who may have been abused or neglected
- Rebel against authority or oppressive conditions; violence is only one part of group behavior
- Grow out of poverty and the urban underclass; strong peer pressure
- Provide strong friendships; become an extension of family

Other Gangs

Chinese Gangs have distinct additional traits:

- "Turf" is less rigid
- Network may be global
- Income is derived from drugs and credit card fraud
- Making money is the motive
- Markings may include scarring
- Do business; have money in legitimate businesses

> **Hispanic Gangs** have distinct additional traits:
>
> - Members are "soldiers," participating in a way of life
> - See themselves as protectors of the neighborhood
> - Nicknames come from physical features; gang names have geographical significance

TRAITS OF SUBURBAN GANGS

- Are composed of affluent, suburban youth: newer versions of organized gang activity
- Unpredictable; not static or long lasting; they change with the speed of popular culture
- Are not driven by desire for money
- Are 10 percent female
- Have power as their goal
- Do not have "turf" that they protect, unlike inner city gangs
- Have concealed or subtle attire and signs of membership

NEW INFORMATION Hate gangs—for example, skinheads—are a variation of suburban gangs. Hate gangs have an ideology that they use to justify their criminal acts. They believe that they have "knowledge" of a particular person/organization/institution/religion that others are missing, and that "knowledge" is their justification.

TRAITS OF OUTLAW MOTORCYCLE GANGS

- Came into being after World War II: Hells Angels and Outlaws
- Feel alienated from society
- Have colors (the official uniform) including a sleeveless denim jacket and club patch
- May wear the patch (13 is a patch worn on a member's colors to indicate that the biker smokes marijuana , deals it, or has contacts in the drug world)

- Expertise with a bike is important
- Require a long probationary period before membership
- Group must come before family; members attend meetings; follow rules

TRAITS OF FEMALE GANG MEMBERS

- Are fewer in numbers than boys
- Are less involved in gang than boys
- Often come from poverty
- Commit the full range of crimes, including violent acts
- Come from homes with unemployed parents and where mothers have been beaten
- Most have children with gang members
- Have strong friendships; are very loyal
- Are brought into gang membership because of association with gang boys
- Use drugs; may trade sex for drugs
- Wear gang clothes and symbols when not at work

TRAITS OF SKINHEADS

Skinheads are different from street gangs (see above) because they are organized around the ideology of racism and are therefore more like a terrorist youth subculture. They:

- Have violence as an integral part of the lifestyle
- Want to produce fear
- Want political change
- Are focused on ideology of neo-Nazism, not turf
- Display deliberate style of shaved heads, Nazi regalia, white power music

CHAPTER

thirteen

Physical Appearance and Communication

IN THIS CHAPTER

• Appearances • Body Language • Verbal and Nonverbal Communication

Dialogue is a major focus in most writers' work. But that is not the only way that characters communicate with each other or with the reader. In addition to the world of words, there is the world of nonverbal communication and characterization through appearances. For example, if a character's appearance is powerful, his face, clothes, movement, and body language all work together to create that impression on others whether he intends it or not.

Nonverbal communication can be illustrated through the senses: sight, sound, touch, taste, and smell. Probably more than 70 percent of information is collected through sight. We pay special attention to nonverbal communication, especially when one sense contradicts another. For example, I hear a man conversing calmly with an associate but then I notice, in his lap, he picks at his cuticles until they bleed.

This chapter presents information about what others perceive from our appearances as well as communication traits, both nonverbal and some verbal. I hope that the ideas will help you to display your characters in some complex ways. Let's begin with appearances and some of the things we see—faces, clothes, and body language—that give an impression of others, whether accurate or not.

The traits that follow are those that have been subject to research and have some accuracy. A word of warning! I have noticed over the years that there is a tendency for people to give great weight to appearances and body language as if they had discovered a secret code. Be cautious: Appearances and gestures can have multiple meanings, or little meaning, or be bound in specific culture, or manipulated for a certain effect.

Facial Expressions

Different cultures tend to identify the same facial expressions as signifying basic emotions, such as surprise, anger, happiness, or sadness. But when a man's expression is ambiguous, he is assumed to be angry, whereas a woman with the same expression is assumed to be sad.

Appearances

FACES

When we learn a face, we rarely forget it. One study showed that people were able to identify faces taken from their own yearbooks as opposed to faces taken from other yearbooks with almost perfect accuracy after fifty years. Artists, authors, and moviemakers all rely on appearance for characterization. An excellent movie can be spoiled by a character who does not look like the person we imagined when reading the book. In a novel, the way you describe a character's face evokes an image in the reader's (and another character's) mind. For example, individuals whose features deviate from the norm (such as very wide eyes or very thin lips) are perceived to also have more extreme character traits. The meaning of a specific interaction is heavily influenced by facial expression, whether sincere, sexy, or serious.

Faces can be constructed along three dimensions: structural (such as size and shape, color, or skin), diagnostic (such as blushing or muscular movements), and artificial (such as hairstyle or makeup).

> **NEW INFORMATION** The number of cosmetic procedures increased by 44 percent from 2003 to 2004. When people are psychologically healthy, they tend to be satisfied with their plastic surgery, feel better about their body image, and like the feature that was altered. When patients have personality problems, they are less satisfied, perhaps because their expectations were unrealistic.

ASSUMPTIONS ABOUT TRAITS

When people read faces, they make assumptions that may be true or false. Certainly, leathery, sagging skin, or facial pouches indicate aging, but other guesses are less accurate. The following are some common misperceptions.

TRAIT	FAULTY ASSUMPTION
People who always look the same; for example, relaxed	stable disposition
People who change appearance; for example, long hair to short; disheveled to neat; glasses to contact lenses	inconsistent personality
Short nose	weak, compliant, gullible
Baby face (round face, large round eyes, high eyebrows, small nose, and small chin)	nonaggressive, nonthreatening, honest, warm, dependent, affectionate
Blond hair	weak, fun, delicate, simple

Dark hair	less fun, intelligent, complex
Light coloring/blue eyes	naive, warm, submissive
Use of cosmetics (women)	popular, sociable, talkative
Excessive use of cosmetics	stereotypically female
Stylish hair	reliable, warm, caring
Low eyebrows	angry
Fine hair, short neck, and fleshy ears	low intelligence
Receding chin	weak
Bald	timid, naive, weak, submissive
Bearded	mature, dominant, educated
Eyeglasses	less attractive but intelligent
Androgynous appearance	homosexual
Sturdy, broad-shouldered	independent, confident

 NEW INFORMATION When an infant looks angry, people conclude that the child is a boy.

APPEARANCE OF THE FACE FOR SIX EMOTIONS

Every writer has been told, "Show, don't tell." Here are some ways to show emotion.

EMOTION	BROWS	EYES	LOWER FACE
Surprise	raised brows; long wrinkles across forehead	wide-open eyes; white shows showing above the iris	dropped mouth; no stretch or tension in lips; lips parted
Fear	raised and drawn brows; flattened brows	hard stare; tension in lower lids	corners drawn back; lips stretched
Anger	brows pulled together; strong deep vertical lines wrinkles between brows	tightening of lids; squinting	lips compressed or slightly open; teeth may show
Disgust	brows down, not drawn together; vertical creases	lower lids raised	cheeks raised; upper lip may rise; tongue may be visible; lips may pull down
Sadness	brows drawn; inner corners raised; bulge above brow	eyes glazed; drooping lids or tense upper lids	trembling lips; lip corners turn down
Happiness	no distinctions; neutral	relaxed or lower lids raised; crow's feet seen	corners raised; lips may be open slightly

ATTRACTIVENESS

THE VALUE OF ATTRACTIVENESS

Generally, high value is put on attractiveness. Beauty is associated with goodness, and people who are seen as attractive are also thought to be kinder, warmer, stronger, more interesting, sexually responsive, modest, sociable, and outgoing. Beauty has power: Attractive people often have more influence on other people than unattractive people. Attractive people are also even considered more fertile. Attractive men are always ranked more favorably than unattractive men in work opportunities. Attractive men and women receive lighter sentences in courtrooms.

There are also situations in which attractiveness is not an asset. Attractive people are underdiagnosed when seeking medical care. Attractive women, more often than men, are considered vain, egotistical, snobbish, and materialistic. For typically masculine jobs high in prestige and power, such as managerial positions, attractive women are rated less favorably than unattractive women; but for stereotypically female jobs, such as clerical positions, attractive women are rated more favorably.

TRAITS OF A CONVENTIONALLY ATTRACTIVE FACE

Different cultures, in general, do seem to value the same basic traits as attractive:
- Straight profile, rather than jutting or receding features
- Orderly face: equal distances from hairline to brow, brow to just under nose, just under nose to tip of chin; eyes not too wide or too close

- Symmetry of features, rather than asymmetry
- Youthfulness
- Large eyes, high cheekbones, full lips, small nose, and light skin (women)
- Rounded rather than angular facial structure
- Smooth, healthy skin, and free of marks or blemishes
- Large chin for men

 WARM UP Write two paragraphs about the same man on the telephone talking to his friend's sister, whom he has never seen: In the first paragraph, he believes that the woman is beautiful, in the second, homely.

CLOTHES

Clothes are certainly observable and often attract notice. It is one thing about a person's appearance that can entirely be manipulated. Clothing may define important aspects of a character without words. For example, clothes may proclaim an affiliation such as a gang beret or a priest's collar. Differently, clothing is one way that a writer reinforces descriptions of weather or has a character define herself, for example, with modesty or flash. Clothing also names groups, such as the Amish's simple black clothing and hats or Hells Angels' vests and leather. Clothing may mark religious affiliation, a subculture, or a peer culture. Religious medals or expensive jewelry can make a statement about permanent values. A walking stick, medical bag, badge, or weapon each conveys a different type of power. Conversely, a character dressed in loose, long garments with no clothing distractions or extremes will be more invisible. And cheap or ill-fitting garb suggests insignificance.

Even colors have power. Up until the 1920s, blue was considered "delicate and dainty" and pink was thought to be "a stronger, decided color."

WARM UP You can prime a person to perceive things in a certain way by manipulating the context. Write two paragraphs: the first reveals your character's response when he bumps into a woman exiting Tiffany; the second paragraph shows his reaction when he sees the same woman limping down the street wearing a shabby coat and torn shoes.

Body Language

In a group, a person tends to orient his body, head, and eyes to one other person or a small group of others who are of interest. Coalitions (for example, partners or lovers) often sit next to each other in a group. Their movements may echo each other; for example, head nodding to reinforce the other person's comments. In the U.S., spouses who are not together in a group, but are in the same area, tend to reestablish contact with an exchanged glance every twenty to thirty minutes.

In a group, a person often signals his intent to speak. This is done by leaning forward; putting a prop, such as a pencil, out in view; by looking at the faces of the others as if to gather them; or by uttering sounds to signal to the group that he wants the floor.

When, instead of a group, it is two people getting on well, one person may adopt the posture, mannerisms, or behavior of the other person. This eases the interaction, and feels more comfortable to the pair. On the other hand, disinterest can be seen when body posture or head and eyes are searching elsewhere.

In a pair, a group, or in larger numbers, speakers often use their hands to depict an action that occurred or an object they wish to describe. This occurs in conjunction with speech. Gestures are also effective in lieu of speech: a wink, showing the middle finger, or a wave.

UNCONSCIOUS GESTURES AND THEIR MESSAGES

Gestures of Invitation/Attraction/Interest

- Tightening muscles; sagging disappears (watch the bodies of people meeting on a beach!)
- Skin color varies, from flush to pallor
- Stroking head and hair; rearranging clothing
- Holding gaze of another person
- Smiling; touching lip or neck; presenting neck
- Licking or puckering lips
- Men: buttoning coat or tugging on socks

- Women: crossing legs, exposing more thigh; placing hand on hip; absently stroking leg; slipping shoe on and off

Gestures of Self-Confidence
- Sitting on the arm of a chair
- Sitting, hands locked behind his head
- Sitting, legs apart

Gestures of Distrust
- Covering mouth with hand

Gestures of Insecurity
- Putting finger in mouth
- Biting nails
- Patting hair

Gestures of Doubt/Disbelief
- Picking imaginary lint off of sleeve
- Looking down, face turned away

Gestures of Deceitfulness
- Rubbing nose
- Hiding hands; for example, putting them in pockets
- Pursing of lips
- Sitting unusually still

Gestures of Power
- Making eye contact
- Sitting at the head of a table in a group setting
- Lowering one's eyebrows
- Using expansive and relaxed body movements
- Maintaining an erect posture
- Walking with powerful gait: quick, leaning forward, swinging arms, and picking up feet

> **Zones of Comfort**
>
> - Intimate Zone (six to eighteen inches): entry is for those who are emotionally close
> - Personal Zone (two to four feet): entry is for social functions
> - Social zone (four to twelve feet): entry is for strangers, workmen, or unfamiliar people
> - Public zone (over twelve feet): for addressing a large group of people
>
> These zones are very different in countries other than the United States (for example, Japanese and Danes stand closer than North Americans; people from the country stand farther apart than people from the city; bosses feel freer to stand closer to subordinates than vice versa). Other interesting occurrences involving space can be seen in public bathrooms, locker rooms, and elevators where people try to keep some distance between them. On the other side of manipulating space, police move into personal space when exerting authority, particularly when they are asking questions.

Verbal and Nonverbal Communication

We acquire essential information through hearing people talk: We hear their diction, their regional accent, their use of vocabulary. We gain insights about them, but we also make assumptions: some correct, some false. We guess their mood by their tone, voice pressure, and choice of words. We guess their education or intelligence; maybe we can even figure out their job. We respond to all of this and more; we react to whether we have heard a soothing voice or an agitated one, a loud voice or a soft one, a calming voice or a jarring one.

When people lose their hearing, they may become more isolated or withdrawn because an essential part of both verbal and nonverbal communication has been lost. Auditory problems, too, cause people to avoid crowds or other conditions that make hearing difficult.

WARM UP Characters respond to information based on whatever goal they are pursuing. For example, your character will attend to and remember different facts gathered from a potential lover than from a job applicant or person on a post office line. Write three paragraphs in which a woman meets the same man under the three conditions described above.

MALE AND FEMALE TRAITS OF COMMUNICATION

Teaching student psychologists, I often remind them that what someone says is only part of the discussion; how they say it and what they omit are also significant.

Everyone has unique patterns of communication, but men and women have some distinctions that can be used to enliven character and dialogue. The following comparisons illustrate the edges of communication patterns. Most people have more flexibility in their communication than the extremes set out below, and fall closer to the center.

Self-disclosure is the willingness to talk to another person honestly. Mutual disclosure leads to greater intimacy. Women tend to disclose more than men and the levels of disclosure change when people's moods change, for example, during anger.

FEMALE	MALE
Asks questions to show interest in the topic or person speaking	Asks questions to gain more information about the person or topic
Talking about problems provides a relief	Talking about problems feels like he is dwelling on the negative
Sharing one's own complaints is meant to show closeness and support	Thinks that sharing complaints does not create solutions
Provides background and detail because she wants to be understood	Too much detail feels like justification: make your point

Continuing to discuss problems demonstrates support	Continuing to discuss problems is useless: make a decision
Can be indirect or subtle; sometimes apologetic	Says what he wants directly
Believes that talking about a relationship brings people closer	Believes that simply talking is useless, unless things can be changed
Enjoys discussion of emotion and relationship	Feels inept discussing emotion and relationships
Apologizes when talking	No apologies
Speaks more quickly	Speaks slowly

DIVERSITY IN NONVERBAL TRAITS

Language, customs, religion, and appearance are obvious distinctive traits, but there will always be subtle differences to attend to. Differences in acceptable personal space, personal greetings, maintenance of eye contact, posture, amount of speech and volume are only a few significant traits. Characters from different cultures will require research to ensure their authenticity.

VERBAL AND NONVERBAL TRAITS ASSOCIATED WITH LYING

- The evidence is mixed.
- There is an association between increased pupil size (an indicator of tension and concentration) and lying.
- Liars are more likely to purse their lips together.
- Liars may pitch their voices higher.
- Liars take longer to start to answer questions than truth tellers.
- In the content of liars' conversations, there is less information and more is withheld.

- Liars are more likely to repeat words and phrases.
- Liars use fewer first-person pronouns, distancing themselves from their stories.
- Liars are generally more anxious and guilty and therefore use more words that connote negative emotion, such as hate or worthless.
- Liars give briefer responses to complex questions and create more perfect stories than is usual with truthful situations.

Liars do not fidget more, blink more, or show less relaxed posture. In fact, when liars are highly motivated and the stakes are high, they may seem unusually still.

People can pick out lying better in others from their own culture because different non-verbal behaviors, such as head nodding, have different meanings. In the US, it is often taken as nervousness; not so in other countries.

NEW INFORMATION Tall people earn more money. Perhaps they have greater self-esteem and social confidence than short people; or perhaps others may view tall people as more leader-like and authoritative. The biggest correlation between height and salary appears in sales and management positions: areas in which customer perception has a major impact on success.

CHAPTER
fourteen

The Big Index

The aim of this chapter is to make the preceding chapters even easier to negotiate. There are eight sections: *Personality Types, Adult; Traits, Adults; Traits, Children and Adolescents; Traits, Groups; Disorders and Problems, Adults; Disorders and Problems, Children and Adolescents; Criminals and Crimes; and Careers.* You can enrich characters with with details of their specific traits. For example, your character is a young woman boxer with bulimia. Look up boxing in the section on *Careers.* Look through *Traits, Adults* for references to anger and aggressiveness. Check out eating disorders in *Disorders and Problems, Adults.* Maybe your boxer has a criminal friend, a minor character who will help her in some way. Look through the section *Criminals and Crimes* and consider the different options for this minor character. These details will lead you to other ideas.

PERSONALITY TYPES, ADULT

Narcissist, 104, 119-120, 138, 181

Passive-Aggressive, 39-40

Perfectionist, 40-42

Personable, 42-43

Problem Solver, 43

Resilient, 44

Show-Off, 44-45

Ultra-Feminine, 38, 45-46

Victim, 5, 46-48

TRAITS, ADULTS

abusive, 23, 39, 48

accident-prone, 26

accommodating, 42

acquiescent, 28

action-oriented, 292

adaptable, 290, 314

adulterous, 184, 189-192

adventurous, 37, 285, 288

aggression, 31, 105, 114, 181, 314
  and careers, 280, 284-287, 289, 293
  in criminals, 132, 137, 144, 146, 155
  and personality types, 21, 23, 27, 33, 37-39, 45
  sexual, 167, 198

aging, 233-236

agreeable, 284

alert, 45

altruistic, 247, 299

ambitious, 37, 41, 168, 285, 291-292, 316

amoral, 113

anger, 7, 30, 81, 190, 200, 244, 247
  and careers, 286, 294
  facial appearance of, 334
  in disorders, 101-102, 106, 108, 112, 256, 266, 269, 271
  in families, 216, 218
  group member, 312, 318
  and memories, 255
  and murder, 151, 155
  parenting, 210, 241
  in personality types, 27, 30, 36, 41, 46-48
  and sexual problems, 162, 166, 198, 273-274, 277

annoying, 40

antisocial, 137

anxiety, 47, 104-105, 113, 121, 184, 226, 258
  adoption, 212
  in disorders, 112, 116
  and drug use, 263
  and illness, 31
  marital separation, 202
  parenting, 207
  in personality types, 27, 32, 40
  sexual, 163, 166

apathetic, 100, 245

appearance, 32, 290, 330-336
  attractiveness, 175-176, 191, 331, 335-336

compliant, 24, 47

compulsive, 106, 115, 177, 192, 260, 299

conceited, 295

conciliatory, 318

confidence, 21-22, 27, 44, 143, 191, 202, 218
  career-related, 285, 287, 301
  gestures of, 338
  leadership, 314, 316
  parenting, 207, 230

confused, 102, 245

congenial, 121

conservative, 25, 282, 287-288

consistent, 25

constricted, 46

contemptuous, 106, 127, 138, 219, 286, 316

content, 26

control, 22, 38-39, 105, 113, 131, 135, 155, 179-180, 195, 197
  self-, 22, 45-46, 105, 162, 282-283, 289

conventional, 31, 282, 287, 289

cooperative, 42

coping, 44

courageous, 20, 296

coy, 46

creative, 20, 283, 286

critical, self-, 41, 100, 105, 194, 283

cultural, 17

cunning, 38

curious, 20, 190, 298, 300

cynical, 294

dangerous, 21

deceit, 38-39, 113, 130, 295, 298, 338

dedicated, 290

degrading, 195, 289

demanding, 37, 41, 47, 101, 181, 282, 314

dependable, 25

dependent, 25, 46, 181, 215, 218, 286

deprecating, self-, 32

depressed, 33, 41, 47, 98, 127-128, 193, 201, 247

despair, 99-100, 243

detached, 36-37, 137, 182, 244

detail-oriented, 105

devious, 33

dictatorial, 289

diplomatic, 291

disagreeable, 21

discrete, 290

disgust, 267, 334

dishonest, 316

disorganized, 34

disoriented, 245

distress, 202

insightful, 42

insincere, 298

inspiring, 314

intelligent, 130, 133

intimacy, 23, 162, 174, 181-182, 184, 190, 205, 208

introspective, 282

introverted, 26, 135, 165-166, 282, 285, 294

intuitive, 26, 34, 121, 287, 315

investigative, 298-299

irrational, 116, 152

irresponsible, 114, 129, 131, 181

irritable, 100, 108, 177, 244, 263

isolated, 29, 302

jealousy, 34, 39, 108, 113, 122, 151, 177, 183-184, 186, 191

judging, 31, 48, 105, 282

jumpiness, 244

kind, 20

knowledgeable, 20

leader, 21, 23, 43, 194

level-headed, 105

light-hearted, 215

logical, 105

lonely, 100, 162, 202, 211, 227, 245, 325

loner, 26, 28, 136, 155

love, 5, 99-100, 105, 109, 135-136, 173-174, 178-179, 240

loyal, 25, 48, 215, 290

lying, 41, 267

malevolence, 111

manipulative, 23, 34, 39, 124, 155, 164, 181, 186, 215, 267, 297, 316
    sexually, 198, 294

marriage, 36, 161-162, 175-178, 185-199, 219-221
    weddings, lavish, 178

masculine, 37, 143, 171, 184, 294, 301

masochistic, 167, 289

masturbation, 161, 169, 276

mature, 42-43, 218, 234

melodramatic, 34

meticulous, 281

migratory, 124, 134

mistrustful, 22

modest, 46, 284, 335

moodiness, 99, 108, 111, 316

motivated, 43-44

nagging, 40, 164

naïve, 33, 46

negative, 47

neurotic, 285, 295

nonassertive, 32, 48

nonconforming, 26, 114, 302

nostalgic, 25

numbness, 102, 244-245

nurturing, 46, 214, 315

objective, 292

observant, 26

obsessive, 155, 157, 260, 286

omnipotence, 167, 290

omniscience, 290

one-dimensional, 38

open-minded, 20, 297

opportunistic, 132

oppressive, 318

optimistic, 22, 29, 169, 174

orderly, 289, 292-293

ostentatious, 45

outgoing, 29, 45, 180, 297, 299

overprotective, 207, 217

panic, 202

paranoid, 6, 115, 183, 263, 265

parenting, 28, 34, 50, 52, 57, 64,
    68, 83, 163, 206-213, 217-221
    and divorce, 76, 205
    fathers, new, 207
    lesbian and gay, 208
    step-, 209, 219-221
    and trophy children, 74

partnering, romantic, 175-176

passionate, 120, 180

passive, 36, 40, 46, 101

passive-aggressive, 31, 39-40

patient, 121, 284, 300

peacemaker, 215

perfectionist, 284

persistent, 20, 26, 289, 294

personable, 121

persuasive, 297-298

pessimistic, 39, 47, 99-100, 214,
    247

philandering, 191

placating, 194

placebo effect, 257

polished, 133, 180, 292

polygamous, 191

popular, 215

possessive, 186

power, 27, 338

practical, 299

precise, 105

problem-solving, 44

procrastination, 27

productive, 44

promiscuous, 34, 115

prostitution, 167

protective, 47, 290, 299

provocative, 299

prudent, 20

quarrelsome, 23

rage, 46-47, 151, 155, 218

reactive, 96

realistic, 292-293, 301

rebellious, 21, 190-191

reckless, 23, 99, 108, 114, 197

reflective, 234

rejection, 103, 293

relationships, 13-14, 34, 176-184, 186
  unhealthy, 179-181

reliable, 43, 301

remorse, 127, 158

resentful, 39, 100-101, 120, 200, 217, 219, 230

reserved, 36, 39, 282, 287, 294

resilient, 216, 247

resourceful, 43

respectful, 25

responsible, 24, 44, 47, 194, 282, 300-301

restless, 96, 185, 263

restrained, 32, 43

revenge, 102, 120, 151, 157, 190

rigid, 24, 105, 194, 217

rituals, 106-107, 154, 210

roles, 12-13, 46

rude, 23

ruthless, 21

sacrificing, 28, 47

sad, 99, 102, 202, 210, 334

sadistic, 23, 167, 289, 320

sadomasochism, 167-168

sarcastic, 23, 45

savvy, 43

scapegoat, 312, 318

scrutiny, self-, 41

secretive, 215, 292

seductive, 33, 46, 317

self-absorbed, 28, 36

self-aggrandizing, 314

self-analyzing, 100

self-awareness, 207

self-care, 48

self-centered, 140, 181, 294

self-defeating, 280

self-denial, 47

self-destructive, 99, 162, 215

self-determination, 46

self-discipline, 24, 43, 191, 214-215, 296

self-esteem, 33, 122, 163, 178, 183, 207, 214
  low, 11, 104, 128, 181, 184, 271

self-indulgent, 129, 131, 133, 181

selfish, 129, 209

self-mutilation, 80, 99, 111

self-pitying, 46

self-righteous, 112, 200

self-sufficient, 43, 112, 177, 181, 215, 285

sensation seeking, 22, 169, 288

sensitive, 26, 32, 96, 100, 112, 115, 247, 294-295, 300-301

serious, 22, 47, 194, 282

sex
  cyber-, 162

confidence scheme, 119

domestic violence, 195-196

murder, 148-158

rape, 143-146

scam, 121

sexual abuse, 34, 140, 294

stalking, 135-137

vigorous, 287

vindictive, 316

violent, 129, 137-138

virility, 275

virtues, 20

volatile, 127, 151, 180

vulnerable, 202, 245

well-liked, 42

wicked, 186

wise, 20, 234, 239

withdrawn, 32, 115-116, 136, 164, 252, 265

workaholic, 280

worldly, 37

worried, 96, 100-101

worth, 100-101, 178, 207, 247, 293

TRAITS, CHILDREN AND ADOLESCENTS

adoptee, 213

advertising, 62, 89

affectionate, 142

aggressive, 64, 84, 87, 89, 126, 203-204

aloof, 82

anger, 67, 74, 85, 90, 93-94, 116, 126

anxiety, 59, 64, 85, 117, 194, 203-204

apathy, 95

appearance, 70, 72, 74-76, 95, 271

argumentative, 73, 75, 83

attention-seeking, 89

birth order, 213-215

blaming, 83

self-, 89, 204

body movement, repetitive, 88

boisterous, 89

bossy, 23

bullying, 56, 68, 83

career development, 281

coercion, 204

competitive, 61, 68, 280

confidence, 64, 82

conforming, 24, 57, 85

control, self-, 59, 89

creativity, 26, 77

critical, 59, 68, 75

cruel, 89

cuddling, 70

curious, 63, 90

daydreaming, 77

defiant, 83, 89, 126

dependable, 224

depressed, 82, 89-90, 95, 117, 194, 204-205, 226

destructive, 89, 126

disabled, 217

disobedient, 89

eccentric, 29

efficient, 43

egocentric, 67

ejaculation, 72

empathy, 90

energetic, 57, 67

enthusiastic, 70

ethical, 73

expansive, 58

exuberant, 58

factual, 59

fearless, 89

fears, 62-63, 65

flamboyancy, 34

friendships, 223-224

imaginary, 60-61

future-oriented, 77

generous, 142

gentleness, 70

global awareness, 73-74

grief, 95, 242-243

guilt, 74, 85, 89, 226, 230

hatred, self-, 93

homosexuality, 225-226, 302

hostile, 83, 95, 126

humor, 57-58, 67, 70, 73

hypersensitive, 82

immigrants, 229-231

impertinent, 89

impudent, 89

impulsive, 87, 126

indecisive, 64

independence, 61, 70, 77, 94, 225

innocence, 32

insecurity, 61

intimacy, 224

introspective, 77

introverted, 62

irritable, 117, 204

isolation, 90

jealousy, 63

judgment, lack of, 90

language development, 56-58

lazy, 69, 87, 129

lonely, 72, 177

loyal, 223

lying, 67, 89

maladaptive, 84

manipulative, 202

masturbation, 69-70, 139, 142, 146

matter-of-fact, 59

mischievous, 58

mistrustful, 89, 194

muttering, 62

negative, 83

noisy, 87

outbursts, 90

overreaction, 70

parenting, 208-209

passive, 88

poise, 66

popularity, 64, 87

promiscuous, 95, 115

quarrelsome, 67

rage, 59

rebellious, 68, 95, 180

reflective, 76

risk-taking, 21, 180

ritualistic, 88

sad, 82, 203-204

sadistic, 126

sarcastic, 71, 73

scapegoating, 230

security blanket, 52

self, sense of, 225

self-centered, 63, 67

self-conscious, 82

self-esteem, 83-84, 89, 205

self-image, 89, 98

sensitivity, 64, 77, 85

serious, 59

sexual arousal, 70

sexuality, 76-77, 126

shame, 94, 204, 271

showing-off, 64, 89-90

shyness, 82, 117

sibling rivalry, 55

silly, 64

sluggish, 87

smoking, 70, 73-74

solitary, 88

stealing, 67

stubborn, 61

sulking, 64

sympathetic, 57

tantrums, 56, 89, 204

thoughtful, 59, 76

timid, 82

touchy, 83

toys, playing with, 54

truancy, 89, 95, 115

trust, 89, 223

twins, 215-216

unafraid, 126

underachieving, 90

underreacting, 70

unforgiving, 126

unhappy, 76

unresponsive, 117

violent, 89, 114, 126

whining, 204

withdrawn, 62, 83, 117, 204, 226, 242

worried, 82, 85

worth, 82, 177

TRAITS, GROUPS

aggression, 321-322

authority, reactions to, 310, 315

autonomy, 308, 311

behavior, 308-309, 322

clothing, 336

cohesiveness, 308, 311

conflict, 309-310, 313, 318

control, 308

crime, 159

cults, 158, 324-326

culture, 312

development of, 310-312

evolution of, 313-314

exploitation of, 318

families, 206-221, 303-308, 312

  adoption in, 211-213

  birth order, 213-215

  blended, 219

  disabled children in, 216-217

  eating disorders in, 269-271

  infertility in, 210-211

  multiple births, 215-216

  relationships in, 217-219

  single-parent, 78, 209-210

  step-, 219-221

  triangles in, 198-199

  types of, 304-307

flexibility, 308

gangs, 89, 129, 326-329, 336

hazing, 304, 320

homogeneity, 308

immigrants, 36, 112, 229-231, 310

intimacy, 308

juries, 318-319

leaders, 158-159, 310, 314-316, 319, 322, 324

members, 30, 32, 42, 110, 317-318

mentality, 312

mind control, 326

minorities, 112

mob, 323

murderers in, 150

participation, 309

permeability, 309

phobia indoctrination, 325

polarization, 309

potency, 309

power of, 324, 335

prison, 156, 323

rape, 145

refugees, 112

secret societies, 153, 322

self-help groups, 321-322

size, 309

skinheads, 328-329

social projection, 309

sorority or fraternity, 310, 320

sports, 320-321

stability, 309

stratification, 309

terrorists, 157-158

transformation, 312-313

unrest, 311

DISORDERS AND PROBLEMS, ADULTS

abuse, 99, 108, 195-196, 221, 255

addictions, 106
  sexual, 161-163

agnosia, 251

agoraphobia, 96-97, 113

alcohol, 22, 100, 118, 127, 169, 180, 226, 301

alcoholism, 101, 192-194, 266-269, 321

Alzheimer's Disease, 252

amnesia, 111, 248-251

androgen insensitivity syndrome, 171

anorexia, 237, 269-270

anxiety/nervousness, 96-98

aphasia, 251

appearance addict, 260

apraxia, 251

ataque de nervios, 80

ataxia, 250

battered wife syndrome, 128

bestiality, 163

bipolar (manic depression), 102, 107-108, 161

body dysmorphic, 259-160

borderline personality, 98-99

Brief Reactive Psychosis, 117

bulimia, 5, 269-271

captivity, military, 243-244, 250

catatonia, 80, 111, 115, 117

communication, 271-273

compulsion, sexual, 161-163, 165

conversion, 258

delusions, 108-110, 112, 115-118, 149, 153, 158, 259
  alien abduction, 109, 116
  erotomaniacal, 136
  types of, 109

dementia, 251-253

depression, 5, 22, 48, 99-102, 108, 166, 169, 184, 190, 216, 229
  in children, 89-90
  flamboyant complaining, 258
  postpartum blues, 232

domestic violence, 195

drug use, 22, 100, 169, 180, 226, 301
  parental, 61, 126
  prescription, 278
  withdrawal, 118

Drug-Induced Psychosis, 118

dyslexia, 272

eating, 106, 113, 248, 269-271

suspicions, 111-113

symphorophilia, 168

terrorism, 16, 246

trauma, 110, 223, 234, 240, 243-246, 250, 258

Turner syndrome, 172

voyeurism (peeping tom), 146, 168-169

DISORDERS AND PROBLEMS, CHILDREN AND ADOLESCENTS

abuse, 56, 94, 162, 255, 259

alcohol, 70, 73-74, 77, 93, 95, 117, 192, 194, 205

anorexia, 269-270

anxiety, 82-83, 86

arithmetic, 92

attachment, 85-86, 177-178

Attention-Deficit Hyperactivity, 86-87, 194

autism, 87-88

birth, 91

body dysmorphic, 259

borderline personality, 98

communication, 271-272

conduct, 83, 88-89

cutting, 93-94, 99

death, accidental, 67

defiance, 83

delinquency, 126

depression, 86, 89-90

Down Syndrome, 90-91

drugs, 70, 73-74, 77, 95, 205

eating, 93

encopresis (involuntary bowel movements), 84

enuresis (bed-wetting), 84, 155

fear, separation, 85-86

fetal alcohol syndrome, 194

firesetter, 90, 155

fragile x syndrome, 91

homicide, 56

infection, 91

lead poisoning, 91

love, spurned, 94

mental, 67

retardation, 90-91

mutism, 80, 91-92

neglect, 52, 56

obsessiveness, 84-85

parenting, 50, 61, 74, 76, 126, 202

perinatal, 91

phenylketonuria (PKU), 91

phobias, 97-98

prenatal, 91

prostitution, 56

rape, 94

reading, 92

rumination, 52

schizophrenia, 92, 115, 117

separation anxiety, 59, 204

skill, 92

sleep terror, 261

speaking, 92

substance abuse, 93

suicide, 90, 93-95, 210

suspicions, 114

Tay-Sachs, 91

tics, 86

trauma, 90-91

writing, 92

CRIMINALS AND CRIMES

accomplices, 119, 121

arsonist, 120-121

child abuser, 7, 139-143

con artist, 22

confidence specialist, 121, 134

counterfeiter or forger, 122-125, 133

delinquent, 126

domestic abuser, 127-128

embezzler, 11, 119

extortion, 134

grifting, 134

habitual petty, 129-130

imposter/pretender, 130

insider trading, 138

kleptomaniac, 130-131

late-blooming, 131

looter, 131-132

marks, 121-122

murderers, 147-158
  argumentative, 148
  domestic, 148-149
  erotomaniacal, 149
  extremist, 150
  female, 150-151
  incidental, 151
  inheritance, 151-152
  passionate, 152
  product-tampering, 153
  professional (hit man or contract killer), 152-153, 280
  psychotic, 153
  school shooter, 154
  serial, 154-155
  sexual, 155-156
  Simmering, 157
  terrorist, 157-158
  visionary, 158

nymphophile, 141

occasional offender, 132

ordinary, 132-133

organized crime, 152, 159

pedophile, 142

peeper, window, 147

pornographer, 142-143

professional, 133-134

psychopath, 134

pyromaniac (fire setter), 134-135, 155

rapists, 139-140, 143-146, 155

scams, 121-123

sexual abuser, 139-141, 147

skyjacker, 135

stalker, 128, 135-137, 149

violent, 137-138

white-collar, 133, 138-139

CAREERS

academia, 39

accounting, 106, 282

actor, 282-283

arborist, 27

architect, 283-284

art, 34, 122-123, 215

artist, 241, 283, 302

assistant, 24, 33

astronaut, 284

athlete, 284-289

bank teller, 28, 289

bookkeeper, 289

boxer, 286

business, 39, 290

butcher, 280

chemist/biologist, 292

childcare provider, 46

clergy, 25, 110, 268

clerk, 28

coach, 147, 289, 320

comic, 289

composer, 27

computers, 29, 139

conference planner, 281

construction, 35

corporate wife, 290-291

corporate woman, 291-292

cost estimator, 113

counselor, 30

dancer, 286

data entry clerk, 139

dealmaker, 292

dean, 106

dental assistant, 46

doctor, 147, 268, 302

domestic worker, 33

engineer, 43, 139, 280, 292

Epidemic Intelligence Service, 280

executive, 23

farmer, 293

fencer, 287

fireman, 135

flight-deck officer (in-air police), 293

football player, 287

forest ranger, 135

funeral director, 293

geologist, 27

golfer, 287-288

guard, 37, 302

guidance counselor, 300

hit man, 152-153, 280

Bibliography

APA Monitor on Psychology. January, Vol. 31 (6) 2000.

APA Monitor on Psychology. January, Vol. 32 (1) 2001.

APA Monitor on Psychology. December, Vol. 32 (11) 2001.

APA Monitor on Psychology. November, Vol. 33 (10) 2002.

APA Monitor on Psychology. April, Vol. 34 (4) 2003.

APA Monitor on Psychology. November, Vol. 34 (10) 2003.

APA Monitor on Psychology. June, Vol. 35 (6) 2004.

APA Monitor on Psychology. July/August, Vol. 35 (7) 2004.

APA Monitor on Psychology. September ,Vol. 35 (8) 2004.

APA Monitor on Psychology. October, Vol. 35 (9) 2004.

APA Monitor on Psychology. November, Vol. 35 (10) 2004.

APA Monitor on Psychology. April, Vol. 36 (4) 2005.

APA Monitor on Psychology. June, Vol. 36 (6) 2005.

APA Monitor on Psychology. September, Vol. 36 (8) 2005.

APA Monitor on Psychology. October, Vol. 36 (9) 2005.

APA poll November, 2004.

Abel, Gene and Osborn, Candice. "The Paraphilias." *Psychiatric Clinics of North America*. Vol. 15, 1992.

Abrahamsen, David. *The Mind of the Accused: A Psychiatrist in the Courtroom*. New York: Simon and Schuster, 1983.

Achenbach, Thomas M. *Developmental Psychopathology*. New York: John Wiley and Sons, 1982.

American Psychological Association practice directorate. "Psychological Series: Essential to America." February, 1995.

Ames, Louise Bates, and Haber, Carol Chase. *Your Seven-Year-Old: Life in a Minor Key*. Gesell Institute of Child Development. New York: Delacorte Press, 1985.

Ames, Louise Bates, and Haber, Carol Chase. *Your Eight-Year-Old: Lively and Outgoing*. Gesell Institute of Child Development. New York: Delacorte Press, 1989.

Ames, Louise Bates, and Ilg, Frances. *Your Three-Year-Old: Friend or Enemy*. Gesell Institute of Child Development. New York: Delacorte Press, 1976.

Ames, Louise Bates, and Ilg, Frances. *Your Four-Year-Old: Wild and Wonderful*. Gesell Institute of Child Development. New York: Delacorte Press, 1976.

Ames, Louise Bates, and Ilg, Frances. *Your Five-Year-Old: Sunny and Serene*. Gesell Institute of Child Development. New York: Delacorte Press, 1979.

Ames, Louise Bates, and Ilg, Frances. *Your Six-Year-Old: Loving and Defiant*. Gesell Institute of Child Development. New York, Delacorte Press, 1979.

Ames, Louise Bates; Ilg, Frances; and Haber, Carol Chase. *Your One-Year-Old: The Fun-Loving, Fussy 12- to 24-Month-Old*. Gesell Institute of Child Development. New York: Delacorte Press, 1982.

Ames, Louis Bates; Ilg, Frances; and Baker, Sidney. *Your Ten- to Fourteen-Year-Old: Middle Childhood*. New York: Dell, 1989.

Arnett, J. "The Psychology of Globalization." *American Psychologist*. October, 2002

Arnstein, Helene. *Between Mothers-in-Law and Daughters-in-Law*. New York: Dodd, Mead & Company, 1985.

Ashcraft, Norman, and Scheflen, Albert. *People Space*. New York: Anchor Press/Doubleday, 1976.

Astin, Helen. Women & Therapy Vol. 20 (1), 1997.

Athens, Lonnie H. *The Creation of Dangerous Violent Criminals*. Chicago: University of Illinois Press, 1992.

Bahrick, H.P.; Bahrick, P.O.; and Wittlinger, R.P. "Fifty Years of Memory for Names & Faces: A Cross-Sectional Approach." *Journal of Experimental Psychology*, Vol. 104 (1), 1975.

Bailey, J. Michael, www.psych.northwestern.edu/psych/people/faculty/bailey, 2005.

Bargh, John. *American Psychologist.* Vol. 54 (7), 1999.

Bartholomew, Kim. "From Childhood to Adult Relationships: Attachment Theory and Research." *In Learning About Relationships: Understanding Relationships Processes.* Edited by S. Duck. London: Sage Publications, 1993.

Baumeister, Roy. *Evil: Inside Human Cruelty and Violence.* New York: W.H. Freeman and Company, 1997.

Becker, S. "The Heroism of Women and Men" *American Psychologist.* Vol. 59 (3) April, 2004.

Bennis, Warren G., and Shepard, Herbert A. "A Theory of Group Development." *Human Relations.* Vol. 9, 1965.

Benson, Leonard. *The Family Bond: Marriage, Love and Sex in America.* New York: Random House, 1971.

Ben-Yehuda, Nachman. *Deviance and Moral Boundaries: Witchcraft, the Occult, Science Fiction, Deviant Fiction and Scientists.* Chicago: University of Chicago Press, 1985.

Berger, Ronald J. "Female Delinquency in the Emancipation Era: A Review of the Literature." *Sex Roles.* Vol. 21 (5-6), 1989.

Berman, Ellen, and Lief, Harold. "Marital Therapy From a Psychiatric Perspective: An Overview." *American Journal of Psychiatry.* Vol. 132 (6), June, 1975.

Bion, Wilfred. *Experiences in Groups.* New York: Basic Books, 1959.

Black, Claudia. *It Will Never Happen to Me.* Denver, CO: M.A.C. Publications, 1992.

Blatt, Sidney. *Psychoanalytic Study of the Child.* Vol. 24, 1974.

Blatt, Sidney. *American Psychologist.* Vol. 50 (12), 1995.

Bondeson, Jan. *The Great Pretenders.* New York: W.W. Norton, 2004.

Borgatta, Edgar F.; Cottrell, Leonard S., Jr.; and Meyer, Henry. *On the Dimensions of Group Behavior in Groups and Organizations.* Edited by Bernard Hinton and H. Joseph Reitz. CA: Wadsworth Publishing Co. Inc., 1971.

Bornstein, Robert, and Bower, Raymond. "Dependency in Psychotherapy: Toward an Integrated Treatment Approach." *Psychotherapy.* Vol. 32, Winter 1996.

Brandon, Sydney; Boakes, Janet; Glaser, Danya; and Green, Richard. "Recovered Memories of Childhood Sexual Abuse: Implications for Clinical Practice." *British Journal of Psychiatry* .Vol. 172, April, 1988.

Brewin, C. "Meta-Analysis of Risk Factors for Posttraumatic Stress Disorder in Trauma-exposed Adults." *Journal of Consulting and Clinical Psychology.* Vol. 68, 2000.

Brown, Mildred L., and Rounsely, Chloe Ann. *True Selves: Understanding Transsexualism*. San Francisco: Jossey-Bass Publishers, 1996.

Bruch, Hilde. *Learning Psychotherapy*. Cambridge, MA: Harvard University Press, 1974.

Burns, Rex. "Characterization." *The Writer*. May, 1988.

Calhoun, George; Jurgens, Janelle; and Chen, Fengling. "The Neophyte Female Delinquent: A Review of the Literature." *Adolescence*. Vol. 28 (110), 1993.

Callahan, Roger, and Levine, Karen. *It Can Happen to You: The Practical Guide to Romantic Love*. New York: A & W Publishers, 1982.

Caprio, Frank S. *Marital Infidelity*. New York: The Citadel Press, 1953.

Carpineto, Jane. *The Don Juan Dilemma*. New York: William Morrow & Company, 1989.

Cattell, Heather Birkett. *The 16PF: Personality in Death*. Champaign, Illinois Institute for Personality and Ability Testing, 1989.

Charlton, William. "Feeling for the Fictitious." *The British Journal of Aesthetics*. Vol. 24, Summer 1984.

Chatman, Seymour. *Story and Discourse: Narrative Structure in Fiction and Film*. Ithaca: Cornell University Press, 1978.

Clifford, C.A.; Murray, R.M.; and Fulker, D.W. "Genetic and Environmental Influences on Obsessional Traits and Symptoms." *Psychological Medicine*. November, 1984.

Clinard, Marshall B. *Sociology of Deviant Behavior*. New York: Holt, Rinehart and Winston, Inc., 1963.

Cole, Sonia. *Counterfeit, Counterfeit*. New York: Abelard-Schuman, 1956.

Cohan, Steven. "Figures Beyond the Text: A Theory of Readable Character in the Novel." *Novel: A Forum of Fiction*. Fall 1983.

Coley, Rebekah Levine, and Chase-Lansdale, P. Lindsay. "Adolescent Pregnancy and Parenthood." *American Psychologist*. Vol. 53 (February 1998).

Curtis, George C.; Magee, W.J.; Eaton, W.W.; Wittchen, H.U.; and Kessler, R.C. "Specific Fears and Phobias." *British Journal of Psychiatry*. Vol. 173, 1998.

Davidson, K. *International Journal of Behavioral Medicine*. Vol.6 (3), 2003.

DeAngelis, Tori. "There's New Hope for Women With Postpartum Blues." *APA Monitor on Psychology*. September 1997.

DePaulo, Bella. *In Deception and Detection in Forensic Contexts*. Cambridge U. Press, 2004.

Depaulo, Bella. *Psychological Bulletin*. Vol. 129 (1), 2004.

Dodson, Fitzhugh, and Alexander, Ann. *Your Child: Birth to Age.* New York: Simon & Schuster, 1986.

Doleys, Daniel M.; Meredith, R.L.; and Ciminero, Anthony R., eds. *Behavioral Medicine: Assessment and Treatment Strategies.* New York: Plenum Press, 1982.

Douglas, John E.; Burgess, Ann W.; Burgess, Allen; and Ressler, Robert K. *Crime Classification Manual.* New York: Lexington Books, 1992.

Douglas, John E., and Olshaker, Mark. *Journey Into Darkness.* New York: Scribner, 1997.

Douglas, John E., and Olshaker, Mark. *Mindhunter: Inside the FBI's Elite Serial Crime Unit.* New York: Scribner, 1995.

Douglas, John E., and Schlesinger, Louis B. "Distinctions Between Psychopathic, Sociopathic, and Anti-Social Personality Disorders." *Psychological Reports.* Vol. 47 1998.

Dudek, Stephanie, and Hall, Wallace B. "Personality Consistency: Eminent Architects 25 Years Later." *Creativity Research Journal.* Vol.4 (3) 1991.

Edelstein, Linda N. *Maternal Bereavement: Coping With the Death of an Older Child.* Westport, CT: Praeger, 1984.

Edelstein, Linda N. *The Art of Midlife: Courage and Creative Living for Women.* Westport, CT: Bergin & Garvey Trade, 1999.

Eagly, Alice and Becker, Selwyn. *American Psychologist.* Vol. 60 (4) May-June, 2005.

Ehrenberg, Tamar. "Female Differences in Creation of Humor Relating to Work." *Humor.* Vol. 8 (4) 1995.

Ekman, Paul. "Universals and Cultural Differences in Facial Expressions of Emotion." *In Nebraska Symposium on Emotion.* Edited by James K. Cole. Lincoln: University of Nebraska Press, 1971.

Erikson, Erik. *Childhood and Society.* New York: W.W. Norton & Co., 1964.

Erikson, Kai T. *Everything in Its Path: Destruction of Community in the Buffalo Creek Flood.* New York: Simon and Schuster, 1976.

Esau, Truman G. "The Evangelical Christian in Psychotherapy." *American Journal of Psychotherapy.* Vol. 52 (1) Winter 1998.

Evans, G. "The Environment of Childhood Poverty." *American Psychologist.* Vol. 59 (2) Feb/March 2004.

Faux, Marian. *Childless by Choice.* New York: Anchor Press, 1984.

Feinstein, John. *A Good Walk Spoiled: Days and Nights on the PGA Tour.* Boston: Little, Brown, 1995.

Field, Tiffany. *Touch*. Cambridge: MIT Press, 2001.

Finkelhor, David. "Victimization of Children." *American Psychologist*. Vol. 49 (3), 1994.

Flannery, Raymond B., Jr. *Violence in America*. New York: Continuum, 1997.

Fleeson, William. *Journal of Personality and Social Psychology*. Vol. 83 (6), 2002.

Fox, Elaine. *Journal of Experimental Psychology*. Vol. 130 (4), 2002.

Fraiberg, Selma. *The Magic Years*. New York: Scribner, 1959.

Frank, Susan; Avery, Catherine B.; Laman, Mark. "Young Adults' Perceptions of Their Relation-ships With Their Parents." *Developmental Psychology*. Vol. 24 (5), 1988.

Friedman, Stanley. "On the 'True-False' Memory Syndrome: The Problems of Clinical Evidence." *The American Journal of Psychotherapy*. Vol. 51 (1,) Winter 1997.

Frieze, Irene. "Female Violence Against Intimate Partners" *Psychology of Women Quarterly*. Vol. 29 (3), 2005.

Freudenberger, Larry, and Bergandi, Thomas A. "Sport Psychology Research in American Football: A Review of the Literature." *International Journal of Sport Psychology*. Vol.25 Oct.-Dec. 1994.

Furnham, Adrian. "Personality and Demographic Determinants of Leisure and Sports Preference and Performance." *International Journal of Sports Psychology*. 21 (3) (July-Sept. 1990).

Galligani, Niklas; Renck, Annika; and Hansen, Stefan. "Personality Profile of Men Using Anabolic Androgenic Steroids." *Hormones and Behavior*. Vol. 30 (2), June 1996.

Garber, Stephen; Garber, Marianne Daniels; Spizman, Robyn Freedman. *If Your Child Is Hyperac-tive, Inattentive, Impulsive, Distractible* … .New York: Villard Press, 1998.

Gardner, Howard. *APA Monitor on Psychology*. November, Vol. 34 (10), 2003.

Gardner, Richard. "Toward a Definition of Stereotypes." *The Midwest Quarterly*. Summer 1985.

Geis, Gilbert, and Stotland, Ezra, eds. *White-Collar Crime: Theory and Research*. Pacific Grove: Sage Publications, 1980.

Gobodo-Madikizela, Pumla. "A Human Being Died That Night: A South African Story of Forgiveness." 2003.

Gold, Steven N., and Heffner, Christopher L. "Sexual Addiction: Many Conceptions, Minimal Data." *Clinical Psychology Review*. Vol. 18 (3), 1998.

Goma, Monserrat Freixanet. "Personality File of Subjects Engaged in High Physical Risk Sports." *Personality and Individual Differences*. Vol. 12 (10), 1991.

Gondola, Joan C., and Wughalter, Emily. "The Personality Characteristics of Internationally Ranked Female Tennis Players as Measured by the Cattell 16PF." *Perceptual and Motor Skills*. Vol. 73 (3, pt. 1) Dec. 1991.

Gonzalez-Crussi, Frank. *On the Nature of Things Erotic*. New York: Harcourt Brace Jovanovich, 1988.

Gortner, Eric; Jacobson, Neil S.; Berns, Sara B.; and Gottman, John M. "When Women Leave Violent Relationships: Dispelling Clinical Myths." *Psychotherapy*. Vol. 34 Winter 1997.

Graham, John R. MMPI-2 : Assessing Personality and Psychopathology. New York: Oxford University Press, 1990.

Granleese, Jackie, and Barrett, Timothy. "The Social and Personality Characteristics of the Irish Chartered Accountant." *Personality and Individual Difference*. Vol. 11 (9), 1990.

Greene, Cherry, and Stitt-Gohdes, Wanda. "Factors That Influence Women's Choices to Work in the Trades." *Journal of Career Development*. Vol. 23 (4), Summer 1997.

Greene, Roger L. *MMPI-2/MMPI: An Interpretive Manual*. Boston: Allyn and Bacon, 1991.

Greenfield, David. *Virtual Addiction*. New Harbinger, 1999.

Griffith, Richard M.; Miyagi, Otoya; Tago, Akiro. "Universality of Typical Dreams: Japanese vs. Americans." *American Anthropologist*. Vol. 60 1958.

Grinker, Roy, and Spiegel, J. P. *Men Under Stress*. New York: Hill, 1945.

Grossman, Dave. *On Killing*. Boston: Little, Brown, 1995.

Gutmann, David. "Deculturation and the American Grandparent." *In Grandparenthood*. Edited by Vern L. Bengtson and Joan F. Robertson. Beverly Hills: Sage Publications, 1985.

Haber, Jon Randolph, and Jacob, Theodore. "Marital Interactions of Male vs. Female Alcoholics." *Family Process*. Vol. 36 (4), Dec. 1997.

Hagestad, Gunhild O. "Continuity and Connectedness." *In Grandparenthood*. Edited by Vern L. Bengtson and Joan F. Robertson. Beverly Hills, CA: Sage Publications, 1985.

Hartup, Willard W., and Stevens, Nan. "Friendships and Adaptation in the Life Course." *Psychological Bulletin*. Vol. 121 (3) May 1997.

Hatch, Marjorie. "Conceptualization and Treatment of Bowel Obsessions: Two Case Reports." *Behavioral Research Therapy*. Vol. 35 (3), March 1997.

Hawthorn, Jeremy. *Multiple Personality and the Disintegration of Literary Character: From Oliver Goldsmith to Sylvia Plath*. New York: St. Martin's Press, 1983.

Heilman, M. *Journal of Applied Psychology*. Vol. 89 (3), 2004.

Henderson, Harry. *Global Terrorism*. New York: Facts on File, Inc. 2004.

Hendrick, Susan S. *Close Relationships*. Pacific Grove: Brooks/Cole, 1995.

Hetherington, E. Mavis; Law, Tracy; and O'Connor, Thomas. "Divorce: Challenges, Changes, and New Chances." *In Normal Family Processes.* 208-34. 2d ed. Edited by Froma Walsh. New York: The Guilford Press, 1993.

Hetherington, E. Mavis; Bridges, Margaret; Insabella, Glendessa M. "What Matters? What Does Not? Five Perspectives on the Association Between Marital Transitions and Children's Adjustment." *American Psychologist.* Vol. 53 (2), 1998.

Higgins, E. *Social Psychology: Handbook of Basic Principles.* New York: Guilford Press, 1996.

Himber, Judith. "Blood Rituals: Self-Cutting in Female Psychiatric Inpatients." *Psychotherapy.* Vol. 31 (4) Winter 1994.

Hogan, R. "What We Know about Leadership." *American Psychologist.* Vol. 49 (6), 1994.

Holmes, Guy; Offen, Liz; and Waller, Glenn. "See No Evil, Hear No Evil, Speak No Evil: Why Do Relatively Few Male Victims of Childhood Sexual Abuse Receive Help for Abuse-Related Issues in Adulthood?" *Clinical Psychology.* Review Vol. 17 (1), 1997.

Holmes, R.M., and DeBerger, J.E. "Profiles in Terror: The Serial Murder." *Federal Probation.* Vol. 49 (3), Sept. 1985).

Holtzworth-Munroe, Amy, and Stuart, G. L. "Typologies of Male Batterers: Three Subtypes and the Differences Between Them." *Psychological Bulletin.* Vol. 116 (3), Nov. 1994.

Hopwood, J.S., and Snell, H.K. "Amnesia in Relation to Crime." *Journal of Mental Science.* Vol. 79, 1933.

Horton, Andrew. *Writing a Character-Centered Screenplay.* Berkeley: University of California Press, 1994.

House, Robert J., and Howell, Jane M. "Personality and Charismatic Leadership." *Leadership Quarterly.* Vol. 3 (2), Summer 1992.

House, Robert J.; Spangler, William D.; and Woycke, James. "Personality and Charisma in the U.S. Presidency: A Psychological Theory of Leader Effectiveness." *Administrative Science Quarterly.* Vol. 36 (3), Sept. 1991.

Hubbard, David G. *The Skyjacker: His Flights of Fantasy.* New York: Macmillan Company, 1971.

Institute of Medicine Committee (IOM). *Report Card on the National Plan for Research on Child and Adolescent Mental Disorders.* 1995.

Ikemi, Y. Kyoshu. *Journal of Medical Science.* Vol. 13, 1962.

Jacobs, David M. *The UFO Controversy in America.* Indiana: Indiana University Press, 1975.

Janis, Irving. *Victims of Group-Think.* Boston: Houghton Mifflin, 1972.

Janet, Pierre. *Neurosis et Idees Fixes.* 2d ed. Paris: Felix Alcan, 1904.

Johnson, Craig, and Flach, Anna. "Family Characteristics of 105 Patients With Bulimia." *American Journal of Psychiatry*. Vol. 142 (11), Nov. 1985.

Johnson, Sheri, and Jacob, Theodore. "Marital Interactions of Depressed Men and Women." *Journal of Consulting and Clinical Psychology*. Vol. 65 (1), Feb. 1997.

Johnson, W. Toward a Typology of Mentorship Dysfunction in Graduate School. *Psychotherapy: Theory/Research/Practice/Training*. Vol. 39 (1), 2002.

Massachusetts Medical Society. *Journal Watch for Psychiatry*. Vol. 3 (4), April 1997.

Judge, T. J*ournal of Applied Psychology*. Vol. 89 (3), 2004.

Kanter, Rosabeth Moss, and Stein, Barry. *Life in the Organization*. New York: Basic Books, 1979.

Kantor, David, and Lehr, William. *Inside the Family*. New York: Harper & Row, 1975.

Karson, Samuel, and O'Dell, Jerry W. *A Guide to the Clinical Use of the 16PF*. Champaign: Illinois Institute for Personality and Ability Testing, 1976.

Kaslow, Florence, and Sussman, Marvin. "Cults and the Family." *Marriage and Family Review*. Vol. 4 (3/4) 1982.

Kassin, S. *American Psychologist*. Vol. 60 (3), April, 2005.

Kirsch, I. *American Psychologist*. Vol. 50, 1995.

Knight, Gareth. *The Practice of Ritual Magic*. New Mexico: Sun Chalice Books, 1996.

Knopf, Jennifer and Seiler, Michael. *ISD: Inhibited Sexual Desire*. New York: William Morrow and Co., 1990.

Kopelman, Michael D. "The Assessment of Psychogenic Amnesia." *In Handbook of Memory Disorders*. Edited by A.D. Baddeley, B.A. Wilson, and F.N. Watts. Chichester: Wiley, 1995.

Korn, Richard R., and McCorkle, Lloyd W. *Criminology and Penalogy*. New York: Holt, Rinehart, and Winston, Inc., 1963.

Koerner, Susan, Wallace, Sara, Lehman, Stephanie, Lee, Sun-A, Escalante, Kristine. "Sensitive Mother-to-Adolescent Disclosures After Divorce." *Journal of Family Psychology*. Vol. 18 (1), 2004

Krause, Neal; Shaw, Benjamin; Cairney, John; "Epidemiology of Lifetime Trauma and the Physical Health Status of Older Adults." *Psychology and Aging*. Vol. 19 (4), 2004.

Krueger J. *Political Psychology*. Vol. 25 (1), 2004.

Krug, Samuel E. *Interpreting 16PF Profiles*. Champaign: Illinois Institute for Personality and Ability Testing, 1981.

Laird, Joan. "Gay and Lesbian Families." In F. Walsh (ed). *Normal Family Processes*. New York: Guilford Press, 1993.

Lampinen, James; Neuschatz, Jeffrey; and Payne, David. "Memory Illusions and Consciousness: Examining the Phenomenology of Tone and False Memories." *Current Psychology: Developmental, Learning, Personality.* Social Vol. 6 (3/4) Fall 1997/Winter 1998).

Leman, K. *The Birth Order Book: Why You Are the Way You Are.* New York: Dell, 1985.

Lemert, Edwin. "The Behavior of the Systematic Check Forger." *Social Problems.* Vol. 6, 1958.

Lerner, J. *Journal of Personality and Social Psychology.* Vol. 80 (1) 2001.

Levin, Jack, and Arluke, Arnold. *Gossip: The Inside Scoop.* New York: Plenum, 1987.

Levinson, Daniel; Darrow, Charlotte; Klein, Edward; Levinson, Maria; and McKee, Braxton. *The Seasons of a Man's Life.* New York: Ballantine, 1978.

Lichter, Erika. *Psychology of Women Quarterly.* Vol. 28 (4) 2004.

Livingston, J. "The Role of Sexual Precedence in Verbal Sexual Coercion." *Psychology of Women Quarterly.* Vol. 28 (4), 2004.

Locke, Edwin. "Building a Practically Useful Theory of Goal Setting." *American Psychologist.* Vol. 57 (9), 2002.

Loftus, Elizabeth. "The Reality of Repressed Memories." *American Psychologist.* Vol. 48 (5), 1993.

Loftus, Elizabeth, and Ketcham, Katherine. *Witness for the Defense.* New York: St. Martin's Press, 1991.

Lyubomirsky, S. "Why Are Some People Happier Than Others?" *American Psychologist.* Vol. 56 (3), 2001.

Ludwig, Arnold M. "Creative Achievement and Psychopathology: Comparison Among Professions." *American Journal of Psychotherapy.* Vol. XLVI (3), 1992.

Ludwig, Arnold M. "Mental Illness and Creative Activity in Female Writers." *American Journal of Psychiatry.* Vol. 151 (11), 1994.

Mann, Coramae Richey. *When Women Kill.* New York: State University of New York, 1996.

Marano, Hara. "Rocking the Cradle of Class." *Psychology Today.* October, 2005.

Marchant-Haycox, Susan E., and Wilson, Glenn D. "Personality and Stress in the Performing Arts." *Personality and Individual Difference.* Vol. 13 (10), 1992.

Margolese, Howard O. "Engaging in Psychotherapy With the Orthodox Jew." *American Journal of Psychotherapy.* Vol. 52 (1), 1998.

Masters, R.E.L. *Sex-Driven People: An Autobiographical Approach to the Problem of the Sex-Dominated Personality.* CA: Sherbourne Press, Inc., 1966.

Masters, William, and Johnson, Virginia. *Human Sexual Inadequacy*. Boston: Little, Brown, 1970.

McCready, William. "Styles of Grandparenting Among White Ethnics." *In Grandparenthood*. Edited by Vern L. Bengtson and Joan F. Robertson. Pacific Grove: Sage Publications, 1985.

McDavid, Joshua D. "The Diagnosis of Multiple Personality Disorder." *The Jefferson Journal of Psychiatry*. Vol. 12 (1), 1994.

McDonald, S. *Neuropsychology*. Vol. 18 (3), 2004.

McNulty, J and Karney, B. *Journal of Personality and Social Psychology*. Vol. 86 (5), 2004.

McRay, Leslie, and Schwarz, Ted. *Kept Women: Confessions From a Life of Luxury*. New York: William Morrow and Co., 1990.

Mehrabian, Albert. "Interrelationships Among Name Desirability, Name Uniqueness, Emotion Characteristics Connoted by Names and Temperament." *Journal of Applied Social Psychology*. Vol. 22, 1992.

Mehrabian, Albert. *The Name Game: The Decision That Lasts a Lifetime*. Maryland: National Press Books, 1990.

Mehrabian, Albert, and Piercy, Marlena. "Positive or Negative Connotations of Unconventionally and Conventionally Spelled Names." *The Journal of Social Psychology*. Vol. 133 (4), 1993.

Merckelbach, Harold; de Jong, Peter J.; Muris, Peter; and Van den Hout, Marcel A. "The Etiology of Specific Phobias: A Review." *Clinical Psychology Review*. Vol. 16 (4), 1996.

Michaels, Gerald Y., and Goldberg, Wendy A., eds. *The Transition to Parenthood*. Cambridge: Cambridge University Press, 1988.

Millon, Theodore. *Disorders of Personality: DSM IV and Beyond*. New York: John Wiley and Sons, Inc., 1996.

Minor, K. *Journal of Abnormal Psychology*. Vol. 113 (2), 2004.

Mintz, Steven. *Huck's Raft: A History of American Childhood*. Belknap Press 2004.

Mitchell. D. *Psychology of Women Quarterly*. Vol. 28 (3), 2004.

Moglia, Ronald Filiberti, and Knowles, Jon. eds. *All About Sex: A Family Resource on Sex and Sexuality*. New York: Three Rivers Press, 1993.

Molloy, John. *John T. Molloy's New Dress for Success*. New York: Warner, 1998.

Mones, Arthur. "Oppositional Children and Their Families: An Adaptational Dance in Space and Time." *American Journal of Orthopsychiatry*. Vol. 68 (1), 1998.

Money, John. "Myths and Misconceptions About Sex Offenders." *Canadian Journal on Human Sexuality*. Vol. 7 (1), Spring 1998.

Monger, George. *Marriage Customs of the World*. CA: ABC Clio, 2004.

Morris, Betsy. "It's Her Job Too." *Fortune Magazine*. February 1998.

Moss, Howard B.; Panzak, George L.; and Tarter, Ralph E. "Personality, Mood, and Psychiatric Symptoms Among Anabolic Steroid Users." *The American Journal on Addictions*. Vol. 1 (4) Fall 1992.

Mouradian, V. "Battered Women." *Research & Action Report*. Wellesley Centers for Women, Fall/Winter, 2004

Muris, Peter; Merckelbach, Harold; and Claven, Michael. "Abnormal and Normal Compulsions." *Behavior Research Therapy*. Vol. 35 (3), 1997.

Nansel, T. "Bullying Behaviors Among US Youth." *Journal of the American Medical Association*. Vol. 285 (16), 2001.

National Institute for Occupational Safety and Health.

National Institute of Child Health and Human Development Journal of Family Psychology Vol. 18 (4), 2004.

Nelson, A. "The Pink Dragon is Female." *Psychology of Women Quarterly*. Vol. 24 (2), 2000.

Nuwer, Hank. *Broken Pledges*. GA: Longstreet Press, 1990.

Oates, Joyce Carol. *On Boxing*. Dolphin/Doubleday: New York, 1987.

Osipow, Samuel H. *Theories of Career Development*. New Jersey: Prentice-Hall, 1973.

Ozer, E. "Predictors of Posttraumatic Stress Disorder and Symptoms in Adults." *Psychological Bulletin*. Vol. 129, 2003.

Parker, Patricia S., and Ogilvie, D. "Gender, Culture, and Leadership: Toward a Culturally Distinct Model of African-American Women Executives' Leadership Strategies." *Leadership Quarterly*. Vol. 7 (2), 1996.

Parkin, Alan J. *Memory and Amnesia: An Introduction*. Great Britain: Blackwell Publishers, 1997.

Patterson, Marcus; Rapoza, Kimberly; Malley-Morrison, Kathleen. *An Examination of Four Subtypes of Jealousy*. American Psychological Association 103rd Annual Convention, CA, 1998.

Pease, Allan. *Signals: How to Use Body Language for Power, Success and Love*. New York: Bantam Books, 1984.

People Magazine. March 23, 1998.

Peterson, Marion and Warner, Diane. *Single Parenting for Dummies*. Indiana: Wiley Publishing 2003.

Pines, Ayala M. "Romantic Jealousy: Five Perspectives and an Integrative Approach." *Psychotherapy.* Vol. 29 (4), 1992.

Polivy, Janet. "If at First You Don't Succeed." *American Psychologist.* Vol. 57 (9), 2002.

Powers, Diane C. *Stalking: A Form of Disordered Attachment and Mourning Variant.* An unpublished dissertation, 1977.

Prentice, Deborah. "What Women and Men Should Be, Shouldn't Be, Are Allowed to Be, and Don't Have to Be." *Psychology of Women Quarterly.* Vol. 26, 2002.

Prochaska, James. "Stages of Change." *Psychotherapy.* Vol. 38 (4), 2001.

Quarantelli, E.L., and Dynes, Russell R. "Property Norms and Looting: Their Pattern in Community Crises." *Phylon.* Vol. 31 (2), 1970.

Quay, Herbert C., and Werry, John S. (eds). "Residential Treatment." *In Psychopathological Disorders of Childhood.* 2d ed. New York: John Wiley and Sons, 1979.

Radkowsky, Michael, and Siegel, Lawrence. "The Gay Adolescent: Stressors, Adaptations, and Psychosocial Interventions." *Clinical Psychology Review.* 17 (2), 1997.

Reddy, Betty. "How We Help the Alcoholic Drink." *Illinois Bar Journal.* (September 1984).

Reik, Theodor. *On Love and Lust.* New York: Farrar, Strauss & Cudahy, 1949.

Revich, E., and Schlesinger, L.B. "Murder: Evaluation, Classification, and Prediction." *In Perspectives on Murder & Aggression Violence.* 138-64. Edited by I.L. Kutash, S.B. Kutash, and L.B. Schlesinger. San Francisco: Jossey Bass, 1978.

Richardson, Ronald, and Richardson, Lois. *Birth Order and You.* Washington: Self-Counsel Press, 1990.

Roe, Anne. *The Psychology of Occupations.* New York: John Wiley and Sons, 1956.

Rogler, L. "International Migrations." *American Psychologist.* Vol. 49 (8), 1994.

Romano, Maria Luisa. *Family Update, Online!* Volume 18 (10), 2005.

Rose, Robert; Fogg, Louis; Helmreich, Robert; and McFadden, Terry. "Psychological Predictors of Astronaut Effectiveness." *Aviation, Space, and Environmental Medicine.* Vol. 65, 1994.

Rosenberg, Elinor. *The Adoption Life Cycle: The Children and Their Families Through the Years.* New York: The Free Press, 1992.

Rubenstein, Ruth P. *Dress Codes: Meanings and Messages in American Culture.* Boulder, CO: Westview Press, 1995.

Rubenzer, S. "Personality and the President Project." *PubMed.* Vol. 7(4), 2000.

Sachs, Rachel; Chrisler, Joan C.; and Devlin, Anne Sloan. "Biographic and Personal Characteristics of Women in Management." *Journal of Vocational Behavior*. Vol. 41 1992.

Sampson, Anthony. *Company Man*. New York: Times Business Books, 1995.

Saudine, L. *Journal of Personality and Social Psychology*. Vol. 87 (5), 2004.

Scheflen, Albert. *How Behavior Means*. New York: Anchor Press/Doubleday, 1974.

Schlesinger, L.B. "The Catathymic Crisis (1912-present): A Review and Clinical Study." *Aggression and Violent Behavior*. Vol.1 (4), 1996.

Schlesinger, L.B. "Distinctions Between Psychopathic, Sociopathic, and Anti-Social Personality Disorder." *Psychological Reports*. Vol. 47, 1980.

Schlossberg, Nancy K. *Counseling Adults in Transition*. New York: Springer Publication, 1984.

Schlossberg, Nancy. *Retire Smart, Retire Happy*. APA Publishers, 2004.

Schmich, Mary. "Shadow Moms Deserve a Hand for the One They Give." *Chicago Tribune*. May 10, 1998, sec. 4.

Seligman, Kurt. *The History of Magic and the Occult*. New York: Random House Value Publishers, 1997.

Shahn, Ben. *The Shape of Content*. Cambridge: Harvard University Press, 1957.

Simon, Rita James, ed. *The Jury System in America*. CA: Sage Publications, 1975.

Sleek, Scott. "Is Impotence Only a Biological Problem?" *APA Monitor on Psychology*. Vol 28 1998.

Solomon, Michael A. "A Developmental, Conceptual Premise for Family Therapy." *Normal Family Process*. Vol. 12 (2), 1973.

Sommers, J.V., and Yawkey, T.D. "Imaginary Play Companions: Contributions of Creative and Intellectual Abilities in Young Children." *Journal of Creative Behavior*. Vol. 18 1984.

Sorenson, Susan. and Taylor, Catherine. *Psychology of Women Quarterly*. Vol. 29, 2005.

Stapel, D. *Journal of Personality and Social Psychology*. Vol. 87 (4) 2004.

Stern, Daniel. *Diary of a Baby*. New York: Basic Books, 1990.

Stern, Daniel. *The Interpersonal World of the Human Infant*. New York: Basic Books, 1985.

Sternberg, Robert. (ed) *Why Smart People Can Be So Stupid*. Yale University Press, 2002.

Sternberg, Robert. *APA Monitor on Psychology*. Vol. 34 (10), 2003.

Storr, Anthony. *Sexual Deviation*. Baltimore: Penguin Books, 1964.

Strier, Dorit Roer. "Coping Strategies of Immigrant Parents: Directions for Family Therapy." *Family Process*. Vol. 35 (3) 1996.

Sutherland, Edwin H. *The Professional Thief.* Chicago: University of Chicago Press, 1937.

Suyemoto, Karen. "Self-Cutting in Female Adolescents." *Psychotherapy.* Vol. 32 (1), 1995.

Talland, George A. *Deranged Memory.* New York: Academic Press, 1965.

Taylor, Pamela J., and Kopelman, Michael D. "Amnesia for Criminal Offenses." *Psychological Medicine.* Vol. 14, 1984.

Tiedens, L. *Journal of Personality and Social Psychology.* Vol. 80 (1) 2003.

Tiefer, Lenore. *Sex Is Not a Natural Act and Other Essays.* Boulder, CO: Westview Press, 1995.

Tiger, Lionel. *Men in Groups.* New York: Random House, 1969.

Torrey, Fuller E. *Witchdoctors and Psychiatrists: The Common Roots of Psychotherapy and Its Future.* New Jersey: Jason Aronson Inc., 1986.

Troupp, Cathy. *Why Do We Fall In Love? The Psychology of Choosing a Partner.* New York: St. Martin's Press, 1994.

U.S. Department of Education and Secret Service Report on the 37 School Shootings,www. ed.gov/news/pressreleases/2002/05/05152002a.html

U.S. Department of Health and Human Services. *Marijuana: Facts Parents Need to Know.* National Institutes of Health, 1995, NIH Publication Number 95-4036.

van Kleef, G. et al "The Interpersonal Effects of Anger and Happiness in Negotiations." *Journal of Personality and Social Psychology.* Vol. 86 (1) 2004.

Visher, Emily B., and Visher, John S. "Remarriages, Families and Stepparenting." *In Normal Family Process.* 2d ed. Edited by Froma Walsh. New York: The Guilford Press, 1993.

Vitaro, Frank; Ladouceur, Robert; and Bujold, Annie. "Predictive and Concurrent Correlates of Gambling in Early Adolescent Boys." *Journal of Early Adolescence.* Vol. 16 1996.

Waehler, Charles A. "Relationship Patterns of Never-Married Men and Their Implications for Psychotherapy." *Psychotherapy.* Vol. 31 (4), Winter 1994.

Wallace, Cameron; Mullen, Paul; Burgess, Philip; Palmer, Simon; Ruschana, David; and Brown, Chris. "Serious Criminal Offending and Mental Disorder." *British Journal of Psychiatry,* Vol. 172 (6), 1998.

Wallerstein, Judith, and Kelly, Joan Berlin. *Surviving the Breakup: How Children and Parents Cope With Divorce.* New York: Basic Books, 1980.

Walters, Glenn D. *The Criminal Lifestyle: Patterns of Serious Criminal Conduct.* Newbury Park, CA: Sage Publications, 1990.

Ware, Susan. *Still Missing: Amelia Earhart and the Search for Modern Feminism.* New York: W.W. Norton and Co., 1993.

Weiss, Robert. *Marital Separation*. New York: Basic Books, 1975.

Wells, Leroy, Jr. "The Group As-A-Whole: A Systemic Socio-Analytic Perspective on Interpersonal and Group Relations." *In Advances in Experiential Social Processes*. Edited by C.P. Alderfer and C.L. Cooper. New York: John Wiley and Sons, 1980.

Weinberg, Martin. "Sexual Modesty, Social Meaning, and the Nudist Camp." *In Observations of Deviance*. Edited by Jack Douglas. New York: Random House, 1970.

White, Kathleen M.; Speisman, Joseph C.; Costos, Daryl. "Young Adults and Their Parents: Individuation to Mutuality." *New Directions for Child Development*. Vol. 22 1983.

Whiteman, Dorit. "Holocaust Survivors and Escapees." *Psychotherapy*. Vol. 30 (3), 1993.

Wiley, Carol A., (Ed.) *Women in the Martial Arts*. Berkeley: North Atlantic Books, 1992.

Wills, Anne, and Olivieri, S. "Anorexia Nervosa in Old Age." *Aging and Mental Health*. 1998.

Wilson, James Q., and Herrnstein, Richard J. *Crimes and Human Nature*. New York: Simon and Schuster, 1985.

Wisniewski, Mark. "The Vital Element: Are Your Characters Breathing?" *The Writer*. Vol. 107 1994.

Woodzicka, Julie. "Perceptions of and Affective Reactions to Prejudice and Discrimination." *Journal of Social Issues*. Vol. 57 (1), 2001.

Woititz, Janet Geringer. *Adult Children of Alcoholics*. Deerfield Beach, FL: Health Communications, 1983.

Zebrowitz, Leslie. *Reading Faces*. Boulder, CO: Westview Press, 1997.

Zimbardo, Philip. *APA Monitor on Psychology*. November Vol. 33 (10), 2002.